NUREMBERG IN THE SIXTEENTH CENTURY

City Politics and Life between Middle Ages and Modern Times

GERALD STRAUSS

Indiana University Press / Bloomington & London

Manufactured in the United States of America

Library of Congress Cataloging in Publication Data

Strauss, Gerald, 1922-
  Nuremberg in the sixteenth century.

  Includes bibliographical references and index.
  1. Nuremberg—History.   I. Title.
DD901.N94S78   1976   943'.32   76-12379
ISBN 0-253-34149-3
ISBN 0-253-34150-7 pbk.   2 3 4 5 80 79

Nuremberg in the Sixteenth Century

PREFACE

Not until one tries to write about it does one fully understand how manifold and complex is life in human communities, and how subtle are the relationships of men to each other, to their institutions, their environment. In order to portray the conditions of life in one community at a certain moment in time, it is not enough to describe places, situations, and events. Actuality at any given instant includes the influence of the historical past upon the present, the interplay of the old and the new, and the encounter of inherited ideas and traditions with unfamiliar contexts. Only where the sources are plentiful is it possible to render a description which in its diverseness and complexity is true to reality.

Medieval Nuremberg offers the historian its abundant archives as raw material for a faithful representation of a historical community in action. Nuremberg was a large city (by medieval standards) and one of European importance, and in the late fifteenth and early sixteenth centuries it experienced its golden age. Nuremberg was not only free and sovereign, lord of its domain and destiny; it also thought of itself as having developed a distinct character, a way of life reflected in politics, architecture, law, religion—in fact in every aspect of municipal existence. As a place of prodigious industrial and commercial activity and as a center of long-established patrician wealth, Nuremberg had connections with governments throughout the Holy Roman Empire and wider Europe and found itself drawn into most of the political, religious, and military troubles of the time. All this deposited a mass of documents in official and private archives, enough to illuminate nearly every facet of Nuremberg's society and culture in the late Middle Ages.

My object has been to give as full and accurate a picture of

the life of this city as my abilities and the publisher's format
allowed. I have used not only the sources but most of the large
body of specialized literature as well. Though I have tried to
keep my text unencumbered by the problematics that have
agitated the scholars, I have noted references where the point
is of some general interest. I have also given the best authorities
on most subjects, even though few wrote in English. I should
like the book to be useful to advanced students who may wish
to pursue the history of Nuremberg, or of German cities in
general, or of one or another of the many particular topics a bit
further. If they do, they will soon discover how much more
there is to say than I have been able to set down here. But if I
have stimulated an interest in the medieval city and if I have
been able to suggest something of the richness and fertility of
life in that distant age, my book will have served its purpose.

Bloomington, Indiana   GERALD STRAUSS
September 1966

In the ten years since this volume was first published scholarship
has made great strides in urban history and related fields of re-
search, and several important studies have appeared on aspects of
society and culture in sixteenth-century Nuremberg. I have
brought the book up to date where it has seemed necessary to do
so and added appropriate titles to its bibliography. As I reread my
decade-old text, I find that although I would express myself
differently now on some points, I can stand by the picture I
endeavored to convey of a German city in the epoch between
medieval and modern times.

Bloomington, Indiana 1976   G.S.

CONTENTS

LIST OF ILLUSTRATIONS

Nuremberg in the Sixteenth Century

ONE

Nuremberg: The City and Its History

The Holy Roman Empire—Cities in Germany—Imperial Cities
—Nuremberg: Appearance and Descriptions—The Countryside
and the Forest—The Walls—Churches, Public Buildings,
Houses—Art and Craftsmanship—The Castle—Population Sta-
tistics—Original Settlement and Early History—The Charters
of Privilege—Struggles with the *Burggraf*—The Independent
City—Nuremberg and the Emperors—Bishop and Margrave—
City Leagues and War—The Rebellion of 1349—The Territory
—Robber Barons—The City in the Sixteenth Century.

On a political map of central Europe in the fifteen hundreds,
Germany appears in the motley colors of innumerable juxtaposed
and interpenetrating territorial divisions. The Holy Roman Empire of the German Nation was, throughout the centuries of the
late Middle Ages, a political patchwork of lands only feebly
linked in common acceptance of a nominal imperial authority.
Territories belonging to the great and ancient stem duchies
rubbed the frontiers of bishoprics and archbishoprics whose domains often dwarfed them in power and wealth. Margraviates
and landgraviates, counties and monasteries and abbacies, city-
states and baronies crowded each other and contended for every
spot of ground and clump of cottages. A structure shaped in the
accumulation of a thousand years' historical traditions, the Empire had neither coherence nor focus. Its thirty or so secular
princes, fifty church lords, three thousand cities and towns, and
its legion of imperial knights, counts, and prelates consorted,
competed, and negotiated with constitutional devices and admin-

istrative practices so out of tune with changing times that they occasioned little but complaint from Germans and scorn from foreigners. Every attempt at adjusting this outworn inheritance to the imperatives of political reality seemed destined to fail. All proposals to make the Empire a functioning state or a viable confederation, to reform its cumbersome legislative and administrative institutions, came to grief in the clash of the opposing forces of centralization and particularism. The Empire did not, as did the western nations in these years, undergo a political development in the direction of the centralized state. None of its sovereigns fitted Machiavelli's model of the New Prince who seized all opportunities to convert his throne into a seat of power. Instead, the Empire remained rooted in its traditional ways, "medieval" in structure and operation and in the rhetoric of its self-appraisal.

Still, the land possessed wealth and power in abundance. In population and area Germany was the largest country in Europe. Advances in mining, metal working, and textiles brought the benefits (and also many of the trials) of rapid economic expansion. German merchants were becoming Europe's leading overseas traders; their very names were synonymous with big business and the accumulation of great wealth. The Rhenish gulden and the *Joachimsthaler* stood among the most respected of international coinages. Technological innovations created new industries and transformed old ones. If the Empire itself was powerless to harness these energies, lesser authorities stood ready to make use of them. Princely territories were tautly governed by rulers and bureaucrats bent on creating in their respective domains the very institutions the absence of which made of the Empire a Leviathan without bones. Cities and towns, dispersed throughout the land but most numerous in the west and south, raised their walls and their fine churches as proud signals of autonomy and affluence. If too few men paid serious attention to all this, if the stereotype of the feeble Empire and its shadowy government tended to disparage the entire land in its rich variety, it was not because Germany's attractions were inferior. It was because they were insufficiently known. But from about 1500 on this deficiency, too, was being repaired. Chroniclers, geographers, artists in all parts of the Empire wrote descriptions of towns and regions to

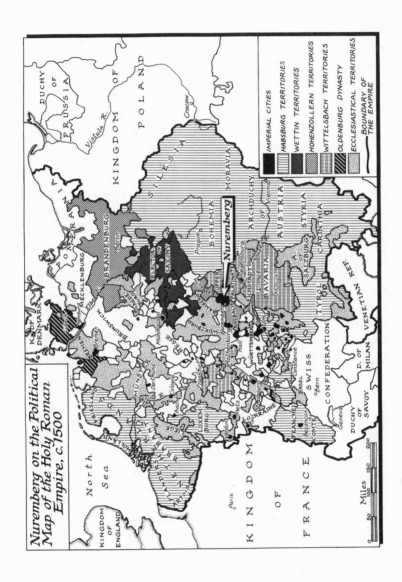

Nuremberg on the Political Map of the Holy Roman Empire, c.1500

inform men of the character of the land, of its natural beauties, its resources, and its sturdy citizens who had made a flourishing society out of the rude country once inhabited by barbarians clad in bearskins.[1]

On one fact, at least, all observers, domestic and foreign, were agreed: the brightest spots in the German landscape were its cities. The delight with which Germans themselves regarded the splendors of their great cities is evident enough in the magnificent city portraits displayed in the geographical and historical volumes that, from about 1500 on, became one of the specialties of the German book industry. First in woodcut, later in copper engraving, the towns appear before the reader in profile to show a striking skyline or in composite view to point out the great public buildings. And it was not only the Germans who took notice. Few visitors to the Empire failed to speak of the magnificence of its larger cities. Some, indeed, wrote at length about them and in detail. If truth were told, said Enea Silvio Piccolomini the Italian man of letters and ecclesiastic (later Pope Pius II), everyone would know that in all Europe no cities equal Germany's in beauty and cleanliness. No grander place than Cologne exists on earth. Strassburg is not inferior to Venice in magnificence and far healthier and more comfortable to live in. German burgher houses would make fine residences for kings and emperors. As for Nuremberg: "What a splendid appearance this city presents! What beauty of location, what learning there, what culture, what a superb government! Nothing is missing to make a perfect civic community. How clean the streets, how elegant the houses!" These are not mere effusions. Enea knew what he was talking about, for he had traveled the length and breadth of the land and seen all that he described.* Half a century later, his compatriot Machiavelli added a political judgment to Enea's compliments. "The power of Germany certainly resides more in her cities than in her princes," he wrote in his *Report on the Affairs of Germany*. These cities he says, "are the real nerve of the Empire." They have plenty of money and they enjoy stable governments; hence they are powerful and free to act. They do

---

* These favorable comments formed part of a treatise that demonstrated how well Germany had fared under the benevolent aegis of the Roman church. See Gerald Strauss, *Manifestations of Discontent in Germany on the Eve of the Reformation* (Bloomington, Indiana, 1971) No. 3.

as they please, fearing neither emperor nor feudal lord. They are self-sufficient, and their excellent political and military institutions render them all but inviolable, while their laws preserve an equitable, public-spirited society.

Machiavelli's reference is not, of course, to all the cities and towns in the Holy Roman Empire. There were more than three thousand of these, though most, at least twenty-five hundred, were townlets of a few hundred inhabitants each. Machiavelli means the imperial cities, more than sixty of them in the late Middle Ages,* which were vastly different each from the other in size, character, organization, and history but identical in the possession of regalian rights that rendered them independent except for a few stipulated and not very burdensome duties to the emperor, such as tax payments, hospitality, a formal oath of allegiance. Theoretically the imperial cities belonged to the Empire, that is to say, not to the person of the reigning sovereign; this is what the designation *civitas imperialis* or *Reichsstadt* was meant to convey: a privileged, practically autonomous body standing in the same immediate political and legal relation to the Empire as the great princely estates. Although imperial cities in this sense had existed in Germany since the early thirteenth century, their constitutional position in the Empire was even in 1500 by no means clear. They were usually invited to participate in imperial diets, but their presence there was not required for proceedings to be valid. Nor did their deputies to the Diet enjoy clearly formulated voting rights. To some extent this inferior status was due to the cities' own unwillingness to place the common interest ahead of the demands of local politics. The narrow and parochial particularism that remained long the bane of German politics was especially pronounced in the habits of those tough, suspicious, secretive urban politicians who remembered so well the long history of bargaining, manipulating, and occasional bloody fighting that had won for their communes their precious freedom of action. Nor did the other estates see fit to welcome the cities on terms equal to those of the older members.

---

* The rolls of the Diet of Worms in 1521 listed eighty-five cities as "free and imperial cities." But of these only about sixty-five were imperial cities in the legal and political sense, that is, immediate subjects of the Empire.

In the feudal assemblies of the *Reichstag*, the burgher representatives were still new men. Their relations with princes secular and spiritual gave them frequent cause for remonstrance. Thus the cities kept to themselves; in fact each kept to itself alone; for aside from occasional agreements to enter a league or form a temporary association, the city preferred to be unfettered by alliances that might compel it to surrender even a small portion of its jealously guarded sovereignty. Its political horizon was narrowly bounded by what its ruling circles considered the city's self-interest. Energies were concentrated on internal affairs: the strengthening of political authority, the maintenance of an economic system providing for all a fair portion of the common wealth, and the preservation of a distinctly urban way of life.

In the long historical view, it would be wrong to see the history of Germany in the late Middle Ages as the history of her major cities. Not only were cities ultimately absorbed in the great territorial states (though in Germany this happened much later than in France and England), but even during the golden age of the medieval city, Germany never had the face of an urban civilization, as did northern and central Italy in its age of Renaissance. City and court were at odds in interests and outlook, in demeanor and style. When the independent city was finally ingested by the aggrandizing princely territory, it fell victim to a power which, however eager to adopt urban techniques of political and economic administration, was alien to the whole spirit of urban culture. However, for a time in the history of the Empire —and this a time of profound and sometimes convulsive changes in German politics and society—the cities arrest the historian's attention. And not the social historian's alone. To the student of political institutions, of public administration, of law and legal process, of financial, military, diplomatic affairs, of church-state relations, and of art, music, letters, and learning, the German city is a fascinating phenomenon.[2]

Of the several hundred cities in the Empire (not counting now the merely nominal ones), perhaps a dozen were real metropolises: Ulm, Cologne, Nuremberg, Strassburg, Augsburg, Lübeck, Hamburg, Frankfurt, and a few others. Among them Nuremberg held a prominent place. No one questioned Nuremberg's standing as one of the two or three preeminent cities in the Empire. Nuremberg's institutions and laws were widely copied, her wealth universally envied. Her politics occasioned interest in the chancelleries of princes and the council chambers of fellow towns. Ambassadors, delegates, businessmen, scholars came from all over Europe to attend imperial diets, to view the display of treasures and relics, confer with the government, buy and sell, consult men of learning, observe Nuremberg's renowned artisans. But while Nurembergers proudly displayed their more obvious municipal attractions, they also kept much to themselves. Contemporaries knew Nuremberg only from the outside: they paced round her walls, conversed with her burghers, tested her products, admired her artifacts. The modern historian is more fortunate in this respect. He can still visit the city (though the fearful destruction of the Second World War has left very little of the old town standing), inspect the handiwork of artisans (this must now be done in museums), and meet citizens in their chronicles, diaries, letters. But he has even richer sources at his disposal: the mass of documents of all kinds accumulated by a government and citizenry to whom orderly procedures had always been habitual and who were sufficiently interested in themselves to save what they had recorded. Using this abundant material, we can know the city from within, as it were. We can sense its moods, even relive the civic life in the minute details of day-to-day existence. This book is based, directly and indirectly, on what has been gathered from these surviving materials. It amounts to a very full story.

We begin with appearances. Let us try to see Nuremberg as contemporaries saw it in the first or second decade of the sixteenth century.

All major cities surrounded themselves with a cushioning ring of rural and forest land, and some towns in Germany attained dominion over a considerable area. Among these, Nuremberg stood in first place. About twenty-five square miles of woods, fields, and villages constituted, at the beginning of the sixteenth century, Nuremberg's territorial domain. Thus a traveler bound for the city entered her administrative jurisdiction a day or so before gaining sight of walls and gates. Throughout the Middle Ages, Nuremberg was enveloped in what natives liked to call a dense forest. Only stands of spindly pines remain of it today, but contemporary drawings do show quantities of deciduous trees among the conifers. This forest, the *Reichswald* as it was called because it had originally been imperial property and been uti-

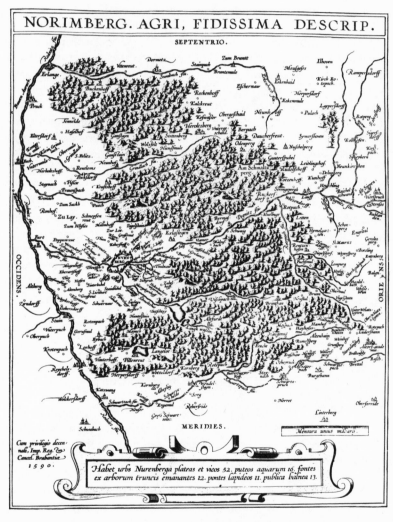

Nuremberg and surroundings in the sixteenth century. From Abraham Ortelius, *Theatrum Orbis Terrarum.*

lized by grant of imperial privilege, came in the course of the fourteenth and early fifteenth centuries into the control of the city, a symbol as well as a prize of her increasing independence. Not only was much agriculture carried on in its numerous clearings, but building stone—the characteristic rose-tinted sandstone of which nearly all the public buildings were made—came from its quarries. The forest harbored glass ovens and charcoal kilns, and it provided firewood and berries and honey from the abundant apiaries scattered throughout. Honey, incidentally, was as early as the thirteenth century the chief ingredient of Nuremberg's famous *Lebkuchen,* and an important source of revenue to the city as well.

Half a mile's distance from the walls the forest comes to a sudden end, and the traveler faces the city. The country roundabout is flat, and the unimpeded prospect must have conveyed an impression of imposing strength and pride. Coming from the north or the northeast, on one of the great commercial roads from Lübeck or Danzig or Breslau, through the northern section of the forest, one saw straight ahead the fortified imperial castle, the *Burg,* set squat on the rocky heights above the city, an enormous pile of fortifications six hundred feet long, surmounted by military and residential structures casting a picturesque outline against the sky. The attractiveness of the scene struck many contemporaries, and the *Burg* on its crest was often painted and described. Beyond the *Burg,* the spires and roof tops of the city appeared closely set within the encircling walls. An even more impressive view, however, offered itself from the south. Approaching from Augsburg or Munich or from the Upper Rhine, through the Lorenz Forest, one saw, as one stepped from the tree line into the open country, the full panorama before one's eyes: the walls with their extensive outworks guarding the gates, the spires of St. Lorenz rising gracefully in the foreground, and those of St. Sebald beyond and to the left, the criss-cross patterns of thousands of red-tiled roofs ascending the slope, and, at the apex of the pyramid, the high gable of the imperial palace in the *Burg* and the huge round keep, one of the oldest parts of the fortress, dominating the entire skyline.

Even in the sixteenth century when men were prosaic about such things, Nuremberg was thought to present an unusually at-

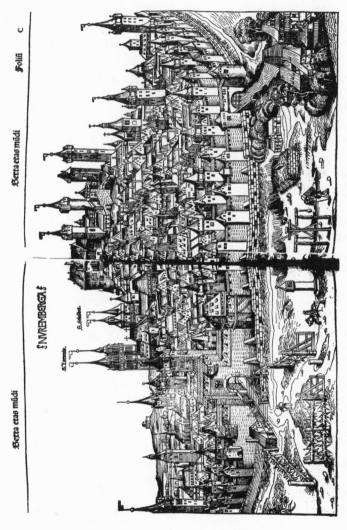

Nuremberg at the end of the fifteenth century. Michel Wolgemut's woodcut for Hartmann Schedel's *Liber Cronicarum* of 1493. The city is seen from the southeast. In the foreground the fortified Ladies' Gate, behind it the two main churches of Sts. Lorenz and Sebald, above the *Burg*. In front of the city walls, the Pegnitz.

tractive appearance. Many visitors and, of course, even more native sons commented on the beauty of the place, an expression much encouraged and occasionally remunerated by the gratified city fathers. Most readers in Germany knew Nuremberg from a really splendid woodcut done in 1493 by Michel Wolgemut for the so-called *Nuremberg Chronicle,* probably the most popular historical book of its time. Its view of Nuremberg is not entirely accurate—a bit of fancy is mixed with much precisely recorded detail—but it does full justice to the city's striking profile. The following decades produced many more such pictures, including some by Dürer who liked to use the view of the *Burg* towering above the town as background for his drawings. And what engravings and woodcuts could not convey was reported in the descriptions of roving city encomiasts who gave to Nuremberg more than her share of flattering words. Much of the praise bestowed on Nuremberg in these verses must, of course, be checked with the facts before it can be accepted at anything like face value. Praising cities was a trade, or at least a profitable avocation, for many an itinerant scholar and artisan, and a city councillor's regard for truth was more quickly outraged by failure to acclaim local attractions than by exaggerating their splendor. A sizable book could be made of the lavish verses in German and Latin addressed to Nuremberg. In fact, it was a local artisan, Hans Rosenplüt, a prolific writer of verse plays and topical rhymes, who is thought to have inaugurated the genre with a lengthy jingle of badly limping verses holding much good description of his city.[3] It is done in the meticulous manner of a miniaturist: glimpses of the one hundred and eighty-seven towers (actually there were not quite that many), the yawning moat, the public granaries, the sixty-seven mills driven by Nuremberg's river, the Pegnitz, the consummate skill of Nuremberg artisans in stone, wood, and metal, and so on.

There are many such poems, some no more than doggerel, others dressed ambitiously in Latin hexameters. Exaggeration and stereotype aside, they are all highly informative. While the native Nuremberger hardly needed to have his blessings counted for him, his government knew that the image cast abroad by these encomia enhanced the city's prestige and speeded the transaction of her far-flung legal and diplomatic enterprises. Thus it must have been highly gratifying that Germany's leading poet and humanist, Konrad Celtis, used his residence in Nuremberg in the 1490's to write a long and wonderfully evocative treatise on Nuremberg, vivid with local color and warmly sympathetic in its description of city life.[4] When the book was put into print in 1502, its author's celebrity assured it wide circulation. Thus, most who came to visit Nuremberg in the sixteenth century expected to see a splendid place, and they were not disappointed. When Jean Bodin, writing in the most important work of political analysis of the sixteenth century, spoke of Nuremberg as "the greatest, most famous, and best ordered of all the imperial cities," he was stating a fact familiar to every informed person.

But back to our exploration of the city. As we cross the open country beyond the forest, our eyes are drawn to the formidable array of walls and towers looming up before us. These walls have a chronicle of their own; indeed, much of the history of medieval towns is contained in the record of their successive fortifications. The protective belt of heavy stone with which the city insured her independence reflected every crisis, every change of fortune in the city's past. Nuremberg's system of walls at this moment in her history was the third in a sequence of circumvallations dating back to the late eleventh or early twelfth centuries. Of the original defenses, linking hilltop fortress and the town huddling on the slope below, not a stone is left, though scholars have been able to trace their probable shape. They fell victim, not to enemy attack, but to the internal pressure of people and dwellings. Knocked down a section at a time they pushed southward across the river, bending in awkward bulges as they strained to include pockets of settlement protruding beyond the old limits. The wider ring shaped by these new constructions was imposing enough: a double wall made of large square sandstone blocks, separated from the surrounding country by a sixty-foot trench. But it was a makeshift system still, nor could it long contain the growing town. Early in the fourteenth century the decision was taken to construct a new belt, the third and, as it turned out, the last, framing the town in the rhomboidal shape it had by now attained. Over a hundred years of building ensued, now sluggishly, now at fever pitch as attack and invasion loomed, in 1427, for example, when the Hussites were feared to be drawing close or in 1449 as the city was locked in a bitter conflict with Margrave Albrecht of Brandenburg. The new walls had a circumference of over seventeen thousand feet, the inner, higher ring was buttressed with eighty-three towers spaced one hundred and fifty feet apart; the outer walls with forty towers. The surrounding trench was one hundred feet wide throughout. Gates and gate towers were added in the 1380's and 1390's; thereafter not a decade went by without some improvement being made or a technical advance incorporated: flanking towers, bastions, pointed stakes sunk at sharp angles into the ground, chains and drop gates, ditches, blockhouses in the grain fields beyond the moat.

In 1452 the great work was complete, and after that it remained substantially intact, except for certain alterations in the 1520's compelled by the increased use of artillery both in attack and defense. Albrecht Dürer's book on fortification, which appeared in 1527, is a reflection of these concerns; indeed, the kind of defenses Dürer proposes and the enormous scale on which he insists they be constructed suggest that his technical grasp, as well as his imagination, were trained by the walls and towers of his native city. The end result of all this building and improving was, even at first sight, so impressive that those who wrote of Nuremberg's fortifications rarely escaped the temptation to exaggerate. Here are the walls as Konrad Celtis saw them, at the close of the fifteenth century:

Nuremberg wears about herself a strong girdle of a three-fold wall and trench. The walls are built of masonry blocks dressed on both sides; the native sandstone used for the purpose is exceedingly soft and easy to break, but once it has been exposed to the air it turns hard as though fired in a kiln. The moat is a good 100 feet wide, and nearly as deep. The ground between the parallel walls is soft and grassy; a little brook runs through it, and deer graze on it. The inner, higher, wall is supported along its entire circumference by two hundred rectangular towers standing equidistant from each other. [Celtis exaggerates here, though other writers inflate the figure even more. Schedel, for example, counts 365, one for each day in the year. Actually, there were never more than 150 towers.] The outer wall stands flush with the rim of the moat, and it has almost as many towers, though they are lower and, where the wall bends, round in shape. The towers are equipped with machines, cannons, and other kinds of artillery. With these weapons the city can withstand any siege. Wall tops are cren-

elated and covered with glazed brick tiles. The inner wall is so thick
that two fully armed men may walk on it side by side. Six large and
two small gates give access to the main roads. Each gate is guarded
by high towers and outworks. The path through the gate is set at an
angle so as to impede enemy advance; it passes an open space surrounded by high walls from which enemies who have penetrated to
this point can be peppered with shot and stones. Heavy chains may
be pulled across the gates and fastened with iron clamps. Vertical bars
and drop gates fitted with needle-sharp bronze spikes can be thrust
down upon invaders and, throwing them to the ground, pierce their
bodies through.

Such gory details illustrating the deadly effectiveness of municipal defenses were expected of city encomiasts, and Celtis was
writing as one. But the picture he presents is, in the main, accurate. Most of its details are borne out by contemporary woodcuts. The moat was wide; the walls and towers were strong and
bristled with equipment ready for battle. If foes should come
near, the city was ready for them, her defenses up to dealing with
the most advanced methods of assault. Yet this was not the only
impression conveyed by walls and towers. The peaceful traveler
was as likely to notice the wooden stairs leading to the upper
tower floors and the balconies marking the stories, the laundry
drying in the breeze, and the household utensils left standing in
the embrasures. For only in emergencies did the defenses accomodate soldiers pointing guns. For peace time they were fitted
out as living quarters, residential space in the city being too
precious to waste altogether on defense.

Thus the city's walls served several purposes and affected her
citizens' lives in many ways. Walls set immovable boundaries to
her interior area and determined property values and the price
of real estate. The need to make repairs and keep the city's defenses abreast of changes in military technology involved all
citizens in labor and taxation. When the Hussites were advancing in the 1420's, all male persons, senior councillors down to boys
of twelve, were called out to do their duty digging in the moat.
In the 1520's, when the trench was widened again and a new
rampart erected, contributions in labor, horses, and money were
imposed on everyone. It was not only that Council and burghers
saw this as a communal duty. They agreed that as little money

as possible should be spent on internal services; for such needs as wall building and trench digging, therefore, citizens were expected to volunteer their labor. To an extent which the subject of a modern state can hardly imagine, the citizen, of a medieval commune was directly involved in the functioning of his community, particularly in its defense. The very presence of an unbroken stone belt, bounding the town and sealing it off against the world outside, was certain to define the citizen's political and social conduct and determine his attitude towards his government. The medieval walled city was an enclave whose citizens lived in a closed and self-contained world, the smallness of which determined their social and political relations, as well as their ideas.

In area, Nuremberg was not large, even by medieval standards. The circumference of the walls, according to a contemporary source, was about eight thousand paces, and a walk from wall to wall, south to north or east to west, across the city took well under half an hour. But within this small space, there were over five hundred streets and thousands of public and private buildings in and around which the city's life unfolded. We must look closely at these buildings if we are to understand the city as a matrix for the thought and actions of men. Let us therefore make our way through Nuremberg, approaching the city from the south and entering at the southeastern gate, the *Frauentor*, or Ladies' Gate, so named after a convent situated nearby.[5]

The moat guarding the walls was, according to most eyewitnesses, wide enough to allow five carts to drive in it side by side. In the early fifteen hundreds it was not as yet protected by the thick clusters of outer bulwarks it was to boast in the next century. On one's way to the city one passed first a small guard house and barricade. The barricade rises and one crosses the moat on a bridge of stout oaken planks. When drawn up by its chains, the bridge fitted into a recess in the gate walls, shutting the opening tight. Heavy beams could be pulled out of holes deep in the walls to bar the doors. But normally one proceeded without hindrance, entering first a walled anterior courtyard, then, passing through a second gate, a spacious inner yard framed by the double walls. This in turn led to the gate tower proper with its twin doors and drop gates.

Plan of Nuremberg in the middle of the sixteenth century. From Matthäus Merian and Martin Zeiller, *Topographia Franconiae*. The Ladies' Gate is in the foreground, just right of center.

Having negotiated this zigzag course and passed the obstacles, we find ourselves in the city. To our right, now, stands
the little convent church of St. Martha; to our left the walled
complex of buildings and yards belonging to the convent of St.
Clara. A number of ways of reaching the inner city lie before
us. We may turn left and walk through narrow alleys by the
wall, under the covered sentry walks and close to the arcaded
arches. It would take us past the Carthusian monastery, Nuremberg's largest, a walled compound including a church and extensive gardens, to the Spittler Gate at the southwestern side of the
city. Or we can walk east, past the convent of St. Catherine
where, in the sixteenth century, the mastersingers held their singing schools. The river enters the city in two branches there,
leaving between them a little island, the Schütt, a sparsely settled elongated tongue of land serving the citizens as park and
common for walking and for games. The entrance of the river
necessitated a breach in the walls at this point, but an ingenious
system of devices had been constructed to meet the dangers of
invasion. Bastions of square stones support the walls, and iron
bars stretch across the water from tower to tower, while posts
sunk in the river bed, and long rails affixed to them, protect the
defenses from enemy attack by water as well as from natural
damage by drifting ice. Looking upstream from the top of the
bastion, a more peaceful scene meets the eye: neatly tilled acres
stretching to the edge of the forest, the fields separated by low
walls and picket fences. The river shore is dotted with grist and
saw mills utilizing this natural source of power.

The most direct way to the inner city lies along the broadest
street of the southern half of the city, called Königstrasse today,
but then not bearing a particular name. Streets, unless associated
with one of the town's distinctive economic or social groups—
Blacksmiths' Street, Tanners' Street, Basinmakers' Street, Jews'
Alley, Clothmakers' Street, and so on—were named after well-
known public places or structures located on them, as "at the
brewery," "below St. Lorenz's." Or they bore simple descriptive
tags: Long Street or Broad Street. The main thoroughfare from
the Ladies' Gate to the center of the city was referred to as "at
the Ladies' Gate" in the vicinity of the gate, then it became "near
St. Martha's," and "above St. Lorenz's" as it approached the parish

church. A most imposing structure stands on the lower part of this street, the enormous pile of the *Kornhaus,* a storage building put up around the year 1500 by Hans Behaim, the city's *Werkmeister* (the master mason in charge of the technical aspects of municipal construction) to assure the city of an adequate supply of wheat at all times and enable it to control the price. It stands rooted in the bottom of the older moat and has extensive cellar halls with vaulted ceilings to accomodate loaded carts and their teams of horses. The huge gabled roof holds six storage floors for laying out the grain.

Moving on, we pass the great municipal arsenal, also anchored in the old moat. The street narrows considerably where it crosses the line of the old wall belt and reaches the older part of the city. We pass a block of private houses, and then, ahead of us, rises the church of St. Lorenz.

Nothing in Nuremberg represents as well the fusion of civic pride and religious devotion so characteristic of medieval cities as the two parish churches built in the thirteenth and fourteenth centuries. Of the two, the *Lorenzkirche* is the younger. Its nave and choir were built in the late thirteenth century; the façade with its grandiose rose window and the two towers date from the fourteenth. The east choir was not completed until the very late 1400's. One must sit in this church for an hour or two in order to see Nuremberg's lovely reddish sandstone at its best. The changing light refracted by the colored prisms in the windows imparts to the stone a subtle and warm glow that mitigates the forbidding dimensions of the church and warms the atmosphere. Side naves hold numerous small chapels, placed there in the late fourteenth century by patrician families who considered private services more appropriate than participation in public worship to their position in the town. There the Imhofs and Rehlingers prayed at handsome altars carved and painted by some of Nuremberg's best artists, enjoying a privacy and splendor befitting both their station in life and their gratitude to God for having secured it for them. It was patrician munificence, also, that brought to the church an abundance of plastic and painted decorations: scenes of sin and salvation above the great entrance portals, a sixty-foot tall limestone tabernacle by Adam Krafft, a lovely Annunciation by Veit Stoss, and much else. No citizen

Church of St. Lorenz, façade.

could kneel long in this edifice without acknowledging, grate-
fully, the twin obligations that defined his loyalty and directed
his conduct: to God in heaven and to the great ones of the world
whom God had set over him.

From the Church to the river the ground descends rather
steeply, a fact not unimportant in the life of the city, as it prevented the flood waters of the Pegnitz from rising to the houses
of the southern parish. At least once a year, near the end of winter, the river rose above its bed, forcing the inhabitants of the
northern bank, where the ground is level, to retire to upstairs
rooms, where they received supplies by boat until the flood sub-
sided. Along the sloping street north of St. Lorenz, a large group
of buildings extending to the river comprises the Franciscan
monastery, founded in the thirteenth century on this spot, which
was then just outside the walls but had gradually been engulfed
among the houses of the growing city. Monks and priests did not,
of course, hold themselves aloof from the noise and the smells
and the traffic of the town, and their churches and monasteries
were not then hushed and serene places set apart. The Gothic
church of the Franciscans towers above a host of shops and
booths and trestle tables that announce the proximity of the main
market square just across the river.

Before crossing over, we may turn west for a moment and
walk along the tiny tributary of the Pegnitz called the *Fischbach*.
This rivulet had since the thirteenth century made its way
through the southern parish, running in an artificial bed lined
with slabs of sandstone and strengthened by transfusions from
suburban ponds. Its purpose was to bring water to butchers, tanners, dyers, and other crafts depending on it. The *Fischbach* runs
through several busy streets, driving a score of mills and crossed
by numerous footbridges. Bucket wells line its sides. In the west
it approaches one of the relics of Nuremberg's former wall, a tall
rectangular tower, the so-called White Tower. Still further west
and on the site of what used to be a suburb before the final extension of the walls, stand the extensive properties of the Knights
of St. John, originally a hospital dedicated to St. Elisabeth (hence
the name of the gate nearby: *Spittlertor*, or Hospitaler's Gate).
The Order's church, St. James, is surrounded by a walled yard; a
long enclosed bridge connects it with the main building in the

A group of artisans' houses. Such extremely narrow street frontage was not uncommon. It was due to the high ground taxes imposed by the city.

Order's compound. A high wall surrounds the entire enclave, shutting in living quarters, stables, storage barns, several court-yards, a small arsenal, orchards and gardens, in other words, a self-contained little community.

Between these splendid buildings and the western wall rise blocks of more modest burgher houses, many of them presenting a peculiar aspect in their extremely narrow frontage, sometimes barely wide enough for one vertical row of windows, three stories high. The streets, however, are broad and airy, and lined with trees.

Most of us harbor entirely wrong notions about the conditions of life in a medieval city, misconceptions probably derived more from reading about working class slums in the eighteenth cen-tury than from the evidence of the Middle Ages. In fact, though people lived in a state of proximity unacceptable to modern suburbanites, density was not high. The great majority of houses in Nuremberg, as in other cities, were one-family dwellings, and an average household probably included not more than four or five persons. While many streets were narrow, and an occa-sional crooked alley left something to be desired in freshness of air, there were also many open spaces and, within a few minutes' walk from every house in the city, grassy plains, shrubs and lime trees, groves to refresh eyes and restore lungs. The city architect was expected to keep his eye on these places of recreation: dis-eased trees were quickly replaced, and a man was employed to care for the deer and other animals grazing in the open areas of the trench.[6] At the point where we had just stopped, the wall turns sharply northeast toward the river, and if we mount to its top and look out, we will see that the entire moat has been planted with fruit trees. It makes a pretty picture, as do the walled orchards and summer houses belonging to burgher fam-ilies. On holidays this was the scene of shooting matches and athletic contests, and it was a favorite place for walking, as the remaining sections of the moat are to this day.

But let us go to the other side of the river now. Immediately to the right of the bridge we see one of the handsomest build-ings in all Nuremberg, the Hospital of the Holy Ghost founded in the early fourteenth century by a wealthy philanthropist as a refuge for elderly people who through no fault of their own had become indigent. When space in the old building became inadequate in the early decades of the sixteenth century, Hans Behaim produced here one of the most successful of the many alterations of existing buildings which were his specialty. Crossing the bridge (a wooden bridge: Nuremberg boasted only one stone bridge in the sixteenth century) and continuing straight on, we reach in a few steps the center of the city's business life, the main market square. In all likelihood, a market place had existed on this spot from the earliest days of the town's history, but the big square required by the commercial and political needs of a large and industrious population was the result of a number of clearing actions, the most radical of them performed in the middle of the fourteenth century, the destruction of the old Jewish quarter and synagogue which had occupied the eastern part of what then became the market. A description of the old market before these alterations were made pictures it as cramped and cluttered with stalls and small booths. All this was swept away. Where the synagogue had stood, a chapel, dedicated to the Virgin (as in all such cases where a Christian church replaced a razed synagogue) was built in the 1350's, partly with money collected as pious donations from people who had been spared from the terrible plague of the previous decade. Behind the church are long, low masonry halls for the use of produce sellers. Stalls and sheds stand about everywhere. Only the great square itself is left unobstructed. Some of Nuremberg's stateliest houses line its sides, the homes of the Pirckheimer, Schürstab, and Frey on the west, others on the south.

Here, too, stands the town hall, on the northern rim of the square, built there in the middle of the fourteenth century after several moves from less satisfactory locations in smaller buildings. Only a labyrinthine system of subterranean passages and cubicles, prison cells bearing the fitting name of *Loch* (hole), is nowadays evidence of the earliest structure, for in the fifteenth century the building was subjected to many renovations. Around 1500 the street floor accommodated various shops; above them was the Council Chamber, the administrative heart of the city. There, on narrow benches along the walls of the rectangular room, sat the members of Council when meeting; facing them from behind a table covered with green baize sat the two governing mayors and their secretaries. Next door was a magnificent eighty-foot-long great hall giving more evidence of Nuremberg's wealth and influence. In this splendid room, in the glow of hundreds of candles and amid the opulence of tapestries and paintings and frescoes designed by Albrecht Dürer, the government staged receptions, the gentry held their dances, and patrician offspring celebrated their weddings. We even hear of tournaments mounted there and in one instance of a horse race to entertain a distinguished guest. In this hall, also, the elections to the Council took place at Eastertime each year, and Holy Roman emperors held court when visiting the city. Adjacent to the great hall was a chamber for the exclusive use of elder councillors, a superbly appointed room lined with hangings and paintings, among them Dürer's "Four Apostles", which the master presented to the Council in 1526. Other rooms contained the treasury, archives, and space for the building's steward.

From the outside, the town hall was plain and undistinguished, in keeping with the city's prevalent domestic architecture and its ruling class's general disinclination to make a display of wealth. On the market square too, there is only one conspicuous structure, the *Schöne Brunnen,* a tall gilded ornamental fountain in the shape of a pyramid decorated with stone figures representing heroes and prophets from the Old and New Testaments and pagan antiquity. At this point, turning east, we enter a residential quarter of comfortable artisans and well-to-do burghers. Draw wells stand at intervals in the middle of the streets. (According to contemporary accounts Nuremberg had over a hundred of these cisterns, not to mention the dozen or so *"Röhrkästlein",* or pipe fountains.) The streets themselves justify the compliments which they elicited from many visitors. They form picturesque intersections and bend in graceful arcs, often shaped by the custom of medieval builders to advance the façade of each house a step beyond its next-door neighbor's in order to accommodate a side window or two in each story. All this may be seen on any one of the street maps and models that have come down to us from the fifteenth and sixteenth centuries. What the plans and models do not show are the compost heaps and the swarms of scavenger pigs being driven to the Pegnitz to drink, the latter a traditional public nuisance turned into private good fortune when chimneys were hung with a year's supply of hams and bacon. In any case, the squealing and the smells and the debris underfoot did not seem to distract visitors from the attractiveness of the street scene.

It was not the street itself, of course, that was beautiful but the houses lining the roadway on both sides, especially patrician houses. From the outside these dwellings look simple enough. A plain façade of square stones, only occasionally broken by a small belvedere or corner effigy, gives little notice, except in its generous dimensions, of the wealth and position of the occupants. To one who penetrates inside, however, the position and affluence of these burghers is immediately obvious. A large outer gate generally opens onto a courtyard from where one sees that the house in whose center one now stands is in reality not one, but several structures: an anterior building facing the street, a posterior one to the rear, separated from the first by the courtyard and connected to it by means of open galleries or, often, a third, lateral building. Each component has its own roof, the courtyard is left open. Wooden balconies admit light and, by way of stairways, access to the two or three stories above the ground. Standing on the cobbled pavement of such a yard one can sense even today the activity, the coming and going that must have characterized life in such an elaborate domestic establishment: members of the family giving directions to the servants, gates opening and shutting to admit wagon loads of goods for the master's firm whose offices and storerooms were located on the street floor and in the cellars beneath. Seen from the courtyard, the house must have presented the aspect of the self-contained little community it was, having within its compound all that was necessary to life and business, even its own well. Behind the ornately carved ballustrades of the galleries lay dozens of rooms and corridors ranging from narrow passages and closets and servants' cubicles under the eaves to state rooms where the family entertained, and to lavish bed chambers fitted out to indulge a desire for comfort tempting even to our modern taste for luxury. Most of the city's houses were, needless to say, simpler than this —street-floor rooms nearly always holding a workshop (Albrecht Dürer's ground floor, for example, held a printing shop), above them two stories of simple wood-paneled living and sleeping

Dürer House. Albrecht Dürer purchased this house in 1509 and resided in it until his death in 1528. It was built some time after 1400.

rooms. But most were snug and comfortable, and roomy enough for a family with two or three children, a servant or two, and space to spare.[7]

What is most striking to the modern mind accustomed to accepting the claims of speed and efficiency as paramount, is the loving, time-consuming care lavished on the little objects of daily use. Hinges, locks, door panels, weather vanes, stove tiles are works of art—not art, of course, in the modern sense that makes the artist's handiwork an object of reverence rather than use, but art in the tradition which finds the beauty of an object in the pleasure derived from handling it. Everyday things were endowed with as much dignity and grace as fine materials and carefully nurtured, unhurried craftsmanship could bestow on them. It was a source of great pleasure and boasting to Nurembergers that their city gave employment to so many makers of fine objects, and this pride engendered the civic sense that led burghers to give commissions to native artisans to decorate the city and its public buildings with the best products of their workshops. Among these commissioned objects were some works of genius: the tomb of St. Sebald by Peter Vischer, and Adam Krafft's "Tabernacle", and Veit Stoss' "Annunciation". But even more characteristic, and in their unpretentious ways equally attractive, are corner madonnas and saints and Adam Krafft's relief sculpture adorning the gate of the public scale near the market square and illustrating the weighing process, or the "Stations of the Cross", seven large stone reliefs commissioned from Krafft at the end of the fifteenth century by a private citizen and posted here and there within the city and on the way to St. John's cemetery beyond the northwestern gate. A walk around the town brings discovery of innumerable such objects, the products of a characteristically medieval combination of private devotion, civic mindedness, and seasoned craftsmanship.

But to return to our exploration. Just north of the market place and west of the town hall, we see rising ahead of us the great east choir of St. Sebald, the parish church of the northern half of the city. Sebald himself was, according to the traditional version of his life, an eleventh-century Danish prince who, turning his back on country and bride, obtained a preaching mission from the Pope and appeared in the forest around Nuremberg

Church of St. Sebald, façade.

Church of St. Sebald from the south, showing the great hall choir, surrounded by the houses of the northern parish.

where he performed a number of miracles. When he died, the legend goes on, his body was placed on an ox cart and the draft animals encouraged to proceed on their own. Where they stopped, a chapel was erected to honor the holy man. Even in the fifteenth century considerable doubt touched the facts of this matter. Sebald had never been canonized, nor his relics everywhere accepted as genuine. In 1425, on the occasion of the transfer of the imperial regalia to Nuremberg, the government made a renewed effort to have its local hero recognized by a papal bull of canonization, and this time successfully. Notwithstanding the many previous denials, the city's request was now granted, but the grounds on which the affirmative decision was based were largely practical: the Church of St. Sebald is Nuremberg's chief house of worship; the anniversary of Sebald's death has been annually commemorated, on August 19, for many years; his name is already listed in prayer books and breviaries among those of the other saints; churches and shrines bearing his name have received papal indulgences. Thus Martin V agreed to make official what had long been popularly accepted, and the remains in their ornate silver casket were now declared to be relics of a saint.

The church which bears Sebald's name and holds his tomb dates in its earliest parts from about the middle of the thirteenth century, the grand purpose of sponsors and builders being to erect a structure large and splendid enough to match the great charter which Emperor Frederick II had awarded the city's merchants in 1219. Of this original structure, the central basilica with its narrow nave and squat pillars still stands. Apostle figures, stiff and inexpressive in the old style, cling to the pillars. The pressure of population, however, soon led here as elsewhere to expansion: two Gothic side naves were added in the early fourteenth century, and, in the 1360's, an immense east choir, a hall choir of grandiose proportions opening from the nave like a forest seen from the mouth of a cavern: three broad naves and ambulatory, lit by tall windows of beautifully colored glass to make the rose-colored sandstone glow like fire, in sharp contrast to the pallid limestone of the old basilica. Late in the fifteenth century the two old towers were raised by the addition of belfries and these topped with peaked caps to balance the roof of the east choir towering above the old steeples. The resulting edifice presents the spectator with the usual mixture of styles and proportions. But this casualness toward the dictates of form is the strength of the medieval church, and one never really realizes it until one sees the building in its setting. Having walked through the town, enter St. Sebald by its side door and walk down the nave toward the great choir. The impact will be striking, and this, of course, was intended by those who designed the building and its extensions. Material, decoration, light, and above all space, combine to praise the Creator who makes all things possible, acclaim the achievements of the commune, and record its insoluble link with the past.

Outside, however, all refers to the present. The great portals of the church face the wine market, the nucleus of the northwestern quarter of the city. To this large square come the carts of vintners from the Main and Neckar regions, entering the city by the New Gate in the western wall. The wine itself was, in the sixteenth century, stored in the halls of a capacious building beside the river. Several footbridges cross the river southward to the St. Lorenz parish, and there are a number of mills along the banks. A tiny island in the middle of the stream holds the *Säumarkt* where the pork butchers work on trestle tables. All the slaughtering and trimming was done there and in sheds along the north bank of the Pegnitz (which received and carried off the blood and waste parts of the carcasses), until the construction of a large municipal slaughterhouse in the late sixteenth century removed these gory activities from sight.

Moving on northward through a rectangular square bordered by substantial burgher houses and, directly behind, some narrow streets of small two-story artisan dwellings, we reach, ascending, one of the best residential quarters of the city, the streets around the dairy market. Here stand commodious town houses inhabited by some of Nuremberg's most substantial merchants, superb buildings with arcaded ground floors and three tall stories above, broad enough for four or five windows on each level, the whole building surmounted by tall tiled roofs with corbie-stepped gables and three tiers of dormer windows. From this point on the streets and alleys rise sharply to scale the rocky heights of Nuremberg's eminence, the Castle Rock. Turning about face before

View of the northwestern section of Nuremberg toward the *Burg*.

beginning the ascent, one sees the panorama of the city spread out below: criss-cross lines of sharply angled brick roofs descending in tiers to the river, then rising again, step-like, on the other side. The field of tiled roofs makes a deep impression on the spectator; many visitors described it, a feast for the eyes, ever changing in its colors and shadows as the clouds pass across the sky.

Turning north again we face, close up now, the pinnacle of the city's sky line, the *Burg*. From such proximity, what impress one most are the gigantic fortress walls rising vertically from the natural rock to the level of the castle. Above the walls beckon the towers and roofs of the castle buildings, familiar as our landmarks during the entire walk northward through the city. Though architecturally undistinguished, the *Burg* has an interesting history. Its origins go back to the eleventh century when the Salian emperor Henry III built a rude fortress on top of the hill and installed a castellan or *Burggraf* to look after his interests. Utilizing the many opportunities available in that time of self-help, this official soon emerged as a potent lord with substantial territorial possessions roundabout. Frederick I, recognizing the facts, left him in permanent possession of the original fortress. For himself, the emperor ordered built on the western ledge of rock above the city, a new castle and a mausoleum.

In 1377, unsure of the intentions of the ambitious *Burggraf*, and to provide themselves with means of action should their suspicions prove justified, the citizens erected a lookout post near the wall on the eastern slope of the rock, tall enough for an observer standing on top to spy on activities in the *Burggraf's* residence—an expedient leading to a great deal of bickering between *Burggraf* and town. Of the original structures on the hill, only a pentagonal keep, queerly shaped to suit the contour of its site, gives evidence of the fortress' antiquity. In the fifteenth century it was equipped with a peaked roof and wooden balconies from where the *Burggraf's* men could inspect the city while the city's men on their look-out were watching the *Burggraf*. This tower is the only remainder of the eleventh-century fortress. The other buildings of the *Burggraf's* residence were burned to the ground in 1420, and never restored. Later in the fifteenth century Hans Behaim constructed another one of his big storage buildings on the open space between the keep and the look-out. It is an imposing edifice and looks like an integral part of the *Burg*, as Behaim intended it should. But it really has nothing to do with the castle, though its ground floor occasionally accommodated the horses and equipment of visiting dignitaries.

Nearby stands the tallest structure in the *Burg*, and the highest point in the city, a lofty round tower built in the twelfth century as a second and larger keep, hence originally accessible only through an opening halfway up. Its upper stories offer an imposing view of the country, a point of military importance, for, as Dürer wrote in his book on fortifications, from the top of such a tower "the whole plain can be seen afar in every direction, so that nothing can stir unperceived, and signals can be given from there by hoisting baskets, smoke, gunshots, or fire."

The *Burg* proper, or *Kaiserburg* as it is called, after its imperial occupants, lies west of the round tower. Stables, kitchens, living quarters, and turrets built into the fortifications surround an outer courtyard in the midst of which stands a structure housing the castle's only well, driven one hundred and fifty feet straight down through the rock. A gate admits into the walled court. On the left, we see the imperial residence, a late Gothic building put up in the 1440's for the Emperor Frederick III and frequently enlarged and altered thereafter. Here Maximilian I lived for nearly six months in 1491, and the expected arrival of Charles V in 1520 set the burghers to renovating the private and public quarters thoroughly. But despite all this up-dating the castle's rooms never lost their spartan character. Compared to the size and comfort of the burgher houses in the city below, the rooms in the castle—even the great hall with its fine open beam ceiling—are bare, uncomfortable, and cold. There is a double chapel, one above the other, the upper level for the emperor and his party, the lower for lesser men. From the top of the castle walls outside, one gets a good look at the castle hill's strongest defenses, huge solid intersecting triangles of square blocks of masonry with overhanging ledges, protected by a wide curving moat. In the 1530's and 1540's, the City Council brought in the Sicilian military enigneer Antonio Fazuni to construct these walls in order to protect the western exposure of the *Burg* where the ground rises gently almost to the level of the castle yard. A network of subterranean passages inside the casemates connects the *Burg* with the town hall and various points inside and outside the city.

We leave the *Burg*, walking by Behaim's granary and the look-out, down the eastern slope of the rock. Just south, at the foot of the hill, lie the thirteenth-century monastery and church of the Benedictines, a square court surrounded by a cloister. Immediately behind rises a former gate tower, popularly called the "*Schlagturm*" after its mechanical clock which activated a bell to sound the hours of the working day. The descent continues to the easternmost bulge of the city, a quarter in which large solid patrician houses alternate with gardens and orchards. Not many years earlier, this quarter had been a suburb with farms and herb gardens and pavilions belonging to the well-to-do, but in the early years of the sixteenth century, the garden houses had grown into stone mansions designed according to Renaissance ideas now making their way up from Italy to merge, sometimes rather strangely, with the native building tradition. Most notable among these mansions is the Tucher House, built in the 1530's for Lorenz Tucher, member of one of the stellar commercial and political families of the city. It is a concrete symbol, one among many such, of the slow passage of the burgher patriciate into a titled aristocracy. From the Tucher House, a short walk through gardens and orchards brings us to the eastern wall in the vicinity of the Lauffer Gate. A few steps south and we reach the river again. Across it and continuing along the wall, a few minutes' walk brings us back to the Ladies' Gate where we started our exploration.

So much for streets and buildings. What of the men and women living and working in them? It seems fairly certain that around 1500 Nuremberg numbered some 25,000 souls, but a few words of explanation are needed before this figure becomes meaningful. There is nothing in the history of German town life to compare with the frequent population counts to which the medieval Italian communes subjected their citizens.[8] The lists of arms bearers and grain consumers, the thirteenth-century *Libri focorum* of Perugia, Padua, Pistoia, the property assessments and inventories of real estate holdings, the registers of baptisms and funerals—these have no equivalents in the Empire, at least not before the seventeenth century. Not until the Protestant Reformation were parish registers kept; only after the greater princely territories had succeeded in depriving municipal governments of much of their autonomy in the course of the seventeenth century was demography considered a part of political responsibility. Thus early population statistics are generally unreliable and fluctuate wildly from source to source, some vastly exaggerated, like Celtis' 52,000 for Nuremberg, given in his *Description* of 1502 and derived by him from the known annual grain consumption of the entire city, divided by the assumed amount eaten by a single individual in the course of a year. How naively even the learned men of the time thought about such matters may be seen from Celtis' additional figure of 4000 births a year. If true, this would have implied a total population nearly double his own reckoning, which is itself more than twice too large.

Actually, few German cities in the early sixteenth century could claim a population larger than 20,000. Cologne may have had about 30,000, but it was the largest city in Germany. Ulm, Strassburg, Hamburg, Lübeck, Nuremberg had 20,000, slightly more or less. Most other towns were much smaller. Augsburg had about 18,000, Frankfurt on the Main some 10,000, Mainz 5000 or 6000, Leipzig less than 5000, Dresden perhaps 2500. For large cities in the modern sense, one must go outside the Empire to Florence (80,000 in 1520), Milan (about 85,000), London (over 50,000 in the reign of Henry VIII), Paris (more than 200,000 in 1500), Naples (some 230,000 at the same time). Beside such metropolises, German cities were midgets, a contrast reflected not only in area and appearance but also in institutions, as we shall see. Population size and characteristics exert, of course, a direct bearing on society. It is not only the formal structure of a community that reflects demographic facts and trends but also the habitual and instinctive ways of a human group, its mood and outlook, the varieties of social coalescence. All these are influenced, some scholars would say determined, by the relationship of space to numbers of people.

As it happens, one of the few precise censuses taken in

medieval Germany was done in Nuremberg in the middle of the fifteenth century. The occasion was provided by a military threat, usually the impetus to count bodies for manning the walls and mouths to be fed. Thus in 1431, after an imperial diet meeting in Nuremberg had declared war on the Hussites, the City Council ordered the six municipal quartermasters to count all males between the ages of 18 and 60. The city was covered house by house and men capable of bearing arms were listed, altogether 7146 of them, a figure from which students of population can determine with fair reliability the total number of people in the city, probably 22,000.

Much more precise, however, than this enumeration, in fact outstanding among early German censuses for its accuracy, is a population count undertaken in 1449 and 1450 when Margrave Albrecht Achilles of Brandenburg, Nuremberg's traditional enemy, began a war of attrition against the city by cutting off all access to it. As soon as the Margrave's declaration of feud had reached the city, the Council placed a ceiling on the price of grain and instructed each home owner to store a certain amount of it under his roof. Six months later, when no end to the conflict was in sight, the Council further ordered a precise numbering of citizens and other residents to discover how long the accumulated stores would last. Once again the city, now divided into eight administrative "quarters," was surveyed door by door. Information based on sworn evidence was obtained in each house and drawn up in registers. All men, women, and children who inhabited the city at this particular time were listed: male and female citizens and their children, male and female servants, peasants fled behind the walls from their exposed villages, clerics, Jews, resident aliens. The resulting official count must have been exceedingly accurate, for in this particular situation no householder would have reported fewer individuals than he had to provide for, while the census takers must have taken great care to check suspiciously high figures so as not to be deceived into allocating excessive supplies. The grand total thus obtained came to 28,378 or, if one adds to this the number of infants not included in the survey, a sum of 30,131 people. Of these, however, 9912 were refugees without permanent residence in the city. Subtracting these, one gets a permanent population of 20,219, of which, the census informs us, 446 were members of religious orders and their retainers, 150 were Jews and their servants, and 1800 were resident aliens, itinerant artisans, and day laborers with permission to live and work in the city.

In all likelihood, this figure of 20,219 represented a decline from the population of the early part of the century, but the 1430's and 1440's had been a time of wars and epidemics and consequent population loss to the city by death and emigration. It seems, indeed, that the villages and hamlets outside the walls had collected a good many of the stricken who fled the city or were driven away. In 1407, following a Council decision to levy a common penny upon all subjects, three patrician commissioners spent two months riding through Nuremberg territory counting heads. In all they found and listed 14,576 adults. Something like 5000 under 15 should be added to this figure for a total rural population of about 20,000 subjects. Some of them lived very close to the walls and came to the city daily to ply their trades; day laborers, beggars, free-lance prostitutes and an amorphous floating population inhabited the villages nearest the city. For these rural subjects the City Council was no less responsible than for its cocitizens. Indeed, the dependent countryside had not long before been organized into districts and given an administration to bind it more firmly to the city's purposes and the Council's direction.

A population of 25,000 or so, with another 20,000 living in close proximity and tied to the city's life in many ways, made Nuremberg one of the half-dozen major urban centers in the Empire, an eminent position reflected, as we have already observed, in architectural splendor, and expressed abundantly in the self-confidence that characterized business and political life. Elsewhere in the Empire, critics and apocalyptic preachers intoned a call for self-examination and a change of heart. In Nuremberg the voices of doom were muted. And no wonder. Never had the city's fortunes stood higher or her future looked so bright. While reformers and prophets searched the past for an Eden of lost opportunities and abandoned innocence, the burghers of Nuremberg saw no reason to doubt that the sixteenth century would be their city's golden age.

When projected against the historical past, especially the distant past, Nuremberg's rise to wealth and power does seem remarkable.[9] Inconspicuously and unfavorably situated in an infertile region whose hills bear no vineyards, on a stream that supports no shipping, the town owed her existence to nothing more than that red sandstone rock rising above the firs and the swampy soil. Just who and what it was that first occupied the rock is something of a mystery. Much controversy has been stirred up by local chroniclers over this question, and each generation of scholars has had its favorite founding fathers. To the humanists, classical or at least tribal Germanic foundation was axiomatic: a Roman fort built on the rock by Tiberius Claudius Nero, hence Neronberg; a settlement established by one Norik or Noricus, an alleged son of Hercules; an asylum built by the Narisci or Noriker, a Celtic tribe uprooted by the Huns. As facts were hard to come by, legends sprang up to fill the void: Attila was said to have sacked the town. St. Boniface erected a chapel on the future site of the Church of St. Sebald. Charlemagne liked to hunt in the surrounding woods and used the town as his lodging place. Otto I held an imperial diet there in 938. And so on.

Actually, nothing is known of Nuremberg's ancient history, even the meaning of its name is problematical; its root has been variously identified as Slavic, Celtic, and Germanic. The most likely explanations derive the name from Germanic *Nurung*, cleared land, thus *Nureberg*: cleared mountain; or from *Nuorringberg*, a sacred mountain, a place consecrated to Odin in Germanic times. Shadowy as these pieces of information are, Nuremberg chroniclers were not disposed to abandon any claims to the antiquity of their town. It was the Prussian historians of the eighteenth century, arguing on behalf of Hohenzollern claims to Nuremberg, who dispelled these mists of wishful mythology by laying bare the total silence of medieval chroniclers before the late eleventh century on matters relating to the town. The earliest written reference occurs in 1050 in a document issued by Emperor Henry III while residing at Nuremberg. The place could not have been only just founded; on the other hand, twenty-five years earlier another emperor, Konrad II, had taken up residence in a nearby village, which he probably would not have done had there been a better abode nearby. All this seems to suggest that the first crude structures later to be enlarged into the *Burg* were erected around 1030 as a military and administrative nucleus for the surrounding regions.

What probably happened was this: the territory in question belonged to the Salian emperors. In order to protect their interests, they ordered a fortified residence built on the steep sandstone rock above the Pegnitz River. The pentagonal tower described above dates from this earliest phase of the building history of *Burg* and town. Into this outpost the emperors placed an official, called *castellanus* or *comes* or *burgravius,* to govern the strong place, keep its ramparts in repair, conserve and enforce the imperial rights in the region. To do this job he needed a small band of men stationed with him, also servants and retainers. This little establishment, in turn, required the labor of peasants, and these were soon found among Bavarian and other settlers who had moved into the region sometime in the early eleventh century when the Bishopric of Bamberg was organized to undertake the colonization of the Slav-infested territories of Franconia.

Around this nucleus of fighting and farming men the town began to accrete, the functions of its oldest citizens recorded in the names of the passageways framed by their cottages close to the *Burg:* Soldiers' Alley, Blacksmiths' Alley, Shopkeepers' Alley, and so on. Merchants tended to settle down in groups (Henri Pirenne has shown how this habit originated in the commercial demands and opportunities of the tenth and eleventh centuries[10]) and always attached themselves to some already existing center of activities, an episcopal seat, a monastery, or a fortress. This happened in Nuremberg. Houses rose on the slope from the base of the rock down to the Pegnitz. Walls were built and a moat excavated. As the original strong place on the hill became inadequate, and also in order to allow his by now hereditary *Burggraf* to inhabit the old *Burg* as his own residence, Emperor Frederick I built a larger castle-like structure on the western plateau of the rock, including residence, chapel, crypt, and fortifications. This imperial castle was placed in the charge of another official, whose office, however, was confined to the management of the buildings. The *Burggraf* himself held on to his governing and judicial role in the territory roundabout. Since he could not be expected to live on the dignity of his office alone, he was awarded certain rights and incomes guaranteed in imperial charters, a portion of the fines collected in the town courts, a penny's tribute from every smithy, rents and harvest help from every household south of the Pegnitz, every third head of game, every third tree cut in the forest, a portion of traffic tolls, and a few others. The *Burggraf* also held direct jurisdiction over a number of villages, monasteries, and fortified places in the neighborhood. No wonder that Nurembergers began to resent this network of carefully defined and hereditary rights, which hemmed and restricted them, while the *Burggraf* scorned the shopkeepers of the town below his perch as grasping schemers and upstarts and sought to protect his interests by using all means, from war to legal chicanery, to keep the burghers in their place. It was not the fault of the *Burggraf,* nor the merit of the burghers, that changing times favored merchants and artisans rather than feudal barons.

The stages in Nuremberg's ascent from settlement to city are marked by grants of privileges gradually transforming a motley cluster of dependent persons into a self-governing and practically independent commune. As an imperial foundation, the town and its residents belonged to the reigning emperor; administrative functions were considered to be carried on by his delegation; moneys collected were his; authority and essential prerogatives remained in his hands. Artisans worked at their trade and merchants shipped their goods under the emperor's protection, a benefit for which they owed him fees, and this relationship defined not only their activities but their legal standing as well and that of their town. Being by law the emperor's men, the townspeople could do what they did and be what they were or wanted to be only by grant of privilege.

A number of factors converged to make it necessary or advisable for emperors (and, in the case of other communities, for bishops and territorial rulers) to allow their powers to slip away from the crown into the hands of townsmen. Economic developments, disputed successions and investiture struggles, contentions between emperors and territorial nobles, the perennial need for large sums of money at critical moments—these and others created the milieu for the rise of cities in Germany in the eleventh, twelfth, and thirteenth centuries. The gradual emancipation of Nuremberg tells this story as well as that of any other city. Shortly after Nuremberg's first mention in the documents in the middle of the eleventh century, we note the first sign of an emerging municipality: the transfer from neighboring Fürth of the right to hold markets, collect tolls, and mint coins. Though this privilege was later temporarily rescinded, it provided the economic base for the growth and diversification of the population. Artisans from neighboring courts and manors came to sell surplus products, and many remained, protected from their lords' attempts to recover them by the maxim *Stadtluft macht frei*— town air makes free—a rule specifically declared by the emperors for a number of cities and a revolutionary twist of a traditional principle which had it that the air you inhaled made you the property of the man on whose land you breathed it. The market right was significant also in its legal aspect, for out of this *ius fori*, out of the permits and warrants granted to the merchants by their lord, developed the institutions and statutes of the medieval city. Bits of solid information gleaned from the chroniclers allow us to piece the story together: the chapel of St. Sebald as the goal of numerous pilgrimages, visits of emperors, the construction of the new imperial residence on the hill, expansion of the town to the river and beyond. It was a slow process, but by the middle of the thirteenth century Nuremberg evidently had become not only a city in the physical sense but juridically and socially as well. Referred to as *civitas*, it enjoyed the status of a privileged corporation, its residents organized as an association of citizens with collective rights and mutual responsibilities.

A charter granted by Frederick II in 1219 seems to recognize the status of the new *civitas*. It guaranteed security of person and of property, exempted burghers from any and all litigation save before the imperial *Schultheiss* in the city, allowed taxes and other fees due to the emperor to be levied not on individuals but on the citizen body collectively. It also granted various commercial, legal, and monetary privileges: toll freedom in a number of cities, no dues to be paid on the Danube between Regensburg and Passau, and so on. These were important rights, to be sure, but former interpretations of the Privilege as a Magna Carta of liberties have been modified by recent historians. The Privilege, it appears, was not intended to mark the beginning of the city's autonomy as a self-governing commune; it merely provided the merchants and artisans with a legal basis for their business activities, to enable them, as the Privilege put it, to pursue those trades on which their livelihood altogether depended, the situation and soil of the city being so unfavorable. The Emperor was not yet inclined to let go of his political rights. Throughout most of the thirteenth century these in fact remained in the hands of his agents, the *Burggraf* on the hill, and the *Schultheiss* in the town.

It was the aggrandizing ambitions of the *Burggraf* which ultimately compelled emperors to build up their city as a countervailing force. Since 1192 the office of *Burggraf* had been hereditary in the house of Hohenzollern. Able and ruthless men on the hill making good use of the emperors' discomfiture in their desperate struggles with the papacy, succeeded in extending their sway in both city and countryside. Indeed, for a time it seemed as though the *Burggraf* was on his way to converting his privileges and immunities into the personal domain of a territorial prince. In the face of this threat to its life as a commune, the city took up the struggle, led by its communal officers, the *consules* and *scabini*, and supported actively now by the emperors. The balance of power soon changed. From about the middle of the thirteenth century the citizens won the right to call themselves an *universitas civium*, meaning a corporation with increasingly sweeping rights and powers. They possessed a seal of authority. Their executive body devised effective governmental procedures: tax collecting, police power within the city, regular meetings of the Council, and majority rule within it, military and administrative organization.

The great Privilege issued by Emperor Henry VII in 1313 acknowledged and codified these advances. It ended the legal impediment represented by the *Burggraf* by granting the city the right to occupy the castle during periods of imperial interregnum and by naming citizens as assessors to the *Burggraf's* court in the country, in criminal as well as civil cases. Even more important, the imperial office of *Schultheiss* in the city was shorn of its powers. *Consules et scabini* were specifically empowered to supervise and enforce peace and order within the walls. The

Schultheiss himself was obliged to swear an annual oath before the Council, promising to pronounce fair and impartial justice "in accordance with the verdicts of the jurors," and "to preserve and advance the city's privileges and laws." The Council, a collegiate body of wealthy citizens whose emergence in the guidance of municipal affairs can be traced to the early thirteenth century, is left in sole charge of internal government.

Thus the relationship between city and imperial agents had been reversed in less than a century. Before long now, the councillors were to bring remaining imperial possessions and jurisdictions under their control. In 1320 Emperor Ludwig the Bavarian granted the Council sweeping judicial powers, including the right to put a man to the sword, "if it appear to them that, because of his depravities, the man be better off dead than alive." Ten years later the right of asylum in *Burg* and monasteries was abrogated, closing the last sanctuaries from the Council's authority. Furthermore, the imperial *Burg* was to be open to the city at all times, excepting only during the emperor's residence there. In 1347 Charles IV affirmed an earlier custom of appointing only Nuremberg citizens to the office of *Schultheiss*. Ultimately the office was altogether transferred to the Council. All these cumulative privileges ("Graces, Freedoms, Rights, Charters, Privileges, Contracts, Donations, Immunities, Statutes, Laws, and Good Customs" in the swollen language of the chancelleries) were frequently and explicitly reaffirmed by emperors, especially at the beginnings of their reigns, as *quid pro quo* for receiving the customary oath of allegiance from the city's government. In 1350 the Council won from the emperor a further guarantee that all privileges, issued or to be issued, that might tend to weaken any of the established rights and liberties of the city, were to be held automatically void.

Little now remained to be added to what the Council already held. Since the 1380's it had been in possession of the *Burggraf's* right to a fee from the city's smithies. This had been acquired by purchase. Already the citizens had isolated the *Burggraf* in his castle by means of a specially built curtain of walls and portcullises. At the end of the fourteenth century they had built the tall look-out tower "so that they might see what was going on in the *Burggraf's* castle," as a chronicler put it. In the middle of the fourteenth century the city managed to crowd the *Burggraf* from his country courts by substituting her own peasant tribunals. Finally in 1422, shortly after his castle had been burned down in the course of one of the *Burggraf's* many private feuds, Emperor Sigismund awarded the entire hill, imperial castle and all, to the city. The reason given was the decrepit state of the buildings and the expressed willingness of the Council to restore them. From now on, the deed states, "our fortress shall never be separated or alienated from the city of Nuremberg." The rest of the burggravial prerogatives were sold to the city in 1427 by the *Burggraf* Frederick VI who, as the first Margrave of Brandenburg of the house of Hohenzollern, had a bigger game to play than quarreling with Nurembergers over judges' fees and convoy rights. Only some hunting rights (traditionally the last relics of aristocractic privilege), a few escort responsibilities, and the county courts were exempted from transfer to the city. At the same time, however, the county courts were denied jurisdiction over Nuremberg citizens. The purchase price for all this was a handsome lump sum of 120,000 gold gulden. Emperor Sigismund ratified the transaction. As an outward manifestation of her autonomous standing, the city received the right to maintain trumpeters and trombonists to sound flourishes at solemn occasions. This was in 1431 a small matter in itself, but an important symbol in an age that set great store by these ceremonies of authority.

Nuremberg's emancipation from dependence and obligation was now virtually complete—so complete, in fact, that the aggregation of privileges collectively known as Nuremberg's constitution came to be a model for the privileges claimed by, and granted to, other municipalities in the Empire. In their proliferation of rubrics and articles, these charters described precisely the relationship of town to emperor and to imperial officials. They defined the extent of legal and political autonomy enjoyed and practiced by the town. We have seen how the significance of these charters was physically expressed in the masonry of Nuremberg's great churches and expanding ring of walls and gates. Thus the city as it acquired its constitutional form of a community of collectively free citizens, took on a physical shape fit to reflect this historic attainment and to turn it to good use. The vast ransom paid the *Burggraf* for his remaining prerogatives shows the economic power now concentrated in the Council's hands. By the early fifteenth century, Nuremberg was well on the way to that status which was soon to make her one of the leading cities in the Empire.

Despite the apparent facility of this progress to power and independence, there was nothing inevitable about it. Shrewd bargaining, constant alertness in grasping and making opportunities, and above all the promise given of the city as a strong and reliable ally in politics and war—these were necessary to win concessions of privilege from the emperor. Just what it was the city had to offer in this coalition will become clear presently. The partnership was real enough; of this there is abundant evidence. Citizens never forgot, nor wanted to forget, that their liberties and rights were, legally and historically, privileges and that the emperor was the sole source of this bounty. Only the emperor could establish or guarantee the nationwide conditions of peace and order, the *pax imperialis*, on which the city's economic growth depended. Indeed, the very existence of the independent city was linked to the survival of the Empire. For the alternative to the Empire was the territorial state with its ambitious and aggrandizing prince, its more or less centralized bureaucracy, its leveling laws, and its nascent mercantilism. The demise of the Empire would mean the triumph of the territorial state and the end of autonomous cities.

Later epochs were to see this development come to pass, but in the fifteenth century it was seen only as a threat and one to be militantly opposed. And in this opposition emperors and free cities were natural allies. Only when the burghers suspected that monarchs were using their imperial office to pursue personal or dynastic ambitions did the cities contravene their policies, and then their spokesmen did not mince words in letting the sovereign know where the power really lay. But if his pursuits were in the interest of the Empire, even if they were not crowned with success, the cities' support could be relied upon. For the local observer this support revealed itself in the spectacles which accompanied imperial visits to the city. Nuremberg especially did not lack opportunities to display the goodwill of its govern-

ment and people, for it was a favored place to hold meetings of
the Imperial Diet; indeed Nuremberg had been designated in
the Golden Bull as the city where a newly elected emperor was
to hold his first congress with his Estates. The chronicles and annals describe these imperial visits in minutest detail: how many
horses in the imperial retinue, at what time of day and at what
gate the distinguished guest was received, who walked in the
procession to greet him, who held his stirrups as he dismounted.
Municipal account books list expenditures for appropriate festivities: "Item, 8 pounds 8 Heller for free wine issued to pipers,
for ringing all the bells in the city, for pipers and trumpeters to
play from the steeple of St. Sebald, for bonfires to be lit in all the
quarters of the city." In this way the link with the sovereign was
kept alive, as well as the link with the past during which the
present relationship of city and monarch had been established.
Formal allegiance was not begrudged the emperor; on the other
hand, no monarch was under any illusion about the location of
power or the whereabouts of money in his realm.

Power and wealth are, of course, troublesome properties to
guard. Frequently the city was forced to take to arms, look for
confederates, and resort to repressive action in the maintenance
of its newly won position. From one source, at least, little resistance was forthcoming. Nuremberg was never an episcopal seat;
therefore she had no trouble defending her growing autonomy
from her spiritual overlord. The bishops of Bamberg, to whose
diocese Nuremberg belonged, being the southernmost of the
four archdeaconates into which their territory was divided,
offered only token opposition to the slow but sure progress that
placed effective ecclesiastical control into the hands of the municipal government. In this instance, too, the emperors assisted
their city. Henry VII, for example, specifically forbade his judicial officer in Nuremberg to deliver any citizen to the bishop for
trial. By about 1500 the Council enjoyed the right of patronage
over the two town parishes, and its agents managed the revenues and expenditures of all churches, hospitals, and convents
in the city. The few contentions that arose were compromised
but always in a way to satisfy the crucial demands of the Council. Thus before anyone had heard of Brother Martin Luther, the
Reformation in Nuremberg was far advanced.

But if the Church was docile other contenders were not. Bavarian attempts to make good their claims on Nuremberg had to be frustrated. Enemies common to the western and northern German cities had to be taught a set of facts which historians now recognize but contemporaries were slow to grasp, namely, that times were changing and the economic and political character of society was moving toward a new alignment of forces. Hence the city leagues of the thirteenth and fourteenth centuries, both defensive and organizational in purpose, Nuremberg belonging to several. Frequently these leagues were the Empire's best hope of stability. But it was not devotion to an abstract ideal of peace and order that prompted Nuremberg or any other city to join. Action always followed calculation of concrete advantages. Thus Nuremberg held herself aloof from the great league of Swabian and Rhenish cities founded in 1381, until her own situation vis à vis the *Burggraf* and the dukes of Bavaria appeared precarious enough to warrant the expense of membership. (Nuremberg, as the leading city in Franconia, was assessed with a heavy contribution to the common treasury and supplied a large body of pikemen to the common army.) When war broke out late in 1387, the city's military activities were largely confined to destroying nearby townlets and villages from which the *Burggraf* drew income. As a local chronicler saw it: "Also that day, the city took over a fortified place about a mile distant from Nuremberg. . . . On the Wednesday following the city captured the fortress at Schönberg. That same day the city burned the town of Bayersdorf. Also that day we burned down Wöhrd near Nuremberg. A large number of dyers worked there from whom the *Burggraf* got more than 900 gulden annually . . ." Destruction and conquest were meticulously recorded in a paper sent round to all the allies; the war must have weakened the *Burggraf* considerably. But when the conflict ceased to serve a clear purpose, Nuremberg pulled out. To cover the enormous costs of the war, extraordinary sources of revenue had to be tapped. Loans and new taxes on wine and grain provided some of the cash, but most of it was squeezed out of the city's Jewish population in a particularly nasty bit of extortion which will be described in another place. It was a dog-eat-dog world in which the city had risen to power; magnanimity and kindness were not the ways to hold on to it.

This maxim held as true in civic affairs as in external business. The most serious threat to the stability of constitution and internal politics which Nuremberg had to sustain, and the last one as things turned out, arose in the middle of the fourteenth century. This was a rebellion of some of the city's workingmen against the by now comfortably entrenched regime of men of wealth and family who constituted Nuremberg's governing class. Just what the circumstances of the uprising were is difficult to determine. Documentation is scanty, much of it may have been intentionally destroyed at the time, and the chroniclers' accounts reflect the bias of ruling circles and clergy. The general cause must have been the self-perpetuating character of patrician government, but the crisis was perhaps brought on by the eroding economic position of certain artisans, aggravated by heavy rural immigration into the city following the plague (at least this is what happened elsewhere). The rebels' immediate complaint was a conciliar refusal to tolerate artisan participation in city management.

Nuremberg's civic tumult was not an isolated occurrence.[11] Many German cities experienced unrest at this time. Results varied. In Worms, Augsburg, Mainz, Frankfurt, and Strassburg, the artisan movement succeeded at least for a time in winning a share of the government; in Magdeburg the guilds captured control of the city; in Regensburg, Rothenburg, Bern, and Nuremberg the old ruling groups were able to crush the rebellion and restore the *status quo ante*. The Nuremberg uprising was not a proletarian insurrection nor an explosion of resentful masses striking in blind fury against their oppressors, though there was a throng gathered before the town hall and the mob broke some doors and locks and destroyed documents and registers. The rebels were skilled craftsmen who demanded recognition as corporate groups and a share in the city's government. During the brief time they held power they encouraged the formation of artisan guilds but otherwise left the laws unchanged. Mismanagement, lack of support in the city, and opportune meddling by neighboring barons soon brought the rebel government into disrepute. In September 1349 Emperor Charles IV appeared with an army, and the usurpers submitted. Once again in power, the old patricians reacted swiftly and with firmness. Though bloodshed seems to have been held to a minimum, there were expulsion and repressive action; above all, guilds and other craft organizations of whatever kind or purpose were dissolved, banned, and forbidden in perpetuity.

Thus the rebellion came to be of lasting significance in the internal affairs of the city. In fact, it was customary for a while to refer to municipal events as having taken place "before the tumult" or after. Nuremberg's artisans never suceeded in forming independent corporations; what organization there was and such administrative and police functions as had to be carried on issued from the Council and were controlled directly by it. This fact influenced political and economic affairs in Nuremberg in many ways, as will be seen later. The rebellion of 1348–1349 remained in the collective memory of the upper classes, colored by the legends which soon sprang up; reference to it was useful as justification for keeping things as they were and as warning of what might happen if changes were made. In fact, the political structure of the city changed very little after the middle of the fourteenth century, except to bring even more far-reaching powers into the hands of the patricians and their Council.

Nor were these powers restricted to the immediate limits of the city. It was not only that authority tends to expand but Nuremberg's fortunes as a center of political and economic strength were bound too closely to its environs to permit anything less than absolute control. The result was the creation of a *Territorium*, a state governed from its nucleus and firmly tied to the city's political and economic interests.[12] The process of attachment began with the forest which surrounded the city. By rights the emperor's, by delegation originally under the jurisdiction of the *Burggraf*, the forest with its proliferation of offices and courts and benefices gradually came under the authority of the Council. In the old days the *Burggraf* had named foresters, assigned cleared land for cultivation, presided over and profited from the special courts of beekeepers and charcoal burners and quarry men and other forest dwellers. All this was now the city's. A prominent burgher officiated as the supreme forester, municipal forest riders roamed the woods to investigate trouble, and fortified country houses were sold by their owners or conquered from them. At the same time, the Council strove to extend its protection over monasteries and churches in neighboring villages: *Tutela et defensio,* as it was called in the papal charters confirming this right, which in practice meant supervision of revenues and inspection of conduct. Similarly, the Council managed to acquire a number of privately owned townlets and villages formerly held as fiefs or acquired through purchase by Nuremberg citizens. Throughout the fifteenth and early sixteenth centuries, the government added to this growing territory by treaty, purchase, and, occasionally, conquest. Decisive measures attached the rural population to the central government. Peasants were taxed, judged, and conscripted in times of need. A militia regulation of 1442 listed 424 villages and hamlets whose residents owed obedience to the government at Nuremberg. The word *"Untertan"* (subject) came into use at this time to define the new relationship of authority and obedience. Sixty years later Nuremberg joined Bavaria in a war against the Palatinate solely in order to push out and consolidate her eastern border. Imperial privileges were promptly issued to secure the conquests, and in 1513 a comprehensive administrative system for the entire territory was worked out and a bureaucracy organized.* Boundaries were marked off with stones. Map makers were commissioned to chart the domain.

Naturally there continued to be trouble. A series of imbroglios with Margrave Albrecht Achilles of Brandenburg-Ansbach and his son Frederick, a pair who saw themselves as the champions of the feudal nobility against the usurper towns, periled the city in the middle and late fifteenth century. Such quarrels usually started in the courts and ended on the battlefield, the bone of contention petty—the income from a quarry or the defection of

---

* The administration was headed by four Council members who also constituted the Superior Court for all cases between residents of subject towns and citizens of Nuremberg. The territory itself was divided into *Pflegeämter,* each headed by a *Pfleger* stationed in the main town of his district.

a retainer—but the root always the shifting positions of towns and feudality, a desperate cause for both parties.[13] Frequently the entire citizen body was placed under arms to defend the city or its dependencies. The scale of these military efforts was enormous, relatively speaking of course, and taxed the city's resources sorely, and there must have been many moments when the city's whole future hung on the outcome of a battle. A large painting in the Nationalmuseum in Nuremberg records such a moment as caught by an eyewitness: streams of armed citizens are seen marching out of the gates to battle with Margrave Kasimir (it was in 1502, and the battle was fought near St. Peter's before the walls), the supreme commander Ulman Stromer clearly recognizable on his mount, the humanist scholar and patrician Willibald Pirckheimer, astride a white horse, leading the reserves.

Most often, however, conflict was on a smaller scale and more easily handled. Robber barons were the usual source of trouble; the chronicles and documents are full of short-tempered descriptions of the outrages committed by these cutthroats and their henchmen against innocent citizens or dependents.[14] Indeed, the records make it appear as though the woods and hills around Nuremberg were thick with such lawless elements. Not all of them were knights. Many among the most notorious *Placker* were runaway servants or apprentices, unemployed journeymen, or burghers' sons gone bad. Descending upon merchant convoys, they unyoked horses, broke open bales and barrels to see what was inside, intercepted cattle herds, held up traveling businessmen, stole their weapons and carried away their servants, confiscated whole wagon loads of goods, and occasionally declared armed feud on the entire city. Not a year passed without several major disturbances. For example, in 1381: "Appel von Gailingen and his thieving helpers attacked a convoy of Nuremberg carters and stole the teams off thirty-two of their wagons;" in 1384: "Ropreis von Wildenstain caught three Nuremberg burghers, Fritz Muffel, Seyfried Penniger and Hermann Hoffmann, took all they carried with them, and held them for 200 gulden ransom each;" in 1448: "Two henchmen of Klaus von Heldritt stole two horses from the wagon of a Nuremberg burgher. Haymeran Nothaft confiscated several sacks of saffron owned by a Nuremberg burgher, Hans Schlüchter. Konrad von Gumpenberg and his retainers attacked Konrad Baumgartner and Konrad Imhof, but later made restitution of the damages. Hans Kraft, the son of a Nuremberg burgher and henchman of a highway robber lately beheaded in Nuremberg, began to attack Nuremberg citizens. The Council sent off letters describing his misdeeds to all neighboring towns."

These are typical incidents. Nearly always the Council had to intervene, either diplomatically or with force of arms. There may not be much merit to Ulrich von Hutten's observation that German burghers would long ago have succumbed to sloth and soft living had the robber barons not forced them to protect their property, but it is true that cities were not often left in peace. In the 1470's one Hans Schüttensamen, son of a Bayreuth burgher, took over a castle near Nuremberg, gathered a straggling band of proletarian knights, and preyed on traffic until, betrayed by one of his own men, he was caught and burned at the stake. Kunz Schott, *Burggraf* of Rothenberg, kidnapped and murdered couriers and messengers in the course of his feud with the city; in April 1499 he abducted a member of the Council, cut off his right hand and sent him home with the bleeding hand in his pocket; and 409 Landsknechte had to be hired and sent afield before the nuisance was stopped. In 1512 a group of merchants traveling from Bamberg to Nuremberg was intercepted by Götz von Berlichingen, some of the men tortured, all held for ransom.[15] Once again Nuremberg prepared for war. In 1521, a Nuremberg burgher, Hans Rumer Horäuf, returned from the following experience with a band of noble highwaymen, as described in his deposition:

When they got to Brandenstein he was blindfolded and taken up to the castle. There they placed him in a cell in the stable barn and secured his hands and feet in the stocks. Soon after nightfall two of them came to him and told him to estimate his worth. When he said he had no money, they bound his hands behind his back, tied him to a winch, and pulled him up to the ceiling. But he insisted that he was a poor wretch and could give them nothing. Next night four of them entered his cell and again demanded that he name a ransom. He said he might be able to raise fifty gulden. At this, they laughed contemptuously and asked for 1000. When again he pleaded poverty they locked his hands and feet in tension irons and left him that way all night.

On the third night Horäuf raised his offer to 200 gulden, while his captors reduced their demand to 800 and threatened to cut off his hands and feet if he did not pay. Agreement was finally reached on 400 gulden, but the poor man remained imprisoned until his relatives had raised the money and paid up. It took major military efforts to clean out such robbers' dens. The emperor might issue ringing decrees of proscription against these offenders, but only the troops of the city could bring them in. "This we owe to the Holy Empire, to ourselves, and to the common weal, and for this have we been privileged by the Emperors and the Empire": Thus the Council to a Bavarian duke who had sought to prevent action against a disturber of the peace with whom he was allied.

Robber barons were small threats in themselves, but powerful rulers were ready to support or enlist them when the opportunity to despoil the city looked promising. The margraves of Brandenburg especially were rarely content to give the city peace. It was a tough school of politics in which young men born into the governing class gained their experience as statesmen. Constant vigilance was needed and far-flung diplomatic activities and always the readiness to act decisively in moments of danger. But if the challenge was stiff, success was all the sweeter. As enemies were held off and covetous rivals defeated, the city recognized her own image as the guardian of order and the champion of lawfulness in the Empire. There was righteous pride, not merely malice, in the glee with which Nurembergers heard the verses of a vicious satire written in 1557 by Hans Sachs, to celebrate the death of Margrave Albrecht Alcibiades of Brandenburg-Kulmbach, a truculent and depraved noble with whom the city had had no end of trouble.* The Margrave has died and is on his way to the world beyond. Sachs hears bells and sees sad faces: surely, he remarks to a bystander, they re-

* Always cautious, the Council refused Sachs permission to have the poem printed.

flect the population's distress at the noble's passing. Not a bit of it, he is assured:

> The clanging of the bells you hear
> Express our happiness and cheer
> That death at last has taken him.
> The moans, laments, and faces grim
> Reflect our grief that this foul foe
> Did not expire long ago.

The Margrave departs from the world escorted by a throng of peasants, burghers, nobles whose livelihood he had destroyed:

> Without a cause you ruined our lives
> Starved our children and our wives.
> Now you must face the Judgment Day
> And for your misdeeds you will pay.

And he goes off, jeered by a grisly crowd of maimed and broken victims of his wanton cruelty:

> Hacked up, cut open, smeared with gore
> Their death-pale faces sick and sore;
> Like hanged men many, piteous wrecks,
> The rope still dangling from their necks.

At the gates of hell he is received as a brother by a delegation of fearful classical despots including Heliogabalus, Domitian, and Caligula.

Tyrants and disturbers of the peace merited only scorn from townsmen contemplating a dead antagonist from behind their ramparts and their full storage bins. Their city, on the other hand, filled them with pride and with confidence in the rightness of her cause and her strength to defend it. What Hans Sachs, a simple, plain-spoken shoemaker pursuing a placid and useful life in his native city, wrote of Nuremberg might also have been written in praise and appraisal of any of the other flourishing cities of the Empire. Four qualities, says Sachs,[16] distinguish his fellow citizens and help them preserve their way of life. First is the political adeptness of the men who govern them:

> In daily council do they meet
> Of civic business to treat.
> Surrounded by experienced men
> They ask who, what, why, where and when,
> Explore all facts of relevance,
> Anticipate developments,
> Consider all the circumstances,
> And keep a sharp eye on finances.

The second quality is justice and fair-mindedness:

> No man in Nuremberg or abroad
> Need of our city's power be awed;
> His rights, his freedoms are secure,
> Nuremberg hurts no one, rich or poor.
> We ask and take no more than right
> From King, from Prince, Duke, Count, and Knight.
> We use no brute force to compel,
> High-born or low, we wish them well.

The third quality is loyalty:

> Toward our Emperor we have ever
> Been faithful, our friends need never
> Fear that we might abuse their trust
> We keep our word, our deeds are just.

The last is strength and resolution, and firmness of character represented by walls, towers, bulging arsenals and stores; and finally money:

> Thus day and night, good times and hard
> We keep our vigil, stand our guard.

Sachs' limping doggerel barely manages to avoid sounding comic. But the homespun sincerity of his words, coming from one occupying such a lowly position in Nuremberg's society, does give voice to the real feelings of self-satisfaction animating his compatriots. Having looked around their city and surveyed its history, we can surely join them in their pleasure. They were safe, they lived well, their past was honorable and the future looked bright. Was there any reason why they should not regard their city with pleasure and themselves with admiration?

TWO

Politics and Government

A Contemporary Description—Ideological and Historical Origins of Patrician Rule—Nuremberg's Patrician Families—Concentration of Power in the Hands of the Council—The Council as Governing Body: Composition and Procedures—Administration—The Chancellery—Finance: Revenue, the Treasury, Fiscal Administration, Coinage—Craft Regulations: the Sworn Crafts, the *Pfänder*, Supervisory Personnel, Wage and Price Control—Paternalistic Government—Sumptuary Laws—The Purposes of Social Control—Summary: Nuremberg's Political System.

Though now largely an academic concern, the question of how a city-state society like Nuremberg governed itself was in its own time a matter of keen interest. Politics in Germany was carried on by rule of thumb. Few principles existed and no theories. What counted was a nimble wit on the part of statesmen, an astute political realism, and above all experience. Much value was therefore placed on political proficiency attained elsewhere, and frequent attempts were made to draw on it. Eager to learn and adopt, city governments not only scrutinized each other in action but traded information, borrowed experts, copied laws, institutions, and procedures that seemed to work in other places. Not everything was revealed in these exchanges. A reserve of expertise composed of native shrewdness and acquired skill was always kept back.* But the basic facts of urban administration were public property and widely disseminated.

* For example, the Council prohibited the publication of an excellent *History of Nuremberg* by Sigismund Meisterlin, written in the 1480's, because it divulged much inside information about the city's government and foreign policies.

To this interest in the mechanics of city government we owe a handy description of Nuremberg's regime at the beginning of the sixteenth century, written by one who knew it from the inside: Christoph Scheurl, a Nuremberger by birth, doctor of civil and canon law from the University of Bologna, former professor of jurisprudence at Wittenberg, and since 1512 legal adviser to the Council of his native city. It was a fundamental rule not only in Nuremberg that university-trained lawyers could not belong to the city's legislative bodies. Thus amateur statesmen counted on their jurisprudent advisers to steer them through the intricacies of litigation and to help with both substance and form of the business of government and diplomacy. The professional's counsel was invaluable, but only the layman could make policy —this principle epitomizes the burgher's deeply rooted distrust of the arcane phrases, the Latin formulae, and the complicated written codes of the lawyer. As a consequence, men like Scheurl enjoyed enormous influence and power in city governments, although they bore no responsibility.

In December 1516, Christoph Scheurl wrote a concise description in the form of a Latin letter, titled *Concerning the Polity and Government of the Praiseworthy City of Nuremberg,* addressed to his friend and one-time classmate Johann Staupitz, now the Vicar General of Augustinians in Germany. Staupitz had recently been in Nuremberg to preach a series of Advent sermons to enthusiastic audiences at St. Vitus'. At the time he had urged Scheurl to provide him with some information about "the form and character" of Nuremberg's constitution and government. Scheurl at once complied, not with a detailed treatise but informally, limiting himself to "the main points." The letter is in fact an admirable outline of Nuremberg's government and administration, and we may reproduce it here with profit.[1]

"The supreme political body in our city is the Council," Scheurl begins. "It consists of 42 men, of whom 34 are patricians belonging to the Old Families, and 8 are commoners chosen from the multitude. The 34 patricians are further differentiated into 8 *Alte Genannte* and 26 Mayors [*Bürgermeister*]. Of the 26 Mayors, 13 are called Jurors [*Schöffen*], the other 13 are called Mayors; but these same 26 Mayors also fall into two other groups of 13 Senior Mayors, and 13 Junior Mayors. Seven of the 13 Senior Mayors form a separate group of administrators; they are called The Seven Elders [*ältere Herren*], 3 of whom are appointed to the office of Captains General [*Oberste Hauptmänner*] of the city, and of these 3 men two have charge of the treasury and are called [after the name of the city's chief tax, the *Losung*] *Losunger*.° The Senior *Losunger*, that is to say, the man first named to this post, is the highest officer of the whole Council and is regarded as the first man in the city.

"We also have a Greater Council [*Grosse Rat*] composed of honest, brave citizens whose number is not fixed, but usually comes to about 200. The members are called the *Genannte* (or *nominati*)† and they are honorable men who earn their living in respectable business [*Gewerbe*], not lowly manual work, except for a few, whose skills are specially useful to the city. . . . It is from among these *Genannte* that our Council members are elected by specially chosen Electors as I shall describe in a moment. The *Genannte* are consulted whenever a new tax is to be imposed,†† war declared,§ or the subjects [*Untertanen*] warned of impending dangers.‖ . . . In sum: their office consists mostly of being at hand to ratify the Council's decisions and see to the

° *Losung* is a contribution by the citizen of part of his fortune. The word comes probably from *lösen*, to redeem, acquit oneself, perhaps connected with the fact that payment of the *Losung* was made in the form of metal counters purchased by the citizen. The *Losunger* was the official who set and collected the tax.

† Literally, "designated men," originally, perhaps, substantial individuals indicated by name to be consultants or agents to the government, or witnesses to the courts.

†† Especially unpopular taxes, like the irksome duty on grain, imposed after long hesitation in 1576 when the city was in desperate financial straits.

§ "Consulting" is an euphemism here. For example, before the Bavarian war of 1504 the Little Council summoned the *Genannte*, acquainted them with the facts, with Nuremberg's responsibilities under existing treaties, with expected gains and dangers. The decision to go to war had, however, already been taken.

‖ For example, when there was some muttering in the city during the 1524 peasant uprisings, the Council summoned the *Genannte* and told them to use their influence among the people to prevent possible trouble.

observance of its laws. It is considered a great honor for a man to become a member of this Greater Council.

"Now, the election of our Council [i.e., the Small Council of 42], takes place in the following manner: On the third day of Easter, every year, the Greater Council assembles for the purpose of choosing the Small Council. The *Genannte* choose from among the Seven Elders or the Seven Senior Mayors one Mayor and one Juror as Electors, while the Small Council itself names three Senior *Genannte* as the Electors of its choice, for a total of five Electors. The only proviso is that no two members of the same family may serve as Electors, nor a man who has been an Elector the previous year. . . . As soon as the five Electors are inscribed, the Councillors are quit of their offices and duties and rejoin the ranks of plain ordinary burghers. . . .

"Having pronounced an oath to God, the Electors shut themselves into a specially provided room, and proceed to vote for members of the Council, except that they cast no vote for the 8 *Alte Genannte*, who will be appointed later by the new Council. Ordinarily, the Electors simply reelect the incumbent Councillors, but occasionally they replace a younger man or retire an old one whose age might prove a hindrance to him. However, they never refuse to reelect any one without having good cause, and it is considered a great dishonor to be retired from the Council against one's will. Thus, except in uncommon circumstances, a new Council member is chosen only upon the death of an old one. But the power of Electors is nevertheless very great, for they may on occasion raise one of the *Alte Genannte* to the rank of Junior Mayor and, further, they assign to every Senior Mayor one of the Junior Mayors to make a pair (who may, however, not be of the same family) to be the Governing Mayors of the city for the duration of one month. The Electors also choose the 13 *Schöffen* and assign to each his seat on the Council benches, but this must be done in such a way that *Alte Genannte*, Mayors, and the members chosen from the Commoners sit in mixed order. Moreover, they determine the order of precedence according to which men may speak in Council, for it is deemed a great honor to be the first to be called on to give his vote or opinion. The right of first voice usually indicates that a man is on

his way to becoming a *Losunger*. . . . All this done, the Electors
notify the Councillors elect, who then swear their oath of office.

"On the Thursday following, the newly elected Council meets
to name the *Alte Genannte*, then proceeds to appoint all the
municipal officials. No post is so lowly that it is not thoroughly
considered and discussed by the entire Council and each member's opinion solicited on the choice to be made. Finally, the
first pair of Governing Mayors is designated to officiate for a
period of 28 days. When their term expires, the next pair will
take over, and so on, until at the end of the year each of the
26 Mayors will have served his period. . . .

"The two Governing Mayors are obliged to spend nearly all
their time in their office or on the streets. They must hear complaints, settle arguments, urge debtors to pay, make peace between litigating parties. The Senior Governing Mayor receives
ambassadors and emissaries, opens all official letters and reads
them the moment they arrive, day or night, whatever the hour.
He convenes the Council, . . . informs its members about current
business, puts the question and counts the votes, orders decisions
put in writing, and adjourns the sessions. When the Seven Elders
meet separately, as they often do, the Senior Governing Mayor
must sit with them. Only he may put questions in Council and
bring matters up for discussion. . . .

"The government of our city and the common weal rest in
the hands of ancient families [*Geschlechter*], people whose ancestors, even back in the earliest days, were also members of
the government and ruled the city. Foreigners who have settled
here, and common people, have nothing to say, nor ought they
to, for all power is of God, and only those may exercise it whom
the Creator has endowed with special wisdom. Therefore we admit no one into our Council (excepting the eight commoners
already mentioned) whose parents and grandparents did not also
sit in the Council. It is true that some exceptions are now being
made to this rule, and that some newer residents (but they are
men of honest birth and distinguished family) have entered the
Council. However, such men may not occupy a position higher
than that of Junior Mayor. As for members of old Nuremberg
families, they may rise in honor and title from Junior Mayor
to Senior Mayor, to Elder—ultimately to the distinction of

Losunger. The ascent to this highest honor, however, is reserved to very few, for although we have many patrician families, most can aspire no higher than the office of Senior Mayor. The families whose members may be Elders are few in number, and even fewer those who may become *Hauptmänner.* A mere handful only become *Losunger.* But concerning these things there are no laws; still, they are generally observed. . . .

"All our officials receive salaries to enable them to be diligent in the performance of their duties. The *Losunger* receive the highest salaries, because they have no time to engage in any commercial business whatsoever while in office.° The Seven Elders receive 50 gulden each, but all hold in addition several other offices from which they draw income. . . . Each time a member attends Council he receives a token worth 50 *Pfennige* when he cashes it in at the end of the month. However, if tardy, he is fined 4 *Pfennige,* and if absent without excuse he forfeits one of his tokens. Senior Mayors have a salary of 8 gulden a year, Junior Mayors receive 4 gulden.† They are hard-working men, for the Council sessions usually last three hours, and there are nearly always grave matters about which the Seven Elders alone deliberate further, sometimes for half a day, after their junior colleagues have gone home.

"Now I must say something about the positions of the *Lo-sunger.* The two incumbents of this office exercise the highest power and dignity, for to them are entrusted the keys to the city's treasury. A man chosen from among the Commoners in the Council is named associate to them, but this person's sole responsibility is to guard the door to the treasury chamber.†† The *Losunger* work with the help of two experienced secretaries

° *Losunger* received a salary, several gratuities, and special payments. In 1500 their total income amounted to about 400 gulden for the year.

† Considering the wealth of incumbents, these sums constituted little more than honoraria. Only since the middle of the 15th century did Nuremberg remunerate her government officers and then only to meet complaints that official business consumed so much time that private affairs had to be neglected.

†† Actually to sit by the door (double doors, to be absolutely correct; the room was well guarded) in order to watch the goings and comings and keep an eye on proceedings in the room. It was a meaningless but politically sensible concession to public suspicion of patrician rule.

who record everything; they meet three days a week, Mondays, Wednesdays, and Saturdays after noon. They collect the *Losung* tax when it is due, receive and examine the accounts of all the other officials of the city, and they must themselves at the end of their year of office make a full audit of their receipts and expenditures to the Elders. All public moneys spent or taken in by the city flow through their hands, and all documents issuing from the Civil Court must bear their seal. In sum, nothing touching public affairs can be kept from them, no secret is so great that they do not know it.

"The three Captains General [*Oberste Hauptmänner*] have custody of the keys to the imperial regalia and to the city gates. They are also keepers of the city's seals. For the rest, all power lies with the Seven Elders, for these men meet daily to discuss confidential and grave matters before apprising the members of the Council. The real power is therefore theirs alone; their junior colleagues in the Council know and can do relatively little. One thing only is not in their province: the current state of the treasury. Only the two *Losunger* know this, though once a year they must open their accounts to the Elders, as I have said. . . .

"The eight Senior *Genannte* are much like veteran soldiers who have been freed of the burden of military services. They hold no particular office and thus cannot rise to the highest dignity except that occasionally one of them may be made a Junior Mayor. None, however, may ever become a Senior Mayor. Senior *Genannte* are usually men of good family whose brothers or close kinsmen are high officers in the city, for, as has been said, we have a rule that relatives may never occupy the same position at the same time. The 13 men elected *Schöffen* have the following function: Some of them must be in attendance whenever an accused man is put to the torture in order to take down the suspect's confession; all must be present to condemn a guilty man, although, in fact, the verdict they give always accords with the decision previously made by the Council as a whole. Every Council Member has to swear an oath always to follow the majority, regardless of his own opinion and vote. About the eight Commoners, only the following need be said: there are in our city eight special crafts each of which is entitled to have one member elected to the Council. These eight men are at liberty to attend Council and vote whenever they wish, or they may remain at home if they so desire. They hold no particular office, are pleased to accept the decision of other Councillors, and, if they participate in a question, vote with those whose opinion seems worthiest to them.

"To continue: we have a court, called the Court of Five. Its members are the two ex-Governing Mayors whose monthly term of office has just expired and the two whose term has just begun, also one additional member from the Council at large, not including, however, the *Losunger*. This court meets three times a week, on Monday, Wednesday, and Friday afternoons, to hear matters involving slander and injury. Its proceedings are swift and to the point; it tolerates none of the long-windedness and formality of judicial process, accepts no written briefs, and permits no party to appear with advocate. Only rarely are witnesses summoned: most matters are decided on oath.* There is no appeal from its verdict, but if the matter before it is very grave, it is usually referred to the Council.

"There are nowadays so many dangers to the security of our city that we have a total of seven Military Captains [*Kriegsherren*], though it is rare for more than three to be serving at one time. (Generally, you have noticed, we prefer our officials in groups of odd numbers.) The senior member of the group bears the title of War Captain [*Kriegsherr*]. They have an office in the Town Hall, called the War Room; there they meet to deliberate in time of war or danger of war. Each member is paid 100 gulden a year. Their jurisdiction covers everything of military significance; for this reason they have at their disposal a detailed register of all villages, peasants, horses, carts, and so on, in the entire Territory. They deal with many secret matters, and every day receive confidential information, but of these things I cannot speak here. . . .

"Not until two years ago [1513] did we establish an Office of Territorial Administration [*Landpflegeramt*]; before that, each of our towns, villages, castles, and so on had been placed under the protection of a single Council member; but recently it was thought better to appoint from the Council five Territorial Ad-

---

* In other words, this court operated independently of the Roman legal procedures introduced into the other courts of the city.

ministrators [*Landpfleger*]and give them charge of the entire Territory, especially the towns and villages conquered in the late Bavarian war. These regions they govern in the name of the Council. They may not accept any money or presents, no matter how trivial, from anyone.

"The Council furthermore chooses three of its members to be Guardians of Widows and Orphans. This body meets three times weekly, Tuesday, Thursday and Saturday afternoons, but it has no power to issue binding decrees, only to point out the right way and urge the parties to accept it. The Guardians divide legacies, execute testaments, assign guardians to minors, and so on. They also examine guardians' accounts and distribute money left by deceased people for the service of God. The office of Guardians was established twelve years ago on the Venetian model, and since then we have had no trouble with suppressed or fraudulent testaments. Another praiseworthy service of this office is its supervision of the revenues and properties belonging to ecclesiastical benefices, also all moneys donated or left to the performance of good works. Of these they keep a list and make sure that all stipulated masses and other godly offices are performed as directed. . . . There is also an official responsible for settling quarrels between domestic servants and their employers. He is called the *Pfänder*, and is elected from the Greater Council. But he has other duties, too. He sees to it that the streets and alleys are kept clean, that bread and meat and other victuals sold in the public market are of good quality and offered at a fair price. The *Pfänder** also heads a Court of four Councillors which meets Tuesdays, Thursdays, and Saturdays to interrogate artisans accused of violating commercial or other regulations, defrauding a customer, or turning out a bad piece of work. This Court of five also appoints a Sworn Master [*Geschworen Meister*]from each of the city's crafts. In other words, what elsewhere is done by the Masters of the Guild is assigned in our city to the five *Rügsherren* [the members of this Court].

* From *Pfand*, meaning pledge or security. The *Pfänder* was originally a legal officer empowered to take security from the accused and, in certain circumstances, award it to the offended. In Nuremberg he was a supervisory official and presiding officer of a court charged with watching over the observance of laws and punishing transgressions.

"We also have a City Court [*Stadtgericht*], a tribunal composed of eight men selected by the Council from among the *Genannte*. It is divided into two benches and a Council member is assigned as assessor to each bench. This City Court meets on Mondays, Wednesdays, and Fridays for three consecutive hours, and it is competent to interrogate any person, citizen or not, interpret the law, pronounce judgment, receive complaints, and hear arguments, orally or in writing. Small matters involving sums not exceeding 32 gulden are handled summarily. On the other three days (Tuesday, Thursday, and Saturday mornings) the judges read judicial documents, deliberate on judgments to be rendered, and draw up verdicts. And if the matter is great and weighty, both benches must meet together and arrive at a unanimous judgment. In addition to the members mentioned, three or four doctors of both laws are assigned to this court. They advise the judges, especially when some matter touches the provisions of the written [that is, Roman] law. Judgments may be appealed from this Court to the Council, unless the matter under dispute involves a sum of 600 gulden or more, in which case the appeal goes to the Imperial Chamber Court. . . . There is also a Municipal Judge [*Stadtrichter*] charged with the execution of verdicts. He sits over cases involving capital punishment, and he must be present when a man is put to the torture. . . . In addition to these courts, we also have a petty tribunal of four men called *Fronboten* [bailiffs] who hear cases involving sums not exceeding five gulden.

"Finally, we have the Peasant Court [*Bauerngericht*], composed of younger members of the Greater Council. This Court is regarded also as a kind of school for the training of the sons of our distinguished Councillors, and for this reason its number is not fixed, but increases or decreases as it pleases the Councillors. If a young patrician does well on this Court, has learned the speech and procedures of judicial affairs, shows an active and clever mind, he is elevated to the Civil Court, and ultimately, perhaps, to the Council itself. This Peasant Court has jurisdiction over all controversies arising among the rural people of our Territory. It meets on Saturday afternoons for three full hours. . . .

"As I have already said, no doctor of laws is admitted to membership in the Council. If it should happen, and it often does, that the Councillors, in session, cannot come to agreement, or if the facts of the matter under discussion are confusing, or the case itself is extraordinarily grave, then two Councillors are deputized to seek expert advice from the doctors, and to relate this advice to the whole Council on the following day. Ordinarily five or six doctors of law are retained full time by the Council; four additional lawyers are available for consultation, and receive a salary, though they may also handle private cases for Nuremberg citizens, which the former may not do without express permission of the Council. . . . The Council never renders a judgment on appeal without having carefully examined all relevant documents and consulted two, three, or even more of their legal advisers. This shows how thoroughgoing and cautious our distinguished Councillors are in all things. . . . Incidentally, lawyers are held in great esteem here; they rank in dignity with the Seven Elders and the Senior Mayors.

"Finally, the Chancellery: We have two First Secretaries [*Oberste Stadtschreiber*]who are privy to all the secrets of the Council. They are in attendance whenever the Council meets; when the Seven Elders sit by themselves one secretary is always present. They record every decision made by the Council, draft letters to be sent, and read incoming correspondence. In sum: they are the eyes of our government. Each receives 200 gulden a year in salary. The Chancellery employs in addition six clerks; these men are kept busy writing all day long. Each has about 100 gulden a year."

Thus Nuremberg's government as seen and described by Christoph Scheurl. It is an unsentimental document—as indeed is every pronouncement on politics and statecraft in Nuremberg —with no waste of platitudes or saving phrases about popular sovereignty. The only sovereignty that mattered was the sovereignty of the commune, and by 1500, the commune had become too closely identified with its leading citizens to be considered apart from them. This is not to say that there was a fundamental division of interest between patricians and commoners, a schism expressed in contrasting attitudes to the city and reflected in distinctions of manner, speech, dress. There was not, though members of the ancient families had certain privileges and comforts not generally permitted. Common origin, above all a common tradition, linked the classes in a community of interests where the part each group was to play was defined by its role in the operation of the city. It was the role of the patriciate to govern and to lead, but not to dominate, exploit, or reign. To us, today, Scheurl's assertion of a God-given wisdom to rule sounds like a feeble attempt to justify an oppressive oligarchy. But there is no reason to doubt that the principle was accepted by both the governors and the governed. Nor was it ever inflated into a grandiose claim of Divine Right. The difference between Princes by the Grace of God and Nuremberg's practical, penny-counting businessmen-patricians strikes one with special force if one happens to arrive in the city after viewing the ripe baroque splendors of one of the nearby princely residences, like Würzburg. There the sovereign lived an exalted existence amid gilt and marble opulence in his vast palace. Sweeping staircases, cascading hangings, wall-sized Tiepolos combined to create around him an air of majestic isolation. Not so the merchant-councillors of Nuremberg. Their town houses were a bit roomier and better appointed than the dwellings of their humbler fellow citizens, but as men they remained close to the substance of life, mingling with the crowd, speaking its idiom, obeying its laws, sharing its profits and privations in peace and war.

Nuremberg was governed as an aristocracy, though there was no proper term in German to describe it as such. (Scheurl: "The government of our city and the common weal rest in the hands of ancient families".) Jean Bodin recognized the fact; indeed, in his *Republic* he selected Nuremberg as an example of aristocratic urban government, "wherein of an infinite number of citizens there are but twenty-eight ancient families which have power over all the rest of the subjects." Only the members of these deeply rooted families (actually there were forty-three in the early sixteenth century) exercised real political power; latecomers and commoners had, as Scheurl writes, no real political rights. (The point carries more punch in the original lapidary Latin: *"Advenae et plebeii nihil possunt."*) The Council of forty-two, or more correctly its twenty-six Mayors, was the whole government, at once legislative, executive, and judicial. Its membership was self-perpetuating. The Council made all appointments, but it never shared authority with any group or individual. It took advice but never delegated decisions. It bore responsibility for all that happened and was done but was accountable to none. Its members spent long hours in conference over political matters of grave importance and more long hours discussing the length of women's frocks and the script of a salacious carnival play. There was nothing, literally nothing, in the life of the city that was not the Council's business. No corner of a man's personal life was so private as to afford him isolation from the arm of his government. The Council governed totally, its rule solicitous and benevolent, but also severe. The story goes that Emperor Ferdinand I once asked a Nuremberg councillor how he and his colleagues managed to keep so populous a place in such good order. "With kind words and heavy penalties," the councillor answered. The laconic phrase contains the sum of the political wisdom gathered at Nuremberg.

Bodin thought that Nurembergers had modeled their system on the constitution of Venice. But beyond a few features common to all patrician societies and some occasional borrowing, there was little similiarity. Venice was the envy and frustration of all statesmen who sought political stability, in Germany no less than in Italy. But the development of the Venetian state differed too much from Nuremberg's to have provided much ground for adoption. Nuremberg's constitution at the beginning of the sixteenth century was the result of her own history and the achievement of her indigenous amateur statesmen—the same group of men who now occupied the seat of power in government and society.

Two subjects, both historical in nature, must be considered before we can fully understand the character of Nuremberg's regime. The first is the peculiar political quality of the medieval German town as a community of fellow citizens originating as a free confederation and bound by an oath of association. In the course of the twelfth century, first in the episcopal cities along the Rhine, later elsewhere in Germany, merchants and artisans, usually at the crisis point of some controversy with their municipal overlords, formed protective unions the better to guard and advance their economic and political rights.* This act of association was customarily sealed by a solemn oath. In swearing the oath, each member bound himself to maintain the peace, respect public authority, hold himself available for military and other duties, and contribute his share of the public expenditures. The resulting organization was much more than an aggregate of persons living in useful propinquity. It was a community by oath, a *coniuratio*, an *Eidgenossenschaft*, a sworn association held together by a network of obligations tying the individual to the community and, in turn, distributing to him his portion of the gains obtained by common effort. It loosened the old relationships of individuals to overlord and interposed the commune as spokesman and protector. It identified the commune as the agent of the common interest and organized it as an effective instrument for advancing the welfare of all. The immediate object was always the establishment of communal autonomy, as formulated in a classic passage from the annals of Cologne: "*Coniuratio Coloniae facta est pro libertate.*" But in the long run of events, the *coniuratio* came to mean far more. It embodied the idea of a constitution not only by creating the community as a legal corporation but also by giving it a coherent body of statutes and surmounting it with a government that functioned as an organ of the community, not merely as a ruling power set above it. In making the oath an individual act of compliance, it created a society based on voluntary consent. Each of the participating *coniuratores* accepted his responsibilities and declared himself liable for neglect or violation. In fact, the citizen's oath of the medieval town comes closer than anything else to giving some substance to the persistent historical fiction of the social contract.

Even where circumstances did not encourage or permit the formation of an original *coniuratio*—and in Nuremberg they did not—the citizenship oath played an important role in municipal political theory and practice. Often a loyalty oath in form, it was pronounced annually by the assembled citizens in the presence of their Council and pledged them to observe, without reservations, the laws of their city and to obey all that it pleased

---

* The movement has earlier roots in the Low Countries and France. Cf. Henri Pirenne, *Early Democracies in the Low Countries* (Harper Torchbooks, 1963).

their government to order and decree. Sometimes the oath was preceded or followed by a public reading of the fundamental statutes; frequently the formula contained a reminder of the original act of *coniuratio* and its binding force on the present ". . . as it has been the custom from the time of our ancestors down to the present day that all who enjoy the right of citizenship here shall assemble once each year to swear the oath of faith and friendship binding each man to his neighbor." Thus the *coniuratio reiterata,* the annual restatement of the oath, not only handed the government a legal instrument for enforcing civic obedience and punishing delinquency but also preserved the original declaration of mutual interdependence as a political ideology. Municipal statutes made constant reference to the oath, directing a man "by his oath" to do something or not to do it, reminding citizens that "by their oath" they were bound to ungrudging consent and compliance.[2]

In Nuremberg this free compliance expressed and insured by oath took the unusual form of voluntary and apparently unsupervised payment of the municipal tax, controlled by nothing more than a sworn declaration of good faith. Once a year or whenever the *Losung* (Nuremberg's basic source of revenue) was to be paid, propertied Nurembergers estimated their own fortunes, reckoned their taxes, and placed the right amount, unobserved, in a closed chest.* Visitors were struck with an amazement bordering on disbelief at this apparent evidence of Germanic civic virtue. To quote Machiavelli in his *Discourses:*

And that it is true of these republics [of Germany, i.e., the imperial cities] that in them there still prevails a good deal of the goodness of ancient times, I propose to make clear by giving an example. . . . When these republics have need to spend any sum of money on the public account, it is customary for their magistrates or councils, in whom is vested authority to deal with such matters, to impose on all the inhabitants of a town a tax of one or two percent of the value of each one's property. The decision having been made, each person presents himself to the tax collectors in accordance with the constitutional practice of the town. He then takes an oath to pay the appropriate sum, and throws into a chest provided for the purpose the

---

* Actually they bought chits, little metal tabs, from a government office. These they inserted into the chest.

amount which he conscientiously thinks he ought to pay; but of this payment there is no witness save the man who pays. This is an indication of how much goodness and how much respect for religion there still is in such men, . . .

Machiavelli was, of course, familiar with Italian conditions[3] where the art of tax dodging had been refined to the point of virtuosity. (See, for example, the *Ricordi* of the Florentine merchant Giovanni Morelli, written about 1400, instructing his heirs in dissimulation, lying, even fraud, to succeed in the avoidance of assessed taxes.) To someone accustomed to thinking of government and its agents as hostile and grasping powers, the German municipal practice[4] does indeed appear unusual. In Nuremberg, as in many other towns, it worked like this: The decision to levy a tax having been made, the City Council announced the rate and had it posted on church doors and read from pulpits. Next, the tax officer and his staff drew up a tax list, usually a fresh list on each occasion, and ordinarily by means of door-to-door canvassing of households by the quartermasters and street captains. His roster of taxable heads of families complete, the tax officer designated places and announced a date for the deposition of the tax. In the interval, the citizen estimated his fortune (we will see later how this was done) and computed his tax according to the announced rate. Either immediately before or just after this self-assessment, he pronounced his oath before a responsible official. In some cities he did it by himself, in others (including Nuremberg) he was summoned by pre-arranged bell signals for joint swearing with the other residents of his block or quarter.* The oath pledged honest calculation and full payment of the tax sum. It constituted, in law and in fact, a public approbation of the government's policies and the citizen's declaration of full support. It was not merely an oath of truthfulness to enable the government to prosecute in case of fraud; in any case the government had no way of incriminating tax payers as there were no documents to be filed and no witnesses to the transaction. There was only one surety: the citizen's word. No records of individual payments were kept. The scribe simply wrote d or z

---

* The logistics of this was handled by the quartermasters and street captains.

(*dedit* or *zalt*) opposite the tax payer's name in the list, and that was that. The oath made sense only if it was understood, by citizens and government alike, as a conscious reaffirmation of the communal character of society and an approbation of the government's actions as the rightful expression of the will of the entire group. The occasion was the collection of revenue, but the spirit of the act was one of rededication to the ancient purposes of the commune, a periodic return to the pristine principles of the founders of state and society.[5]

This extraordinary procedure has given rise to much speculation. Some scholars refuse to believe that cunning politicians of the Nuremberg patrician type would have been naive enough to place so much reliance on something like natural Germanic integrity or on their fellow citizens' selfless public spirit.[6] They assume that ways and means existed to keep track of individual payments (through the purchase of the metal counters, perhaps) and that the burghers knew it, though they preferred to feign belief in voluntary consent and acted it out as a political myth: oath, formula, hand on relic, and the rest. This may be so. Other aspects of Nuremberg politics show that not trust but suspicion motivated the government in its legislation. But it is a fact that there are no documents to reveal governmental surveillance of taxation, open or secret, though in all the other branches of administration Nuremberg's records and archives were kept in pedantically fastidious good order. In fact there are no tax records of any kind, a gap much regretted by the social historian, but a revealing phenomenon to a student of the political ideology of the German commune. The independent city felt itself to be a body of constituent parts living in harmony of function and interest, whose minor imbalances could be quickly rectified by adjustment, nourished, protected, clothed, entertained, and guided in its affairs by specialized and responsible organs designed for the purpose, sufficiently distinct from feudal court and countryside to have gained a clear knowledge of its identity, and possessing a sense of purpose enabling it to act not only efficiently but consciously. In theory, at least, each segment of society, each class and craft accepted and respected its fellows. All acknowledged the primacy of the public interest, and all, or nearly all, were content to abide by the rule of those members whose standing, wisdom, experience, and skill made it logical and profitable that they should rule.

The historical tradition explains why paternalistic government was not ordinarily resented or resisted and why those who exercised it did so with a keen sense of obligation. But the historical setting also furnishes a second clue to the general acceptance of patrician government. All during the slow uphill struggle for urban autonomy, Nuremberg had found her spokesmen and defenders among the members of her distinguished families. It was only natural, therefore, that these men should take over the direction of the state they had helped establish. This had happened so gradually and so long ago that absolute patrician rule had come to be taken as a fact of life, a principle deeply embedded in municipal institutions; the patrician oligarchy was linked with the very existence of municipal independence and was not to be altered or even questioned without profound peril to the stability of the state.

It was an aspect of the unswervingly conservative nature of urban civilization that problems of the present were always seen in the light of the past. When observed in this rearward orientation, the dangers and opportunities facing a city like Nuremberg in the early sixteenth century did, indeed, appear strikingly similar to the circumstances amid which she had risen to her present position. Would it not be foolish, then, to remove seasoned minds and practiced hands from the helm? Statesmanship was an empirical science, and the knowledge of it was cumulative. Experience counted far more than learning, philosophy, or even native gifts. Men whose forebears had so successfully steered the city through the stormy currents of imperial and territorial politics, who had learned the mechanics of government in lowly jobs and had risen to high office through a rigorous process of selection—such men could and should be trusted. They were the chief makers of the city's political tradition. Tradition is a powerful cohesive in every society and age. In the 1500's, when the ubiquitous call for reform and renewal was sounded not as a demand for innovation but as a plea to return and to restore, the argument from tradition had special force.

No reinterpretation of history or special pleading was needed to present the city's patrician families as the executors of her

emergent autonomy. They had been just that from the very beginning.[7] When thirteenth-century imperial privileges had empowered the city to pay the emperor's tribute collectively, the
responsibility for assessing individual contributions had been
given to a group of consuls already gathered in a college and
meeting from time to time; these were well-to-do merchants regarded by both burghers and imperial officials as representatives
of the citizen body. Such a college of consuls officiated in most
German cities, probably adopted from similiar bodies in the
Italian communes.[8] Unlike their judicial colleagues, the *Schöffen,*
who were bound by oath to the imperial *Schultheiss* and associated with him on the city's civil bench, the consuls were responsible to no one save the community of burghers. As we
have seen, the power of imperial officials waned in the thirteenth century and that of the corporate city grew correspond-
ingly, a transfer of power taking the form of an absorption of
administrative and legal functions by the citizen representatives.
Consuls and *Schöffen* combined to form the City Council, organ-
izing themselves as Scheurl describes it in his *Letter.* There were
thirteen consuls and thirteen *Schöffen,* but the original cleavage
of title and responsibility was soon obscured by a more practical
division of the Council into senior and junior mayors. In any
case, as Scheurl notes, in the one significant function remaining
to the *Schöffen,* namely the verdicts over cases heard in civil
court, they were bound by the vote of the Council as a whole.
From about 1300 on, the Council met regularly, kept records,
built a town hall as the new political center of the commune,
developed an orderly way of doing business, and set up a city-
wide administration. By the middle of the fourteenth century,
the councillors had come to control courts and legal procedure,
they negotiated with towns and princes, set taxes, accepted new
citizens at will, and made all the rules respecting public order.
The Council's statute books *(Satzungsbücher)* where these rules
are recorded—laws about bread baking, weapon carrying, materials and cost of clothing, market police, public demeanor, and
a thousand more—are the best evidence for the sweeping, real,
and arbitrary powers now in the hands of the patrician Council.

Yet this patriciate was no ordinary oligarchy, and its Council
not a committee for the management of the vested interests of

a narrow caste. Since the opposite is now often affirmed[9], this point must be made clear. The questions to ask first are not what authority did the Council possess? (the answer would be simple: its authority was total, in law and in fact), or what were the specific regulations in which this authority impinged on society? (a mere enumeration of these would require several volumes), but for what purpose was it exercised and how was it understood by the city's working population? There was, and this much is certain, general agreement on the organic nature of society (that is to say, of the only society the burghers thought about: urban society, their own city, Nuremberg) and of the contributory function of each of the constituent parts of the social body. Not that this view of society was clearly formulated. Neither in Council decisions nor in legal briefs nor in diplomatic presentations, and certainly not in the records of private discussions, do we find a trace of a considered theory of society and government. But we can sense the existence of the organic view in the procedures and enactments as they have come down to us. In law the theory is familiar enough:[10] the city itself as a legal subject, a legal person embodying its entire population, though in this particular respect inhabitants were considered primarily in their passive roles as beneficiaries of the collective communal effort. In the active sphere, on the other hand, a clear distinction was made between social action, which involved all in their respective trades and services, and political action, which was reserved to those who, by their special status, possessed this privilege and exercised it in addition to their normal social functions. Relics of political activism by the populace at large survived, of course. But these were largely ceremonial. Even the citizenship oath served mainly to assure the burgher's passive compliance.

This must not be misunderstood. We have no evidence to suggest that nonprivileged townsmen resented their enforced passivity as a deprivation of fundamental rights or an imposition of oppressive class tyranny. An occasional Council ruling was attacked because it inflicted loss or penalty in the name of some such claim as *necessitas licitum facit, quod ius illicitum* (culled from the pandects of the Roman civil law and asserting the right of public power to do harm to an individual where the public interest was touched) and because such reasoning apparently violated ancient Germanic ideas of right and justice. But there was no objection to the principle itself of privileged and restricted political authority in the state. Patrician rule was accepted as right, that is, as legal and also as just. It did not degrade the rest to leave the governing in select hands. God had established this order, and the historical tradition had habituated it. There was much else to be done, for oneself and for the city. All that a man could do, and did well and with a cheerful spirit, served the community and thus himself. These were not hollow phrases. In a spatially confined settlement of 20,000 souls with only a few common centers of activity, the communal purpose of a man's work was readily visible. The work of his hands created wealth, and this wealth became palpable to his senses. He took pride in the attractiveness of his city and enjoyed the spectacles which a bustling society put on for his diversion and edification. He lived well, worked in decent conditions, had time and energy for the pursuit of his pleasures. To his neighbors he was attached by feelings of kinship and sympathy. He marveled at the complex social organization which enabled the society to keep itself going, to prosper, to increase in vigor and splendor. In this complex organization he had his place, humble or exalted. Either way he understood his role and observed the direct impact he and his work made.

This is how the burgher interpreted the authority concentrated in his patrician Council. His society, his eyes told him every day, was a complicated and subtle machine most difficult to keep in good order. Only from above could the myriad operations be observed, controlled, and adjusted. He respected his councillors for their skill and foresight. He admired them for their successes. He was not envious and not resentful. The prosperity of the commonwealth depended on everyone's actions. Every role, politically passive though it might be, was endowed with a political purpose. Long before Protestant theology came to speak of simple worldly human activities as intrinsically worthy and holy callings and encouraged men to pursue them faithfully, the medieval city had endowed these activities with the dignity and meaning of civic purpose. The town's business was the individual's business, to work, teach, study, or govern. That the latter was the preserve of a few was no more wicked or unjust or unnatural than that legal opinions should be drafted by academic lawyers or that gun barrels should be bored by skilled gunsmiths. *

Urban aristocracies and the social distinctions on which they depend go back to at least the eleventh century in Germany. Most cities had their burgher nobilities: the documents refer to them variously as *optimi civitatis, primores, meliores, maiores, sapientiores,* or (in German) *Geschlechter.* The term "patriciate" did not make its appearance until the fifteenth century, a humanist word introduced to dress the old families in classical garb. By then they had gained a firm hold on municipal government, more exclusive or less, depending on local constitutional developments.

Who were these ancient families? Their origins differ somewhat from city to city, but in most towns prominent standing was the consequence of money, and money came from commerce. A heated controversy used to divide scholars on the question of patrician provenance, but it seems to be a fact that most of the families rose to distinction not as landowners nor because they had once been imperial *ministeriales* but on the strength of their wealth accumulated through commerce. They did not at once form a closed corporation; for a century or more, local *Geschlechter* gained members by steady influx from below or from abroad into the ranks of the wealthy. Only in the fourteenth

* It may be helpful to introduce Max Weber's terminology here. Of the three "pure types" of authority Weber distinguishes, two would seem to apply to the control exercised by the Nuremberg patriciate. Authority, Weber maintains, may rest on three grounds: (1) "rational grounds—resting on a belief in the 'legality' of patterns of normative rules and the right of those elevated to authority under such rules to issue commands;" (2) "traditional grounds—resting on an established belief in the sanctity of immemorial traditions and the legitimacy of the status of those exercising authority under them." Perhaps there is evidence also of at least a trace of the third source of authority: (3) "charismatic grounds—resting on devotion to the specific and exceptional sanctity, heroism, or exemplary character of an individual person, and of the normative patterns or order revealed or ordained by him." Patricians certainly claimed to possess "exemplary character," though, of course, the magic properties of "charisma" are quite beside the point. See Max Weber, *The Theory of Social and Economic Organization* (translated by A. R. Henderson and Talcott Parsons, London, 1947), pp. 297 ff.

century did this growth stop (though not entirely), and from then on patriciates tended to become exclusive, distinguished by dress and style of life and by membership in *Geschlechterstuben*, closed clubs like the *Richerzeche* in Cologne, or in societies with romantic names like the Association of the Circle in Lübeck or the Brotherhood of King Arthur's Court in Danzig. Patricianship from then on was a matter of birth, as the name *Geschlechter* suggests.

In Nuremberg this closing of ranks did not happen until 1521, but after that it remained unbroken. According to a ruling of the Council made in that year, patricians were all those families entitled to be officially and formally asked to dance at the town hall ("those Families who used to dance in the *Rathaus* in the olden days, and who still dance there"). Members of other families might go of their own accord but were not summoned to attend. This formal distinction divided the true patrician from those who were not quite of that rank; the latter formed a kind of penumbra of *honorabiliores* and *Erbare* around the patricians proper—rich and respected folk but in standing and privilege strictly secondary. However, the patricians were themselves divided into classes, three of them in order of antiquity in the community. We have them all listed by name in that same ruling of 1521, each family in its proper rank, so that there was no chance of confusion and embarrassment. The most prominent of them, the so-called "first old families," are ancient indeed. The Holzschuher turn up in Nuremberg chronicles as early as 1228, the Pfinzing soon afterwards, in 1233, the Ebner in 1255, the Stromair in 1258, the Grundherr in 1265, the Nützel and Muffel in 1276.[11] Altogether sixteen families belonged to these "first old families;" "second families admitted to the oldest ones" included such prominent names as Tetzel, Baumgartner, Pirckheimer, Imhof, Kress, and six others, while sixteen further families composed the "third families, later admitted." There were forty-three patrician families in all, the youngest going back to at least the fourteenth century in the annals of Nuremberg, though not all were indigenous. The Imhofs, for example, came from Lauingen and the Toplers from Rothenburg. But there, too, they had been among the privileged, and ruling groups in the various German cities felt a strong sense of solidarity toward each other.

It is true that there were some nonmaterial (though not any the less tangible) reasons for the all but unassailable hold of the patriciate on Nuremberg. Essentially, however, its position in the city rested on economic power, translated socially into certain group privileges, and politically into nearly exclusive ruling rights.* Invariably patricians were large-scale merchants and manufacturers. The Tucher, Imhof, Ebner, Nützel, Schürstab, and Volckamer (all "first old families") traded with France and Switzerland and had branches in Geneva and Lyons. The Haller imported from Hungary, the Kress and Fütterer from Milan, Venice, and Genoa. The Behaim and Hirschfogel traded with the Alpine lands and the Adriatic. "[Jacob Welser] engages in business dealings with all countries on a scale unprecedented by any citizen in Nuremberg heretofore." The admiring words are Lazarus Holzschuher's, set down in a family chronicle† written in 1511. Welser had only a short time earlier come to Nuremberg from Augsburg. But he was at once admitted to the Council and his sons after him; his family name stands among those "later admitted" in the patrician roster of 1521. By then he had the largest business in the city.

We shall be looking in the next chapter at the sources of patrician wealth and its employment in civic life. Right now the point is political control, and how it worked. Only patricians were *"ratsfähig"*, that is, eligible for membership in the inner circle of twenty-six mayors in the Small Council. The family names designated patrician in 1521 turn up year after year in the lists of members.[12] There were (we have heard Scheurl on this point) no laws concerning these matters, and customs were flexible enough to admit a Welser into the inner circle, though he was a newcomer to the city and its traditions. The Council itself was not bound by any rules. Things were just done that way, owing to crystallizing group consciousness and fortuitous political circumstances that played events into Nuremberg patricians'

---

* Patricians were "Honoratorien" ("amateurs" in the Henderson-Parsons translation of Max Weber) whose status rested, in Weber's useful formulation, on the condition that "the individual is able to live *for* politics without living *from* politics." *Ibid*, pp. 380-382.

    † *The Holzschuher and other Honorable Families in the City of Nuremberg.*

hands, as they had not always done elsewhere.* Carefully arranged marriages linked names and fortunes in ever tightening
bonds, while daily contact in Council and in restricted social
gatherings forged a unanimous viewpoint on most matters. Such
exclusiveness was not so much directed against the citizenry at
large as against the wider band of nonpatrician, well-to-do
burghers surrounding the "first families". This group, also called
"honorable" (Erbare), included not only affluent business men
but professional people too, lawyers and physicians and apothecaries. They were distinguished from tradesmen and artisans by
clothing and style of address ("modestus et honestus vir," "ersam
bescheiden Herr"), but they did not belong, and could not gain
entrance to, the innermost nucleus of the "Ratsfähige". In manner of living, in the comfort of their houses and country places
and the size of their investments in real estate, many of these
wealthy citizens were indistinguishable from the "first families".[13] But political responsibility eluded them.

In view of all this it is not surprising that patricians should
occasionally surrender to the temptation of behaving like a hereditary aristocracy. Though burghers, no matter how rich and
influential, had never been held to be noble in the traditional or
legal sense of that word, they did share with the feudal barony
certain characteristic privileges. They could, for example, be
beneficed—many burghers held hereditary titles to villages, castles, tithes—and they also founded and endowed monasteries and
convents. They were even permitted to hunt (though equestrian
hunting was generally closed to them) and to enter the jousting
lists dressed in their own colors and bearing family escutcheons.
Like feudal barons, they owned land, sometimes a great deal of
it, and tried to acquire more. They also engaged in military
pursuits, led the city troops in manoeuver and combat, and sometimes served as knights in the emperor's armies. Occasionally a
scion of a commercial family turns up, all but unrecognizable, in
the trappings of a feudal warrior. Christoph Kress, for example,
who commanded Nuremberg's troops in 1530, was rewarded by
Emperor Charles with an "improved" coat of arms including the
formidable cognomen "von Kressenstein" to be added to the

---

* Developments in Augsburg, Cologne, and Freiburg, for example, were
very different.

homely Kress, and given a present of an ornate ceremonial sword and velvet beret surmounted by huge black ostrich plumes. The Kress family chronicle depicts Christoph wearing his finery, suited more to an Italian condottiere than a German burgher.[14] Spacious residences in uncrowded sections of the city, or outside the walls, provided a suitable setting for the display of such trophies. Family consciousness was another sign of incipient aristocracy. Almost every patrician dynasty had its *Stammbuch* or *Geschlechtsbuch,* in some cases elaborate and detailed chronicles not only of the family itself but also of the city with whose history the family's career was so intimately linked. No wonder then, that there was no social awkwardness between these elevated burghers and true aristrocrats. Emperors thought nothing of taking up residence in a burgher's house while visiting the city, and in 1491 we find among the guests at a patrician wedding Duke Albrecht of Saxony and Maximilian, the Roman King soon to be chosen Holy Roman Emperor. All that was lacking was the patent of nobility, and this, too, they attained, later on in the seventeenth century.

Escutcheons and plumes and rubbing shoulders with dukes did not, however, mean that the burgher patrician ceased to be a burgher. In fact, one often senses a touch of discomfort in the efforts of solid čitizens to act like the second estate and some reluctance in going to the expense of keeping up appearances. It was artifice more than nature with them, perhaps put on to please their wives, or out of some nagging suspicion that this was what was expected of them. Throughout, their minds were fixed on the two concrete poles of their lives: business and the city. Family chronicles reveal how close mercantile concerns remained to the hearts of leading patricians (though, likę Italian commercial dynasties, German families experienced occasional dissipation of talent into extraneous fields, interesting and fine in themselves, but ruinous for the firm). No ostrich feathers could make the descendant of a German *Kaufmann* ashamed of his father's account books and sacks of raisins. Even petty shopkeeping was not considered debasing, though patricians preferred to lease their retail stores to concessionaires. Nor did they ever develop that air of disdain for other classes which so often disfigures the talk and demeanor of aristocracies. Nuremberg laws

—written by patricians, of course—were firm on the subject. (Ill treatment of servants, for example, was not tolerated.) In many ways patricians had risen above their less privileged fellow citizens, but they never forgot that it was the townsmen who procured their wealth for them by making and using their products. They never separated themselves from the generality of men. Patricians were not outside the common municipal law. They paid taxes, voluntarily, and often very high taxes, too. They helped defend the city, did wall and moat duty; (the substitution of a money payment for such labor was open to all). Patrician law breakers were prosecuted along with lesser men. In the squares and on the streets, patricians mingled with the crowd. They attended the same churches (though worshiping at private altars). On high festival days or when a distinguished preacher like Saint John Capistrano or Johann Staupitz visited, they walked in the processions. They were hard working both in their private enterprises and in the affairs of the city. And they were a frugal lot. Their houses were large but not opulent. Their habits remained simple. Business records, household accounts, and public documents alike reveal patricians as exemplary managers: cautious, shrewdly vigilant, conscientious, bent on putting every penny to good use.

To sum up: custom, ability, and sheer success in the management of private and public affairs explain the acceptance of patrician dominance in the city. From whatever angle we observe the position of Nuremberg's patriciate, we meet the same justification of its well-nigh complete political control. Let us now turn to the mechanics of this patrician government of Nuremberg.

It is clear from Scheurl's description that the very idea of separation of powers was abhorrent to Nuremberg's ruling circles. "Divide and be conquered," they might have said, and with good reason, for in the dog-eat-dog world of sixteenth century politics, lack of consensus, undue delay in arriving at decisions and acting on them, and dissipation of authority, meant swift ruin. Nothing characterizes the Nuremberg Council as much as its steadfast refusal to part with even a minute particle of its powers. Its members held in their hands all the legislative and administrative and judicial functions there were. Tasks were assigned to lesser officials but only to implement; and such commissions carried no powers to make decisions nor to bear responsibility. Where authority was required, a member of Council was in charge. Every branch and twig of administration was in the care of a councillor; he decided and ordered, and answered for his actions to the plenum. He had charge of big matters and little; he might be *Söldnermeister* (civilian head of all armed men) and *Stockmeister* (the man in charge of prisoners of war and of negotiations for their ransom) and also *Weiherhauptmann* (supervisor of the municipal fish ponds). Thus when the full Council was in session, every bureau in the government was represented; when the Seven Elders met separately, as was their custom, informed and responsible colleagues were within earshot.

Discussion in Council was exhaustive and deliberate. Procedures for arriving at a decision were sometimes cumbersome, involving memoranda by conflicting experts and briefs by lawyers congenitally inclined to stress the complexity of matters. But caution and deliberation were the ways of these astute merchant-statesmen who had learned from early youth to step carefully, weigh advantages against each other, and consider every facet of a situation. On the other hand, government itself was characterized by an extraordinary consistency of purpose and, by and large, confidence. The fact that there was almost no turnover of Council members helped enormously in achieving this unity of purpose. Jean Bodin, judging Nuremberg's political processes from afar, thought that there was weakness in annual elections. "I am not of the opinion," he wrote, "that the councillors of state ought to be changed frequently, but rather they should be perpetual, as in Rome and Sparta and now in Geneva. For the yearly election in Athens, and nowadays in . . . Nuremberg and many other cities in Germany does not only reduce the significance of the Senate, but also draws after it the inevitable danger of disclosing and publishing the secrets of the state. . . ." It is strange that Bodin should not have known that practical statecraft had modified theory on this point in Nuremberg. Her statesmen had never enjoyed the advice of political theorists, but the dangers of which Bodin speaks were apparent enough to them.

As we have heard from Scheurl, the annual restaffing of the Council was only in the ceremonial sense an election. The members of Council constituted, in fact, a permanent executive, possessing all the marks of authority demanded by Bodin for the sovereign ruler.

This fact must be understood and its significance grasped before Nuremberg politics make sense. In Nuremberg (unlike some other cities) the Council was not merely the supreme authority, it was the only authority. Of course, this situation suited the interests of the city's thin governing stratum. But it was not really the result of deliberation and planning. The system was not instituted in one piece and at one time. Nuremberg had no Lycurgus among her legendary heroes. The elements of Council government are to be sought among the historical circumstances in which the city acquired her autonomy, each prerogative, authority, and procedure rooted in a special circumstance, coalescing only gradually into a coherent system of power. We have already encountered most of these circumstances: in 1219 *consules* are empowered to impose the tax on individual citizens; in 1285 the *consules* begin to exercise the right to banish undesirables from the town (a power apparently based on everyone's right to censure a fellow citizen); about 1300 *consules* and *Schöffen* are entitled to pronounce high criminal justice; as a consequence of the revolt of 1348–1349 the Council assumes all supervisory powers over artisans and workmen; in 1352 Council takes over the *Judenschutz*, the "protection" of Jews, formerly a prerogative of the emperor; and so on. In the meantime the Council had created ranks of subofficials, had fixed an election procedure, set up administrative bureaus, defined its relationship to the courts, imposed and collected new taxes, and assumed the command of troops. Each incident in the city's struggle for independence brought new powers into the hands of *consules* and *Schöffen*. They now met in a single body and regulated their manner of doing business, created a presidium for the meetings of the College of Consuls, and recorded their talk and decisions in a proliferating mass of *Akten*. By 1500 the end result of fortuitous historical chances and astute opportunism was a plenitude of power wholly concentrated in a handful of men representing a small segment of a populous urban state.

The Council met regularly on Monday, Wednesday, and Friday mornings, though either of the two governing mayors could call extraordinary sessions at any other time by ringing the council bell or sending a messenger.[15] In the meeting, the councillors sat in a prescribed order (cf. Scheurl) on cushioned benches along the walls of the Council Chamber in the *Rathaus*. Men whose opinion was most likely to prove influential occupied the leading seats, so as to be the first to speak.* Meetings were chaired by the senior governing mayor—a rotating office, it will be remembered, going the round of the twenty-six mayors for about four weeks a pair (the last of the year's thirteen terms being shortened or stretched, depending on the date of Easter). Governing mayors were also called *Frager* for it was their job to call on individual Council members for opinions and put the question when discussion was concluded.† No councillor could bring up business without having first cleared it with the senior *Frager*, who placed it on the agenda if he approved. The *Frager* also counted votes and declared motions carried or lost. If a vote yielded no majority, the matter was tabled or referred to a committee. All decisions were announced in the name of the entire Council: no dissenting arguments were ever published, each member being pledged by oath to accept the decision of the majority.

Governing mayors were, during their term of office, fulltime public servants. As Scheurl says, they were always to be seen between sessions talking to citizens on the town hall steps and in the square. They, or their secretaries, opened all letters addressed to the Council and drafted replies. They were responsible for order in the city. To advise them and, to some extent, spread control a bit, a kind of mayors' privy council had come into use. Its members were called the *Ältere Herren* (elders; cf. Scheurl), seven of them, hence sometimes rhetorically referred to as *septemviri*. They were named to this office at election time and specially sworn to their duties. They met in executive session to discuss finance and foreign policy. This body of seven al-

---

* But the two *Losunger* were not allowed to have seats one and two, or else they would have dominated proceedings completely.

† The fact that there were two *Frager* reflects the original division of the Council into a college of mayors and a college of *Schöffen*.

ways included the three most important magistrates, whom Scheurl called the *Oberste Hauptmänner* (in Latin *triumviri*), of whom the top two were the *Losunger*. The governing mayors were not thus, by their office alone, the cynosure of dignity and power (though, of course, for one month out of the year the roles of governing mayor and senior *Losunger* coincided). They led the Council, and they ruled the city, and they represented the state to the outside world, but they did not have the keys to the treasury nor access to the great city seal. These were in the keeping of the *Losunger*.

The Council always met in executive session; even the most highly trusted legal advisers, like Scheurl, were excluded. Two secretaries *(Stadtschreiber)* were the only outsiders present, but these were carefully selected, highly competent and trusted men, not mere scriveners. Lazarus Spengler, for example, was a former law student at Leipzig, whose father had held the same post before him. Spengler was to become one of the major influences on the course of the Reformation in Nuremberg. An earlier secretary, Niklas von Wyle, had made a reputation as translator of classical authors into German. Under men like Spengler, the office of *Stadtschreiber* turned into a veritable secretariat of state. Spengler was often sent on diplomatic missions, and his role in Council (he was made first secretary in 1507) was by no means passive. "He gave his opinion on many matters," a contemporary biographer relates, "and spoke so sensibly that the Council was pleased to follow his advise." Later on Spengler became related by marriage to Andreas Tucher, the senior *Losunger* and head of one of the most distinguished families in the city.

In the Chancellery, Spengler and his colleague directed a staff of half a dozen scribes and presided over a labyrinthine array of cardboard boxes in which archival materials and working documents were kept. As early as the thirteenth century the Nuremberg government maintained more or less systematic records; from about 1400 on, its official papers were kept in exemplary order. All matters of which the Council or the Seven Elders took note were entered in a *Merkbuch*, and the sequence of these *Merkbücher* provides a running account of governmental business, important and trivial, as the items came up. Decrees and dispositions were written in a *Manual*, pamphlets of a few sheets each, recording the Council's decisions in the course of one twenty-eight day period. The *Manual* gave the points made during the discussion, noted the question and the vote, and listed the officials responsible for implementing the decision. For the official and permanent record, there were the *Ratsbücher*, a series of large folio volumes, carefully indexed, containing the Council's decisions in formal language. New laws—and there was a steady flow of these -were entered in the *Satzungsbuch*, the book of statutes. Uncompleted matters, tabled questions, and other pending business were recorded in a special volume so that incoming governing mayors could tell at a glance what needed to be done. Correspondence was copied into letter books arranged by years and, within the year, by the names of governing mayors. Documents used by the councillors in their discussions were filed in labeled boxes. As the business of government became increasingly complex and administrative offices proliferated, departmental records were kept by each of the subordinate organs of the Council; thus, for example, the texts of sumptuary laws and regulations respecting architecture and police matters and such are to be found in the books of special bureaus charged with their execution.

In as large a community as Nuremberg a distinction was bound to be drawn between responsibility and execution. A member of the Council was made responsible for the implementation of each decision, but he could not do everything himself. Hence a large administrative staff was brought into being to take charge of the implementation of Council decisions. At first individuals from outside the Council were occasionally summoned to take care of some task or other. They swore an oath of office to the responsible councillor, and their commission rarely lasted longer than a year. But later on annual reappointment became the rule. It was always made clear that the commission was given only to relieve the responsible councillor of some of his burdens; no authority was transmitted. A commission or appointment was not a delegation of power, merely a shift of the burden of seeing to the details. The Council remained in immediate control and could (and often did) intervene directly. That is why, as a close student of Nuremberg's administration points out, there were no clearly marked and separated channels of authority, not even a table of organization.[16] An *Ämterbüchlein,* a booklet of offices, listed the incumbents for the year, and each man knew his duties.[17] But relationship of positions and exact limits of competence—these were left uncertain.

Any of the branches of government would illustrate what has been said, but it is best to begin with the administration of finance, because no other operation came so close to being the heart of the entire organism. Raising and spending money were, of course, the oldest of the operations of government, as old as the city itself. From the very beginning of its existence as a self-governing commune, Nuremberg (as well as other cities of its kind) required substantial sums for purchasing privileges, maintaining walls and an arsenal, buying off enemies, storing supplies. Fiscal institutions thus arose at the same time and for the same reason as the political ones, and by 1500 they had become orderly and efficient. Not by modern standards, of course. Seen through the eyes of the modern civil servant, medieval financial practices were amateurish and chaotic in their confusion and inconsistency. There was no budget, no single treasury, no uniform fiscal year. Special expenditures were met by special taxes. The Council was not bound by appropriations. A *Losunger* was free to reduce or forgive debts or to convert them into payments in kind. Citizens were permitted to "count in" claims they had against the city, that is, deduct money due to them from taxes. Account books were in use as early as the fourteenth century, but not every transaction was entered. All this is characteristic of the place and time. In judging it, one must remember that government rested with a mere handful of men who saw each other every day and probably talked of little other than civic business. Under these circumstances, a certain informality was perhaps justifyable. And a patrician government like Nuremberg's exclusive, self-perpetuating one, which was sure of its touch in political and financial matters, was bound to grant itself a maximum of flexibility in the management of affairs. Financial records were kept in Nuremberg to ease the strain on memories and speed the handling of current business, not to render an audit to the public. Much was simply kept in mind and disposed of in discussion.

Nuremberg's revenue came from taxes and from various other sources such as ground rents, court fees, and municipal monopolies. Taxes were of two kinds: a tax on fortunes, paid at first irregularly, later once a year; and several kinds of indirect taxes on consumer products. The latter were, in all likelihood, the oldest of the city's sources of income. Indirect taxes consisted of the so-called *Ungeld*, an excise on wine, beer, and spirits, varying with quality (the tax on French wines was three times as high as on native Franconian and nearby Neckar and Tauber wines) and levied on brewers, innkeepers, and private persons who did their own cellaring. A city official, the *Ungelder*, with his staff of barrel inspectors and scribes collected the money. On Wednesdays and Saturdays he went to the treasury to hand the collected money, bundled up in little sacks, to the *Losunger*. Similar deposits were made by other officials (the chief scale master reported every Monday), who often carried chests with locks to which only the *Losunger* had the key.

A much more abundant source of revenue was the *Losung*, the direct tax on capital and income. We have already encountered this tax and the method used for raising it as evidence of the ancient associative character of municipal society. The amount to be paid in taxation was determined by the tax rate, as announced by the Council, and the hypothetical sale value of property (real estate, houses, rents, valuables, including silverplate, and cash) as estimated by the citizen himsef.[18] The *Losung* books contain the tax rate and usually the total sum collected, but not, as we have seen, individual amounts. As all other municipal income was more or less fixed, or in any case could not be made to respond swiftly to the city's needs, the *Losung* had to bear the brunt of extraordinary expenses. Since it touched the well-to-do most, and since, so far as we can tell, they paid freely, the annual *Losung* must have been a persuasive argument for the equity of the existing social and political order. Later in the sixteenth century this ceased to be true. When a conjunction of disturbing diplomatic and economic events plunged the city into a severe financial crisis, the councillors could not summon the courage to tap the fortunes of the rich in order to wipe out the growing annual deficit and reduce the public debt. Too many of the wealthy, it was feared, would prefer to sell their goods and emigrate. Instead, taxes on beer were raised and a duty on grain imposed, an unpopular decision causing much dissatisfaction among the people. But these were desperate means engendered by unforseen and deeply unsettling developments. Before the 1560's, at any rate, the well-to-do could claim to be doing their part in sustaining the city's public expenses, and the justness of this claim was widely accepted. In fact it could be said that the voluntary payment of the *Losung* by the rich was the basis upon which their traditional privileged status could be so long preserved.

Other revenues—some substantial, many trivial—were derived from a great variety of sources. The *Bauernsteuer* taxed the rural population. Rental payments came from lessees of municipal land beyond the walls, especially in the forest and its many clearings. Road maintenance taxes were collected from suburban houses. Other revenue came from the lease of offices, tributes from certain categories of people living in the city, (the Jew tax, admission fees of new citizens), fines collected by municipal courts and imposed by police magistrates, and chancellery fees; other sources included proceeds from coinage and money changing, income from municipal monopolies (such as the manufacture of tallow), various kinds of taxes on merchandise exported from or brought into the city, the cloth tax on all woolens made in domestic shops, scale fees (all traffic in export and import commodities was tied to public scales), proceeds from the sale of charcoal from the forest and of fish from the municipal ponds, and many more too numerous to list here. Not all municipal services were financed with the money thus collected. Medieval town councils, Nuremberg's especially, made every effort to reduce the cost of internal administration by holding private individuals and groups responsible for the upkeep of public property. Thus families with surburban villas were told to pay for the maintenance of nearby bridges, and groups of town houses were held responsible for the cleaning and repairing of public fountains. Sizable amounts were saved in this way, and much municipal housekeeping was done without multiplying officials and red tape.

All sums of money taken in by collection officers were forwarded to the *Losungstube* and the adjoining treasury, located upstairs in the town hall on the market square. There the two *Losunger* and their first secretary, the *Losungschreiber,* presided over a collection of large and small sacks and chests of coins of various denominations, stacks of account books, and boxes of documents. Everything the city owned in money and valuables was kept there. Only a half-dozen individuals were permitted to enter, but these men enjoyed complete freedom of disposition.

Just how informal the arrangement was may be inferred from the affair of Nikolaus Muffel, a sensational case involving indictment for embezzlement, followed by trial and execution by hanging, of a man who was at the time first *Losunger* and head of one of Nuremberg's oldest dynasties. The year was 1469. Muffel had been observed (by the second *Losunger* and the artisan member of Council assigned to the treasury) acting suspiciously in the treasury, spreading his cloak apart as a shield and shuffling the money bags about. Once, while spoken to as he was busy in this way, some gold pieces rolled out of his sleeve and onto the floor. No audit was made, nor could have been made, but Muffel was thrown into prison and under torture confessed. It was revealed he had been stealing money for some time to enlarge his already famous private collection of relics. If the charge was true, it constitutes one of the very few instances of patrician malfeasance on record, and it seems to have shaken his confrères considerably.[19] Muffel could do it and get away with it for so long because of the casual storage of valuables in the treasury and the absence of a running account. But no changes were made in procedures. Once a year, as Scheurl tells us, the *Losunger* presented their books to the seven elders (that is to say, to their five colleagues among the elders, since the *Losunger* themselves belonged to the seven). That was all the accounting there was.

In any case, the intricacies of financial reckoning were such that accounts made sense only to those intimately connected with them. Monetary denominations and values varied wildly, even among coins permitted to circulate in the city (and hundreds of others had to be excluded, sometimes cut to pieces to compel melting them down), and it proved irksome to be obliged to reduce all sums to a single monetary unit. Thus a separate reckoning had to be made and a separate account kept for each denomination. When attempts were made to bring accounts to a common denominator, the product was never more than approximate.[20] Usually accounts were given either in pounds silver (of which there were two kinds: the "old" pound, consisting of 30 *Pfennige* and the "new" pound, worth four times as much; pounds were not actual coins, only coins of account) or in gulden. The gulden, a gold coin, was originally set equivalent to 8 old pounds, 12 *Pfennige* silver, but this ratio constantly fluctuated due to circumstances over which the Council had very little control: cheap silver coins coming into the city, monetary accommodations with neighboring cities and territories, imperial attempts at reform, illegal hoarding by speculators, and so on.* As the *Losunger* were also Nuremberg's *Münzherren*, the supervisors of coinage, a job which kept them in constant vigilance over coins coming into the city and their shifting values relative to each other, they understood these things but few others in the city did.

Computation was carried on by moving stacks of iron or copper counters about on an exchequer cloth where every square had an arithmetical value lent to the counter that occupied it:

XM (10,000)	M (1000)	C (100)	X (10)	I (1)
VM (5000)	D (500)	L (50)	V (5)	I ($\frac{1}{2}$)

This system, incidentally, explains the retention of Roman numerals until the end of the sixteenth century. The reckoning was simple, visual, and concrete. Everyone in the room could see what was going on. Expenditures were easily subtracted from income, and the balance was openly visible in counters left on the cloth at the conclusion of the accounting. But what was plain on the chequer cloth, was confusing in the account books, where addition and subtraction and the transfer of sums were complicated procedures. All this is quite strange when one reflects that the same men (some of whom had studied business methods in Italy) were quick to adopt Arabic numerals and modern book-

---

* For a more detailed discussion of Nuremberg's monetary system, see Chapter 5.

keeping techniques in the ledgers of their commercial firms.*
In the *Rathaus* established usage had paramount claim; tradition
was to be preserved. And the more complex it all was, the wider
the gap between initiates and outsiders.

The *Losunger* and their secretaries worked with a complicated arrangement of temporary and permanent books into which
they wrote and from which they transferred entries representing
the city's financial business. At the beginning of each fiscal year
they began a "small" book wherein items were entered as they
occurred. An abstract of this record then was transferred at the
end of the period into a "large" book in order to provide a survey of fiscal matters over a ten-to-twenty year period. With the
aid of this "large" book (the *registrum receptorum et exposi-
torum*) the *Losunger* made their oral accounting to the seven
elders at the end of the year. But to arrive at a reasonably meaningful idea of assets and liabilities, other books had to be consulted, all of them in the *Losunger's* keeping: notebooks on loans,
debts, credits, payments due, and so on, a register of taxes assessed on individual Jews, tax lists by which to anticipate the
following year's *Losung*, a special book for sums spent on gifts to
the emperor and other notables whose favor had to be bought,
and one or two others. To the uninitiated, the process of financial
bookkeeping must have resembled a kind of legerdemain. No
wonder observers believed that frequent turnovers in office must
lead to administrative chaos.

This was no less true of an aspect of fiscal administration already mentioned: coinage. There the problems and the imponderables were such that even aged and experienced *Losunger*
gave up in despair. The trouble was that neither in the Empire
at large nor in any of its territorial or urban segments did it
prove possible to enforce the few existing laws concerning content and value of circulating coins. Neither adulteration nor
hoarding could be stopped, and minting authorities (of which
a conservative estimate counted about six hundred in the Empire,
each pursuing its own aims) were driven to a progressive reduc-
tion of precious metal in their coins in order to keep them from

* Nuremberg had several teachers of business arithmetic in the sixteenth
century. One of them, Ulrich Wagner, had published in 1482 one of the
earliest reckoning books.

disappearing. Several times the Estates, meeting in the Imperial Diet, tried to improve the situation by passing imperial monetary regulations. More often regional groups strove to establish some kind of order by agreeing to common policies, even establishing agencies for testing coins and destroying bad ones. But none of the expedients worked, and inflation continued.

Nuremberg had been a minting site since the thirteenth century.[21] Like everything else, this was an imperial privilege, exercised at first by an imperial agent, but it was not long before the Council brought it under its control. By the late fourteenth century the Council struck coins in the city's own name and supervised them through its own organization. This organization consisted of three *Münzherren*, two of whom were the *Losunger*, as we have seen, and a technical staff consisting of an artisan *Münzmeister*, a goldsmith or silversmith to cut the dies, and several inspectors of coins. The *Münzherren* decided whether and when to change the silver or gold content or fineness of the *Pfennig, Heller, Schilling*, and two kinds of gulden put out by the city. They determined the rate at which foreign coins could be exchanged for domestic ones. The changing itself was done by private concessionaires sitting at tables in the market square. These men took in coins outlawed by the Council in exchange for local or other good coins; half the difference between the values of the two constituted their profit, the other half went to the city. Rates of exchange and the list of proscribed coins varied constantly so that the *Münzherren* were obliged to have the rates written on tablets and displayed at each changing table. Forbidden coins were depicted on large placards.

The *Losunger* also carried on negotiations with silver producing regions in order to get the metal at a favorable rate, and they were in frequent touch with neighboring rulers to decide on common steps to improve monetary conditions or eradicate a common nuisance. In 1527 they took the weighty decision to issue large silver coins in imitation of the famous and by then ubiquitous *Joachimsthaler* from the silver country in Bohemia. This created new problems, especially the need for stern measures to keep them from vanishing into the chests of burghers who, rightly as it turned out, expected them to increase in metal value as they decreased in face value. In the end the city decided that the problem, being national in scope, could not be solved locally and that the only practical policy was a permissive one. From then on the *Losunger* temporized, a hazardous and not always successful procedure.

We shall notice again this tendency to improvise whenever policy entered the realm of imponderables. When city action was taken in response to pressures not clearly understood and not to be reliably predicted, councillors played it by ear, which shows at least that their mental processes were not congealed in rigid patterns. True, Nuremberg patricians were congenitally averse to experimentation, but they did not deprive themselves of freedom of action when problems proved impervious to traditional solutions.

This holds true of policies affecting Nuremberg's relation to forces outside her own competence, especially economic and diplomatic forces. On the other hand, where the city was self-contained and self-sufficient, improvisation was ruled out, and even change discouraged, by the stubborn conviction that little or nothing could be gained from tinkering with a well-functioning, productive social engine. The period of trial and error associated with the fourteenth century was over. Urban society had now reached a state of equilibrium that might fairly be regarded as an end, not a trial ground for further experiments. A tenacious will to maintain, to conserve, characterizes the internal government of the city throughout the fifteenth and sixteenth centuries, and enabled it to escape all but untouched from the tempests of Reformation, peasant insurrection, economic reverses, and war.

So far as the majority of citizens were concerned, maintenance of the status quo was assured by laws governing every aspect of public and private life. The Council itself was unrestrained by prescriptive law, manipulating in the ample space of its time-honored usages, untrammeled by codes or rules. But everyone else in the state worked and lived according to rules defined by statutes and regulations originating in decisions made by the twenty-six mayors. Nowhere is this clearer or more fully documented than in the ordering (the term nearly always used to announce and justify decrees) of the city's economic life, both in production and consumption.

Nuremberg (we have seen this already) had no guilds, that is to say, no chartered corporations of craftsmen privileged to legislate for themselves and their products and free to bring organized pressure to bear on municipal affairs. All such associations had been crushed in the aftermath of the short-lived artisan revolt of the mid-fourteenth century. Following that, every effort by artisan masters to give themselves the appearance of a craft guild was defeated. Not only political activity but also self-regulation of technical matters, workmanship, procurement of material, and such were denied; even social activities were banned if they resembled the sort of thing done by guilds elsewhere. Nuremberg masters tried repeatedly to gain the right to form *Trinkstuben*, convivial clubs where guild activities in other towns were carried on. But always the Council turned them down. If a group of masters or apprentices met privately in order, say, to fine a man who had violated a custom, the Council, if it heard of the meeting (and it usually did), treated it as a conspiracy, punished the spokesman, confiscated the fines, and admonished those present never to do it again. In 1506 when apprentice pouchmakers, acting without authorization, expelled one of their fellows for being of illegitimate birth and induced their masters to appeal to the Council to recognize the principle of legitimacy in apprenticeship rules, the mayors minced no words in setting them straight: "Masters and apprentices of this craft are reminded that we have no guilds in our city, not in this craft, nor in any other craft." Sworn masters were obliged by their oath to report such illegal meetings to the Council if they heard of them. There was nothing artisans in Nuremberg were allowed to do on their own. The Council wrote the rules for them and saw to it that they were obeyed.

The means employed toward this end were twofold. First, handicrafts in Nuremberg were formed into so-called "Sworn Crafts" (*Geschworene Handwerke*), each a group of artisans under a so-called Sworn Master elected by the members of the craft, but invested by the Council. By no means all the trades in Nuremberg enjoyed this official status of sworn crafts. More than

150 different kinds of craftsmen practiced their skills in the city at the beginning of the sixteenth century, and many among them had no organization whatsoever. These were the so-called free arts *(Freie Künste)* for which the Council had laid down no rules affecting such matters as length of apprenticeship, masterpiece, quantity and quality of products, retail price, and so on. But for all those skills and activities deemed essential to the community, rules and regulations abounded. The sworn master served as technical consultant to the Council when it deliberated on these regulations, and he also played a role in their enforcement as an agent of the government, but these were the limits of his authority.

Secondly, the government intervened directly in the productive process by means of its own agencies. Infractions and disputes came before a municipal tribunal, the *Rugsamt*, a five-man court specializing in industrial and commercial matters. Four of its judges were Council members, the fifth, the *Pfänder*, an official with far-reaching competence (cf. Scheurl), was chosen from the Greater Council (because his was a full-time job and would have left no time for a mayor's many other duties). This *Rugsamt* had powers over everything relating to the making and distribution of products. It censured *("rügen,"* hence *Rugsamt)* and punished violations of Council rules. It settled intracraft contentions and jurisdictional disputes.

The *Pfänder*, for his part, supervised all artisan activity and kept his eye on the sale of goods in the market. Prices, weight, quality, and conditions of sale came under his authority. He headed a proliferating organization of subofficials whose very titles describe the extent of his inspectorial powers. Half a dozen market supervisors represented him wherever products were offered for sale. A score of assistants (fruit measurers, grain, honey, beer, hay measurers) were present at all weighing and measuring transactions. A scale master and six assistants operated the public scale. Two *Visierer* probed the contents of wine and beer barrels, and several *Weinrufer* supervised the cellaring of barrels in inns and private homes. No barrel could be sold until its contents had been sampled by one of a team of sworn wine tasters, and found good. There were four herring inspectors *(Heringschauer)*, six saffron inspectors, (because of the great temptation to adulterate this expensive spice), twenty wood inspectors—in fact there were inspectors for everything: nuts, bricks, horses, lime, meat, game, fish, hay. Thirty-six officials were concerned with the sale of wine alone.[22] Needless to say, the system encouraged, indeed required, a mass of red tape. Paper work, lead seals, cardboard tags, tax sheets, passed from hand to hand. The *Visierer*, having measured the taxable wine in a barrel, informed the *Ungelder*, the collector of excises, who issued a special seal to mark the taxed barrels. To see to it that only barrels bearing this seal were tapped, an official barrel tapper *(Anstecher)* presented himself when and where wine was drawn. All goods sold by the pound were weighed and tagged by municipal officers. Eight tag masters marked the little labels required on all bales of wool cloth, and there were tag masters also for *Barchent* (a specialty cloth of flax and cotton) and other textiles. So large was the number of these inspectors that the swearing in of them had to be transferred from the Council to a separate body, the Assessors of the Register of Offices, who administered the annual oath to officials and recorded their names in the year's *Amtbuch*.

No subordinate, however, made rules. Only the Council did that, not policy directives only, not merely general principles, but rules affecting every step in the life of a craftsman and in the manufacture of his product. Nothing was left to the discretion of the individual, and no distinction was made between his role as a producer and his life as a private citizen. All craft statutes, and all amendments added to them in the course of time, were entered in the *Book of Handicrafts*. Regulations had always been comprehensive, but with the increase of economic competition in the sixteenth century, both within and outside the city, and with the growing tendency to restiveness among journeymen and apprentices, they came to regulate even social activities in minutest detail. The following is an example, from the rules made in 1530 for the officially condoned banquets given by journeymen pouchmakers to visiting foreign journeymen of their craft:*

* These rules show that pouchmakers belonged to the "open" crafts whose members might receive (i.e., entertain with a banquet), and occasionally employ, artisans from outside the city. On the other hand, the so-called

First of all: profanity, cursing, or blaspheming are absolutely forbidden, and will be severely punished by the Council, especially when done with intent and malice.°

When a foreign journeyman visits the city he may be entertained with drink and food, but no more than 5 *Kreuzer* may be spent for wine and bread.

No more than two measures of wine shall be consumed at any one sitting.

No journeyman shall sit armed at table.

No foreign journeyman shall rise from table without permission.

Those present shall elect four journeymen as heads of the banquet. These four shall be obeyed in all matters.

No one may pound the table with his hand, nor call anyone present a liar.

There shall be no toasts spoken at these banquets.

There shall be no gambling.

All must remain present until the banquet is declared over.

Apprentices shall have nothing to drink.

Foreigners shall not be permitted to look into workshops and observe our journeymen at work except with the express approval of our sworn masters.

If the foreign journeyman arrives before noon, he shall not be permitted into the workshops until one hour before noon. If he arrives after noon, he shall not look around until one hour before nightfall.

Visiting craftsmen were not permitted to negotiate for work on their own. Each "open" craft deputized a master to "receive" an itinerant journeyman and assign him to a local artisan in need of help. Before such an assignment was made, local journeymen had the right to investigate their foreign colleague's background and qualifications. This was done at the banquet "during the first measure of wine," as the regulations stipulated, because the inquisition was likely to lead to arguments. Therefore, also, the ban on arms and table thumping. The journeymen had, of course,

---

"closed" crafts (*Gesperrte Handwerke*) were not only barred to all except Nuremberg citizens but also so jealously guarded against leaks of technical information abroad that foreign artisans were not even permitted to associate with their members. Among these "closed" crafts were spectacle makers, thimble makers, compass makers, bell makers, and carpet weavers.

° Laws against cursing appear in the statute books with monotonous regularity. They do not seem to have done much good.

a vital economic interest to protect. They had spent at least four years, and often as many as seven, learning their trade and drudging in the master's shop and home. (Apprenticeship periods tended to be shortened or lengthened in relation to the demands for products and the number of men at work. This, too, was a decision reserved to the Council.) They had another half-dozen or so years to wait until they might apply for a master's patent, and in this interim they must save enough to pay the steep master's fee into the city treasury, and also acquire a bride and establish a household, because although the city insisted that journeymen be unmarried, masters were expected to live in the holy state of matrimony, and none was made master until he was prepared to marry. And they realized that admission to mastership—which only the *Rugsamt*, the city's agency for all commercial matters, could grant—depended on the fluctuations of a market over which no one seemed to have much control and which was unpredictable even to seasoned observers. Theoretically each journeyman in every one of the city's sworn crafts possessed the right to work. But if foreign competition eliminated a local product, or changes in taste altered long-established patterns of demand, or a glut on the market sent prices tumbling, then a well-trained, talented, conscientious artisan might find himself reduced to living off charity money collected from his craftmates lucky enough to have work. It was to prevent precisely this situation, at least to keep it from becoming a threat to the economic and social stability of the city, that the Council sought to solve and anticipate all possible sources of troubles by means of regulations.

Wages were fixed, of course, and so were working conditions and hours. Every apprentice had to be registered with the city and his contract with the master entered in the *Book of Apprentices* kept by the *Pfänder*. Each violation and grievance therefore involved the government directly. Finished products had to meet rigid specifications to be passed for export, even for sale within the city. Prices were standardized, the Council determining maximum prices from time to time. Overcharging was to be reported to the *Pfänder*, who usually acted summarily, confiscating goods and imposing fines. The purchase of raw material was strictly controlled; some crafts bought collectively through a committee of masters. In those matters and in all others, procedures were fixed by the Council, sometimes in collaboration with the sworn masters, but often against their advice and wishes when wider concerns conflicted with special interest. Often the Council's policies were restrictive and, in the event, inimical to the city's best interests. Its deep-seated distrust of innovation, for example, prompted it to discourage new tools, especially novel methods for speeding production. Heavy fines awaited the artisan in a sworn craft brash enough to abandon long-established ways and experiment with new materials or new implements. The inventor of a gadget that was apt to upset traditional methods was likely to be forced to destroy it, and he counted himself lucky if he was not punished to boot. This happened many times, to a needle maker, for example, who had perfected a tool to double his production, and to one Jörg Endtner, a thimble maker, who had developed a new kind of revolving spindle "profitable to himself and his work, but damaging to the other masters," as the Council concluded, ordering him to put it away. Around 1500 a Nuremberg mechanic constructed a kind of turning lathe, but the Council instructed the *Rugsamt* to interdict its use, uncertain and afraid of the economic consequence of so revolutionary a machine.

Let us take a closer look at one of the essential crafts in Nuremberg, the butchers, in order to realize the conditions under which work was carried on around 1500. Butchers were not only a group of respected expert artisans but also the purveyors of a commodity considered absolutely essential to the health and comfort of a population which regarded a meatless diet, except on fast days, as privation. We encountered the pork butchers on our tour of the city in the last chapter. The beef and lamb butchers, a far more numerous and important group, had their stalls in the southwestern corner of the market square, adjacent to the so-called Cattle Bridge over which the animals were driven to the abattoirs located on a pier jutting out into the Pegnitz (for convenient disposal of blood and waste). Government control of the craft began right there, at the bridge.[23] Before the cattle reached the slaughtering place they were examined by a team of inspectors who rejected all that did not meet the standards. No animal under three years of age could be sold for beef, and calves had to be at least three weeks old (as shown by the presence of eight teeth) but no older than ten weeks. Following slaughter, a second inspection eliminated diseased flesh. The rules required that lungs be left attached to the carcass to facilitate probing. Suspect carcasses were thrown into the Pegnitz, though occasionally inspectors permitted objectionable meat to be sold, clearly identified and at reduced prices. Inspectors were instructed to examine each and every carcass in order to foil such frauds as sewing diseased meat into the skin and head of a healthy animal. Two municipal *Fleischmeister* were present whenever slaughtering went on. When the city built a *Fleischhaus* early in the sixteenth century for the display of dressed meat, the Council ordered that it be locked at night with two locks and that one key be kept by the building supervisor, the other by one of the *Fleischmeister*. In the morning, the two entered together and inspected the place closely to make sure that no illegally slaughtered meat had been smuggled in during the night. Meat brought in from the cutting benches outside was examined again as it passed through the door before it was laid out on the tables.

The object of all these regulations and inspections was to see that only freshly killed meat was sold to citizens. The law required that meat be discarded on the second day after slaughter. Inside the meat market another kind of control operated. At least one *Fleischmeister* spot-checked dressed meat for weight. Rules required him to remove occasional packages from the servant girls' shopping baskets and reweigh the purchase to expose a possible fraud. Every customer had the right to demand a weight check from the *Fleischmeister*. Only he could attach the little price tags which cuts of displayed meat must bear. Prices varied somewhat with supply but could move only within the limits set by the Council. Special regulations governed the manufacture and sale of sausages. (Peppered pork sausages were great favorites in Nuremberg.) The *Pfänder* himself was obliged to look in on the pork butchers two or three times a week, and in the meat market the *Fleischmeister* had instructions to weigh sausages (each to be one-quarter pound in weight) and cut them open to test meat and skin. These official procedures, incidentally, were not confined to public slaughter and sale. No burgher could kill the pig he kept in the sty in front of his house without prior inspection by city officials. In this, as in everything else, the Council recognized no protected realm of private concern and personal responsibility. A sausage made from the flesh of a measly pig, albeit a privately kept pig, might find its way into a neighbor's kitchen; thus it presented a public danger, and it was the government's business to protect the citizens.

Actually the government's responsibility for meat began long before cattle and sheep reached the slaughter benches, because the procurement of sufficient beef and mutton to satisfy the demand was a difficult problem and a major enterprise, particularly in the middle of the sixteenth century when there never seemed to be enough of either to go around. Far from leaving the purchase of animals to the butchers alone, the Council tried to obtain advance information on herds and prices in the cattle-producing areas of Hungary, Silesia, Poland, and Bohemia. In 1532 a cattle office was established, with a president, called *Ochsenamtmann*, a secretary, and a member of Council as supervisor. Its job was to scout possibilities of large-scale purchase, to bid for herds, and to extend credit to butchers for smaller purchases when favorable opportunities arose. Arrangements were made to corral herds bound for Nuremberg at various places some distance from the city where meadows were available for grazing. A storage house for hay was built in the city (to feed horses, too, of course) and massive hay purchases made abroad. In times of severe meat shortage the Council took steps to prevent undue inflation and assure equal distribution of what was available, ordering fast days to be observed, for example, even after the city had become officially Protestant.

For the butchers themselves the usual stringent craft regulations operated. A government-imposed organization made certain that butchers practiced their skill for the public benefit, not for private gain. Like every other craft, they were responsible to the *Rugsamt* and its head, the *Pfänder;* their immediate superiors were twelve sworn master butchers, of whom two were responsible for the slaughtering and sale of meat in nearby villages. Along with the municipal *Fleischmeister*, they investigated and punished—severely—every violation of every rule governing quality, weight, maximum price, and so on. Four times a week they reported infractions to the *Pfänder*, who in turn notified the Court of Five of which he was president. Repeated violators were deprived of their place of work. The *Pfänder* himself kept the sworn masters under close surveillance; their double role (practicing butchers as well as government representatives) made them suspect of laxness in enforcing the rules. The *Pfänder*, of course, was responsible to the Council for all that concerned production and products in the city. Thus even the inspectors were inspected and the supervisors supervised.

The butchers, along with the bakers, seem to have been among the very first trades regulated in this fashion in Nuremberg, for obvious reasons. Their oldest craft statutes go back to the earliest period of municipal self-government. Brewers, tailors, shoemakers, blacksmiths, and clothiers soon followed; ultimately all vital activities were organized as sworn crafts. The impetus to the elaboration of this vast and intricate network of interdependent rules arose from a characteristic combination of objectives that justify the term "municipal socialism" often applied to the economic and administrative system of the medieval town. Paramount in purpose was always the common welfare of the citizens, a goal that sanctioned even the severest limitations of individual freedom. Let the laws be fair and fairly enforced, and there could be no ground for complaints. Violators branded themselves as social offenders and merited the severe penalties set for them. Indeed, according to some, no punishment was harsh enough to deal with men who sought to hurt or defraud their fellow citizens. For such cuplrits Hans Sachs invented a little inferno, comic to us for its incongruity between Dantesque tortures and the petty transgressions they were intended to punish, but hardly ridiculous to a sixteenth-century Nuremberger who did not think such offenses trivial. Here is the punishment selected for a baker who cheated on size or weight of his loaves:

> For such a one this fate is fit:
> Think of a deep and gaping pit,
> With stinking filth filled to the brim,
> A pole projecting from its rim,
> A basket swinging from the pole

Suspended high above the hole.
Inside the cheating wretch must sit,
Mocked by the crowd around the pit:
His one escape a knife, to cut
The rope that holds the basket up.
At last he cuts it. Plunk. He plops
Into the horrid mess of slops,
And crawls ashore to jeers and laughter.
He'll bake bread honestly hereafter.

The common good demanded a host of preventive and punitive laws; there was no disagreement about that. For while a person might well chafe under the restraints imposed on his own actions, he also benefited from similiar restrictions placed on all others. He was expected to understand this, and we have no reason to doubt that he did.

But there was another motive at work, too: a deep and nagging distrust of human nature and conduct and an ingrained tendency to expect the worst of men. This is, of course, the reverse side of the noble dream of an equitable society. For if men were generous and rational, they would not need to be forced to act as they ought. The need for laws, thousands of them, showed that men could not be trusted, that their duties to each other had to be made obligatory, spelled out in precise instructions and overt threats, and that "ought" meant nothing, only "must" did. This view, made concrete in the statutes, did not turn the medieval city into Utopia. Governing patricians were neither moralists (though public morality was very much on their minds) nor idealists. The drab and cheerless conformism of Thomas More's ideal society has, one is glad to note, no counterpart in historical actuality. Citizens were not required to match an ideal type; they were expected only to behave unobjectionably as defined by their patrician masters, whose aim was not the perfecting of society but its ordering. And good order was the result of good laws; the more disciplined the order desired, the more complex the web of laws which linked its parts. Men being what they are, it was hardly reasonable to expect them to live by the dictates of good reason. Humanists might speak of a golden age when statutes did not need to be written because "laws were then engraved in the hearts of men," but to the twenty-six mayors in the Council Chamber at Nuremberg this nostalgic myth was no substitute for good, solid, properly drawn-up regulations, instructing men as to what they could not do and what they were obliged to do and when, where, and how. They were not in the business of perfecting men, or even improving them, only of governing them as they were. But even so, the well-ordered community bestowed enough benefits to justify the entire system.

Needless to say, the councillors also looked to the laws for assurance of their own continued supremacy. The preservation of existing class relationships in the city was certainly one of the objectives of patrician law-making. But this motive, too, had its reverse side. For far from looking on its privileged position as a license to grasp and exploit, the governing patriciate thought of its authority as a God-imposed mandate to protect, provide, mediate, impel, and guide. Government was a Christian duty, carried out to discharge obligations assumed with high position. This is why the prescriptive statutes and regulations carry a tone of solicitude and of worried responsibility. They reflect the constant, watchful, and somewhat fussy anxiety of paternal authority over troublesome and often wayward children.

Surveying the totality of rules defining life in a medieval town one gets the impression of a seamless and fine-meshed net of prescriptions and proscriptions, so designed as to cover every single aspect of public and private life. No doubt Pirenne exaggerates when he asserts that this municipal socialism "is as logical in its principles, as coherent in its parts, and as rich in its details, as the finest monuments of Gothic architecture, or as the great *Summae* of the scholastic philosophers."[24] But of the municipal laws of Nuremberg—with their all-embracing comprehensiveness, their efficient agencies of enforcement, and their straight lines of authority to the Council—it would not be wrong to say that they are both systematic and rational. Following the Council's business in a given period by looking through the official books where decrees *(Ratsverlässe)* are recorded, one does not, to be sure, get a first impression of system and order. Important matters alternate here with petty ones; the minute of a major foreign policy decision is followed on the very next line by an order to a peasant about some small property matter. Thus it happened that regulations overlapped and sometimes conflicted. Confusions of this sort never lasted, however, for the Council had the habit of undertaking periodic clearing actions of all rules governing a given activity. For example, in 1455 the Council systemized its customs regulations, some of them a century or more old, into a comprehensive *Zollordnung*. In 1485 a host of miscellaneous rules governing nuptial celebrations were combined into the *Wedding Booklet,* and in 1540 the Council wrote a general reform of all rules governing butchers and their work, summarizing previous legislation and doing away with redundancies. The same was done with clothing ordinances, beverage regulations, building regulations, and most other kinds of legislation. As late as 1561 a *Genanntenordnung* synthesized the many rules governing election and duties of the members of the Larger Council. And since at least one councillor always had his eye on each aspect of city life and spoke to his colleagues about it when necessary, it never took long for corrective measures to be taken. This, too, was justification for the concentration of power in the Council. As long as the relative simplicity of activities, and their spatial confinement within the city or immediately outside enabled the handful of mayors to know what was going on and remain in control of it, the system worked.

Contemporary drawings depict the councillors in session in their long, black, fur- or velvet-trimmed robes and black berets, seated stiffly, each in his appointed place on benches lining the Council Chamber. Portrait medals, much favored at the time not only for their ceremonial significance but also for their extreme realism, show us individual councillors, all portrayed at their most severe, stern, and unbending.[25] It is not hard to imagine them at their daily work: instructing laundresses to refrain from pounding garments on a stone, refusing performance rights to a script of Hans Sachs, or approving marriage arrangements for two illegitimate children. The wording of decrees always spells out the reasons for the decisions; rarely did the Council pass a new law without describing the situation that made it necessary. Everything was explained patiently, sometimes elaborately. (Do not beat wet garments on a stone. It tends to break the fibers of the material.) There was nothing arbitrary about the Council's procedures, all things were most carefully considered and debated. One has the feeling that when the Council fixed the weekly menu for the staff of the municipal hospitals, it spent as much time and care on the choice of meats and vegetables (Wednesdays for the morning meal: milk soup or onion soup, roast meat, white turnips or carrots; for the evening meal: soup, meat, barley or rice in milk) as it did on making far-reaching decisions in matters of war and diplomacy. Big matters and little were indistinguishable to these practitioners of total government.

All this is a natural consequence of political ideas inseparable from an urban patriciate. A lack of discrimination between major issues and trivia (as they seem to us), the steadfast refusal of councillors to delegate, and their anxious jealousy to keep all the reins in their own hands are typical of the kind of paternalistic government the patricians provided and meant to provide. Nothing shows all this more clearly and nothing illustrates better their unbroken power over the lives of fellow citizens than the web of sumptuary legislation with which they regulated all but the most intimately private actions in the city.[26] Controls literally reached from birth to death. "No one shall carry an infant to baptism dressed in a robe of silk, or embroidered in gold or silver, or set with pearls." No more than twelve women might accompany the young mother to church; no parties might be given immediately before the christening nor for two months afterwards. As for funerals: banquets and the like were forbidden; only near relatives were allowed to join the procession to the burial place; no more than two professional mourners were allowed; only twelve candles, none exceeding two pounds' weight in wax; personal shrouds were outlawed; as the need arose, you rented one from your parish, "each according to his class," that is, costly, medium, or plain, depending on your status in society.

The objective in these and other regulations, was a mixed one. Curbing excess and waste was a first concern. The Council tended to see itself as the guardian of Christian virtues and its injunctions as the only bulwark against the sins of pride, greed, vanity, and their evil social consequences: time-wasting, frivolity, covetousness, avidity, the restless search for change. "The Council has noted and considered the extravagance, vanity, and excess nowadays being practiced" is a frequent preamble to new

Portraits of Nuremberg burghers by the medallist Hans Schwarz.

Willibald Pirckheimer by Albrecht Dürer.

statutes. For example, memorial stones or tablets may not exceed a prescribed size or value "for the suppression of vanity, extravagance, and waste." Great gatherings at funerals are forbidden "because from this comes much waste of time in trades and occupations." Life was a serious business; distractions, entertainments, gaiety had their places in it, but as recreations not dissipations. Therefore the fun one might have was also legislated: foot racing, bowling were encouraged; chess and other board games permitted; cards discouraged, and dice frequently forbidden. Gambling could never be entirely outlawed, but limits to stakes and bets were set by the Council.

A strong tone of moral reprobation pervades all these statutes and their circumstantial explanations. Most rules were not preventive but prohibitive; they were imposed after excess or abuse had been noted, and they attempted to apply brakes to a process already underway. The wording is stern, censorious, often huffy, the voice of an offended, sometimes outraged parent correcting his prodigal offspring. The coming of the Reformation to Nuremberg made no appreciable change in either the Council's conception of its role or in the severity of the rules; comparison of sumptuary statutes through the years shows this clearly. Even the earliest surviving regulations of dress, speech, and conduct reflect the government's view of itself as the vigilant guardian of the Christian life. In the course of the fifteenth and sixteenth centuries, rules became vastly more numerous and explicit, but nothing essential changed. Occasionally a touch of permissiveness creeps in. It was futile to expect that the increasing prosperity spreading through all classes of society would not bring on resistance to a Spartan code. The Council was forced to extend the range of approved textiles, increase the licit weight of gold chains, and the standard width of velvet borders. On the other hand, prohibitions originally imposed only on the upper classes, at a time when only they could afford to offend against what the Council considered canons of propriety, were in the course of the fifteenth century extended to artisans and their apprentices. Commerce and manufacture brought increased purchasing power to all and required the broadening of sumptuary legislation to include all. In the late fifteenth century there was no class of persons nor sector of life not covered by the laws.

Moral considerations were primarily responsible for the numerous and very detailed apparel statutes that were issued from the Council Chamber and that faithfully reflected each of the vagaries of taste and style in the fifteenth and sixteenth centuries. In these statutes the persistent distrust of human instincts is most explicitly stated: no man over fifty to wear red buckram, no one under thirty-two to trim his cloak with beaver fur, no male person to part his hair; male jackets to reach at least two fingers' breadth beneath the fly (to eliminate the apparently irresistible practice of calling attention to the genital region by stuffing the breeches in front with a lump of cloth and decorating the trousers with a fly of brightly contrasting color), women's bodices to be cut no lower than one finger's breadth beneath the collarbone, and so on. But considerations of decency were by no means the only ones. Clothes more than anything else responded then, as they do now, to the lust for variety and change, and suspicion of innovation was, as we have seen, a strongly pronounced trait of city government. Hardly a single clothing ordinance fails to deplore newfangledness (*Neuerung, neue Sitten*) and imitation of alien ways, or warn of dreadful moral and social consequences if the invasion is not arrested. Slashed sleeves, perforated or open dress fronts (revealing the chemise beneath), shoes tapering to long, thin beaks were objectionable imports and alien new styles (*fremde neue Sitten*). Having tried in vain to control them by outlawing each as it made its appearance, the Council ultimately issued a summary ban on "Innovation and Unaccustomed Styles in Apparel, Adornment and Shoes," imposing heavy fines on violators (three gulden for every single wearing of a shoe deviating from the standard patterns issued to the cobblers) and compelling offenders to report the tailor or shoemaker who had made the illegal article. Such a man was likely to forfeit his right to a stall to sell his products. This was at the end of the fifteenth century, and from then on styles were under effective government control, the Court of Five (cf. Scheurl) being empowered to determine and declare "what was to be considered an innovation or a new departure." Novelty, however, was never totally excluded. From time to time the Council debated such grave matters as the permissible length of trains and the propriety of silken trim on hems, and occasionally it decided to give in to the way of the world *(gemeinem Weltlauf dieser Zeit)* and permit young men to shorten their jackets a bit from the previous rule ("to the tips of the fingers, if the arm is extended straight down the side of the body"). But here, as in other matters, the Council was in a position to control developments and determine their direction.

Sumptuary rules also maintained class distinctions, of course, though this was never their major purpose. Patrician ladies might own a gown with a silk border, and they could trim their sleeves with a quantity of velvet and sew a few discreet pearl-stud emblems onto their skirts, whereas the wives of honest artisans could only admire this finery from afar. But the distinctions were not great. Even regulations governing servants' clothing speak of good wool stuff and hair ribbons. The somewhat wider choice enjoyed by the well-born was not so much an accordance of privilege as simply the external sign of status that everyone, in one way or another, carried on his person. Fines for patrician offenders were exceedingly steep, and patricians like everyone else were subject to restrictions of all sorts. They could not attend out-of-town weddings (unless, of course, they were the bride or bridegroom or their parents); their gifts to each other were governed by a table of maximum values which was kept in the town hall and required frequent consultation. They could no more wear weapons in the city than could anyone else; they must serve their wedding guests locally made honeycakes rather than exotic pastries; and "new, lascivious, shameful, immodest dances" (twirling one's partner rapidly around the room) were outlawed for them, too. The aim of legislation and its enforcement was always to conserve, to keep things as much as possible as they had always been. The claims of innovation were considered but usually rejected, and only the most painstaking scrutiny persuaded the government to abandon a wonted custom. No idea of progress gave to the new an aura of promise and to the different a touch of hope. Affluent and confident though the city was, it peered into the future with concern and suspicion. What lay ahead was at best problematical. Only the past was certain, and only tried, proven, familiar principles would do in the face of the unpredictable.

To the men at the top, urban society—indeed all human

society—must have looked like a swarming hive of creatures, mutable and fickle, tending to excess and extremes, marred by narrow self-interest, and swayed by passion; excitable, volatile, kept from crossing the brink of turmoil and chaos only by their confinement in a comprehensive order of laws. They never theorized about the state of nature nor spoke of the role of laws in the improvement of men and their education to civic purpose and moral duty. All they wanted was to keep society functioning through the operation of a mutually beneficial system of cooperation. That was what the statutes were for: to define the relations of men to one another and fit them into a state of beneficial interdependence.

Did the system work? It did. As long as it was impartial and close enough to the recent time of struggle with emperor and barons to give meaning to the call for piety to tradition, and as long as the political experience accumulated by its rulers sufficed to steer the city through the currents of sixteenth century affairs, the system continued to work. Nuremberg remained stable in population and size, and the increase in commerce and manufacturing brought a time of general affluence to at least the first part of the sixteenth century, as we shall see in the next chapter. With enough wealth to go around, with an abundance of consumer goods being produced by the city's excellent workmen and also being brought in from abroad, with the system of distribution operating equitably, Nuremberg basked in the euphoria of comfortable prosperity. For any who might still object, resist, or refuse to accommodate themselves to the system, the law provided penalties whose grimness (and, in the case of physical punishment, barbarism) reflect the rulers' determination to protect the social order at any cost. It all seems insufferably despotic to us now. But we may doubt whether the contemporary citizen found it so. Authority as practiced by the Council was unbending and on occasion harsh. But it was benevolent, protective, helpful, and exceedingly personal in its operation. It was also honest, scrupulously so. Above all, it was successful. And no doubt this was the major reason for the Council's lasting hold on the loyalty of Nuremberg's citizens.

THREE

Society and Business: Commerce, Indusry, Handicrafts

Classes and Social Groups—The Jews—The Black Death and the European Economy—Rise of Urban Industry—Critics and Objectors—Nuremberg's Merchant Families and their Enterprises—Extent of Nuremberg's Commerce—Patrician Control of Business and Politics—Commercial Treaties—Traffic and Escort—Craft Specialization—The Metal Industry—Renowned Craftsmen and their Works—Municipal Construction Workers —The City Architect—Inspection and Testing of Products— Economic Objectives and Practices—Control of Specialization —Collectivism—Economic Decline after 1550: Causes and Symptoms—Debts and Deficits—The Social Order and the Management of the Economy—Summary: Politics and Society During Nuremberg's Prosperous Era.

The preceding description of Nuremberg's government and of the far-reaching powers concentrated in the hands of its Council might well suggest that, in the sixteenth century, Nuremberg was a unitary state. But it was not, certainly not if by unitary state is meant a strong government ruling a homogeneous population and applying the law equally to all. Society in Nuremberg was neither uniform in structure, nor uniform in law. Law in the Middle Ages was not concerned with applying rights and duties drawn from a general legal order to the individual. Such an order of objective law did not exist. Law was subjective in the sense that it was granted by the lawgiver to groups of men, and sometimes individual men, in the form of privileges.[1] To be in society meant to be in possession of a body of rules and statutes defining one's life and actions. Society consisted, and was thought to consist, of groups and classes, each a legally provisioned component with stated rights and enumerated responsibilities toward itself, toward other groups, and toward society at large. Each constituent group had its law, as it had its distinguishing peculiarities of dress, habit, manner, style.

All this combined to impart to the members of each class a sense of belonging and a common outlook.* But this attitude was not exclusive and not necessarily antagonistic. Enrollment in a social class did not conflict with citizenship in the community, nor did it cancel membership in larger religious and civic configurations. Legal privileges emphasized the group's contributory role in relation to the whole of society. Group consciousness was meant to be positive in this sense, not negative, not anxious to stake and protect a claim against present and future rivals. This did not always work in accordance with its objectives. There were complaints and not infrequently unrest. And the deep hostility between Catholics and Protestants later in the century put a severe strain on the social order in all communities where the two confessions coexisted. But even there the social cohesiveness was usually strong enough to overcome the divisive forces.

A social investigation of a city like Nuremberg in the late Middle Ages would thus be a study of groups: patricians, artisans in every occupation, consumers and producers, bee keepers, officials, clerics, jurists, servants, women as a sex and women as wives, widows, prostitutes, and so on. Each group had its rules by which it lived and worked and adjusted itself to the rest. We will encounter all these various groups in this and the following chapters, first in their economic relations, later in their manifold activities about the city. Some individuals stand out. But, as we shall see, it is the groups that predominate.

* A useful definition of "class," though a bit too sweeping to fit medieval society, is given by Gideon Sjoberg, *The Preindustrial City* (Glencoe, Illinois, 1960), p. 109: "A social class is a large body of persons who occupy a position in a social hierarchy by reason of their manifesting similarly valued objective criteria. These latter include kinship affiliation, power and authority, achievements, possessions, and moral and personal attributes."

First, however, something must be said about one group of people conspicuous by their absence from the scene in 1500: the Jews. Nuremberg had no resident Jews in the sixteenth century, the entire Jewish population having been driven out two years before the century began. They abandoned their property and much of their fortune and left behind a tradition of prosperity and antagonism going back to the distant Middle Ages.

What happened in the summer of 1498 was both repetition and culmination of an ancient story for the Jews in Nuremberg and elsewhere in Germany. Exactly when it was that Jews made their first appearance in the city is not known, but it must have been some time in the twelfth century, when the emperors—to whom the Jews legally belonged as *servi camerae imperialis* (imperial chamber serfs subject to a protection tribute paid into the imperial treasury)—allowed them to settle in a number of imperial cities, among them Nuremberg.[2] Apparently the little settlement flourished, for by the end of the thirteenth century their wealth proved enticing enough to bring on the first of many civic actions against them. Vague rumors of a sacrilege committed in Rothenburg gave the proceedings a religious sanction, and Jewish massacres in other Franconian towns povided the occasion. But the real objective was clearly a practical one. To quote Nuremberg's chronicler:

At this time [1298] there lived in Nuremberg a great many Jews. They owned the best houses on one entire side of the market square, where their synagogue also stood. And more Jews came every day, from all over the world, and committed many outrages against the Christians. Of all this the citizens suffered grievously, until the Council petitioned the Emperor to be allowed to do something about it. As the Emperor made no reply, the Council, correctly interpreting the sovereign's will, decided what to do. When the Bishop of Würzburg burned his Jews, the citizens of Nuremberg did the same.

How many Jews were burned in Nuremberg is not known, probably most escaped with their lives, though not with their property. Soon, however, the Jews returned, as was their custom. Forty years later we read the names of 212 Jewish citizens in a burghers' register. And again they seem to have done well, because before the middle of the fourteenth century, the authorities struck once more. The Jewish quarter still occupied the center of the city, obstructing the natural pressure of people and activities. It was 1349 and affairs in the city had gone back to normal after the abortive artisans' revolt, the Council now being more firmly in control than ever. An enlarged central square was being planned, and some existing structure had to give way. Naturally the Council turned against the alien element in the city's midst. In any case, resentment of Jews was widespread in those years of plague, civil unrest, and inflation. All over Germany Jews were being slaughtered or expelled. Some time ago, the Council had taken the wise precaution of negotiating a division of Jewish property with the emperor in the event that popular fury should turn against the Jews. Whether there actually was such an explosion in Nuremberg is not clear, but whatever it was the Jews fell victim once again. Ulman Stromer's diary entry notes what happened:

Anno domini 1349, the Jews occupied the middle of what is now our new market place. Their houses crowded the square and the spot where the Church of our Lady now stands. The Jews were burned on St. Nicholas' eve that year.

This sort of thing could not be done without imperial approval, for even though by the fourteenth century the Holy Roman Emperors had sold or pledged to the city most of their protective rights over the Jews, they still owned them. Diplomatic representations had therefore been made to Charles IV. Nuremberg, the Emperor was told, was not nearly so commodious and splendid as his favorite city should be. Nothing easier, however, than to make it the finest town in the realm, "if only the Jews did not own the best and gainliest spots and houses. The Jewish people," the city's emissary went on to say, "are so numerous and so grasping that everywhere on the face of the earth they possess the most precious places, crowding the servants of Christ into mean corners, so that we may wonder whether the victory was won by Christ or by Moses." Charles duly consented, and both Jews and houses vanished.

But only a few years passed before the Jews, survivors and newcomers, were back again. To gain readmittance they had to agree to forfeit all their old claims against city and citizens, but this seems to have presented no obstacles to their inaugurating a time of renewed prosperity for themselves. It is tempting to speculate whether these medieval pogroms were really as ruinous to Jewish lives and fortunes as legend has it. Certainly there were marvelous powers of recuperation at work, and it is reasonable to assume that as often as not the Jews outsmarted their tormentors, burying or hiding their treasure like Barabas in Marlowe's *Jew of Malta* or sending it to safe places abroad. No doubt they could sense trouble long before it crashed down on them; their unhappy history would have come to an end long before the onset of modern times had they not learned the art of survival so well.

Returning to Nuremberg in the 1350's, the Jews settled in a new quarter, a yawning site well away from the center, where a decade earlier a terrible fire had destroyed more than 400 houses. There they built their synagogue and school house and a growing number of dwellings comfortable enough for well-to-do artisans to take over in 1500, after the final expulsion. For the present, however, they were citizens again, swearing the special Jews' oath—a modified form of the regular citizen's oath—and paying the fee of admission to citizenship. They paid taxes and special tributes (for example, they had to provide all the bedding for the retinue of visiting emperors), but these were no more onerous than the burdens borne by their gentile fellow citizens. Many restrictions limited their activities, but these, too, differed only in degree from the kinds of statutes with which the other citizens had to live. A Jewish council, always including the rabbi, was appointed over them to settle internal disputes by the rabbinical law. Special apparel was prescribed, as everywhere in Germany since Pope Innocent III had ordered Jews set apart by clothing and other visible signs. However, the tell-tale *pileum cornutum*, the red peaked hat, was not required in Nuremberg. Citizen Jews wore flat berets, alien Jews bulky turban-like head gear. Yellow rings and their feminine equivalent, blue-rimmed veils, did not come in until the middle of the fifteenth century.

Of course all statutes concerning the Jews reflect the religious and human antipathy aroused in Christian minds by the sight of them. Jews were cursed deicides and stubborn unbelievers; they were a rootless tribe whose plight served as a divine warning and admonition to the rest of mankind. They could not buy Christian houses, the baths were closed to them, and during Holy Week they were banished from the streets.[3] Even common criminals were protected from contamination with them: Jewish thieves hung from the outer end of the gibbet—to suspend them from the center of the beam would desecrate the gallows.

Jews were barred from most occupations; only cattle and horse dealing were open and, of course, lending at interest and pawn broking. But interest was limited by law to 1 heller per gulden per week on sums of 100 gulden or less and to 10 per cent per year on larger amounts. Low-paid workers were not allowed to borrow more than 1 *lb* heller from them, and there was a long list of articles that could not be pawned: grain, tools and weapons, religious objects, nor articles bearing the city's seal. Still, Jews continued to prosper in Nuremberg, and by the late fourteenth century they were again wealthy enough to offer inducement to extortion. To be fair to the Council, it must be said that the city was in dire financial straits in the 1380's. The Council anticipated a war of attrition against the *Burggraf* and allied rulers and was being forced to contribute money and troops to a league of cities organized in south Germany in 1381. Under the circumstances, the temptation to squeeze the Jewish sponge one more time could not be resisted. In coordination with the other members of the Swabian League of cities, Nuremberg arranged to round up all her Jews on a given day in 1385 and compel them, under threat of their lives, to surrender their outstanding claims to the Council, cancel part of the interest as a concession to the debtors, and make the Council the sole beneficiary of the rest. Again Ulman Stromer reports:

Anno domini 1385, the Jews were jailed in Nuremberg and in other Swabian imperial cities, all on the same day. The rich Jews were taken to the *Burg*, the poor were shut in the cellar of the house next door to the Town Hall. Each Jew had to bargain his way out by offering his money. In all, the city got from the Jews that day a sum of over 80,000 Gulden.

It was all done in orderly fashion; the itemized list of individual sums pledged still exists. It came to precisely 80,986 gulden, including 7000 gulden owed by the city itself, now canceled.

Even after subtracting a huge sum given to Emperor Wenzel to move him to condone the transaction, the city netted an amount larger than its annual income from taxes at that time. As for the Jews, they probably counted themselves fortunate to have saved their skins and trusted their luck and their apparent indispensability to medieval urban society to make their fortunes over again.

But in Nuremberg, as it soon turned out, they were becoming dispensable. For a century they remained fairly secure, not counting half-a-dozen confiscations and expropriations, none of which was quite so destructive as the one in 1385. Again their number increased and in proportion the insistency of the voices demanding action against them. Just what it was that made the Council decide in 1498 to move for a permanent expulsion we do not know.[4] Evidently it concluded that the commercial success attending the city's rise to political eminence had now ended the usefulness of the Jews to society. Even their taxes and special fees were no longer needed.* And once again their houses and immovable property beckoned as an immediate and very handsome reward of their disappearance. Emperor Maximilian was agreeable to the idea, asking his cut of the confiscations, of course. All the Jewish houses were to become imperial property. Arrangements concluded, the document of expulsion was issued from the imperial chancellery. Listing a number of grievances of the town and townsmen against Jews (their proliferating number, their "evil, dangerous, and cunning usorious dealings," and their purchases of so much Christian property lately), the decree authorized the Council to expel its Jews, not just for a term, but for always. Within a few weeks all had left the town. Hans Sachs sums up the results:

> A happy thought to close my ditty:
> There's not a Jew left in our city.

The Council, having offered Maximilian a lump sum of 8000

---

* Guido Kisch, *The Jews in Medieval Germany* (Chicago, 1949), pp. 316-22, argues that the rapid deterioration of the position of Jews in Germany from the middle of the fourteenth century on was largely brought about by the assumption by Christians and Christian organizations of many of the necessary economic tasks the Jews had done in the earlier Middle Ages. They had become expendable.

gulden for the Jewish houses, began to sell them to the highest bidders at a fine profit. The Jews moved about for a while; some found a refuge in Frankfurt, others went east. None of their descendants returned to Nuremberg until the middle of the nineteenth century.

It is true that for a time Jews had played a useful role in Nuremberg and other cities, perhaps even a necessary role. But Jews had had nothing to do with creating the wealth and building the economic institutions to which these cities owed their rise to eminence. The vitality of urban economies, so prominent a feature of the German scene around 1500, was the culmination of trends originating in that part of the fourteenth century which, in mercantile no less than in political affairs, was a time of both calamities and opportunities. The Black Death, during its repeated visitations, tore great gaps into a population already weakened by prolonged famine. No epidemic in history had greater economic consequences in countryside and town. Agricultural prices went into an enduring decline, while man-made articles mounted in value as purchasing power rose among city dwellers, for the plague had thinned out urban populations, but it had left their properties untouched. The result of this protracted economic imbalance between town and country was the movement of thousands of men away from the land, to join a class of city-bred artisans rapidly gaining in wealth and standing. In the country acreage returned to grass, but towns made good their epidemic population loss by encouraging the rural influx, especially if those who came could offer useful skills. Proximity and competition in and among the city workshops brought specialization in crafts. To escape underselling by newly come rural artisans, municipal craftsmen concentrated on technically more advanced crafts not found in the country. Thus manufacture became variegated, skills increasingly refined, and methods perfected. Heightened productivity in turn animated existing trade and encouraged the search for new markets and more exciting opportunities.[5]

This is the economic base of the political ascent of the German city in the later fourteenth and early fifteenth centuries. It is also the soil wherein the great burgher fortunes flourished, especially in the south and west of the Empire. In the north, the Hanseatic cities, for more than two centuries the commercial barons of northern Europe, sustained in the early fifteenth century a series of reverses from which they never recuperated. In Scandinavia, the Low Countries, England, and Russia there arose a surging economic nationalism which fragmented the Hanse's cosmopolitan trading empire by subjecting the claims of commerce to the dictates of politics.[6] South German merchants were quick to respond to this opportunity. Burgher-merchants of Strassburg, Augsburg, Ulm, and Nuremberg cut themselves in on the lucrative and prestigious transactions so long monopolized by the international traders from Hamburg, Lübeck, and Bremen. Businessmen whose fathers had been content to import salt herring and barley to augment their towns' local products now directed from their counting houses a European traffic in articles of mass consumption: textiles, timber, skins, metal ore, spices, and exotic fruits. They mined copper in Saxony and Hungary, tin in Bohemia, and lead in the Duchy of Limburg. They moved iron ore to refineries, bargained with metal workers for their finished wares, and stocked the fairs of Frankfurt and Leipzig. They shipped flax to Westphalia and Swabia and sold linen in Italy. They supplied the wealthy with sable and ermine and the less demanding with squirrel. They bought silk from southern France and fine cotton from Egypt and Cyprus. Saffron, ginger, anise, figs, and sugar cane came from the Levant. And in exchange for all this there flowed out of Germany (but first through the hands of the merchants) a host of products of native soil and native skills, things grown of wood and fiber and fashioned of metal, glass, leather, paper, and clay.

All who worked to raise or make or handle goods participated in this traffic and to some extent benefited from it. But a creeping inflation throughout the fifteenth century tended to concentrate wealth and purchasing power. Those who gained from this could seize the chances for galloping profits from increasingly imaginative ventures. At the end of the fifteenth century, the voyages to India and the unlocking of the new world brought the promise of fresh sources of supply and new markets. They also brought, and this more immediately, upsetting changes in established trade patterns. When the Portuguese caravels and

carracks replaced Italian galleys in the Orient trade, the previously unrivaled positions of Venice and Genoa began to shrink,
and Antwerp became the nerve center of European trade. This
brought a difficult period of readjustment for the German merchants of Memmingen, Augsburg, and Nuremberg,'who had long
made it their special function to channel eastern and Mediterranean wares to the north. In the long run, the new routes to
India and the discovery of America did not advance the urban
economy of Germany, though the Hanse found a new role sup-
plying ships' timbers to the Portuguese, and south German firms
sent textiles and hardware to European residents in Central and
South America. But the worst of the ill effects did not appear
until the later sixteenth century, as we shall see. Earlier, the era
of opportunities and profits seemed destined to continue un-
checked into the future.

Not all men regarded this promise with delight. At least
eighty-five per cent of the Empire's population was agricultural
at the opening of the sixteenth century, and bewilderment was
widespread among the rural people, mostly at the movement of
prices and the stagnation of their own position compared to the
improvement of townspeople.[7] To traditionalists in all classes
of society, the outlook was bleak. The rich would get richer while
the rest languished. Since no one looked for explanations in the
underlying economic trends now so obvious to the historian, cul-
prits were sought and found among one's fellow men. Merchants, notably large-scale entrepreneurs and speculators, came
in for the lion's share of opprobrium. Ulrich von Hutten lumped
them with clerics, lawyers, and predatory barons as the worst
of robbers, and Martin Luther thought it axiomatic that the businessman, whose buying and selling could hardly be carried on
honestly, corrupted not only himself but his whole society.[8] Imports of luxuries and fine materials sapped the nation's strength
and made Germans effeminate and complacent. Give a merchant half a chance to tickle the common man's taste, says Hutten, and there is no way of stopping the decline. Soon we will be
carrying all our money to the Fugger.

Nearly all critics agreed that unremitting inflation was the
worst of the evils, and every government tried to think of something to do about it. Town Councils fixed wages and prices and

stored staples to cut the market price when necessary. The Imperial Diet issued stern but ineffective decrees against monopolies and cornering. Some comfort was perhaps obtained from the knowledge that hard times had existed before. Indeed Luther noted that the true word of God had never been preached except in a time of need. "There was inflation in the days of Abraham, Isaac, Jacob, Joseph, Elijah, and Elisha—cruel inflation along with the bright light of truth. And in the time of the Gospel there was terrible inflation in the whole world."[9] But that was small consolation for people whose livelihood was affected—the inhabitants of Wittenberg, for example, where prices were rising steeply and inexplicably in the early 1500's. Confusion and resentment over all this were only too apparent in the Empire as a whole, voiced with rising impatience in the many reform manifestos, from the so-called *Reformation of the Emperor Sigismund* in the 1480's to Luther's *Letter to the Christian Nobility of the German Nation* of 1520.[10]

But in the commercial cities such bitterness, if it existed, was muted by the portents of favorable prospects for all. By 1500 there had come into being a substantial class of middle-income people whose lives as workers and consumers were tied in too many ways to the dominant merchant patricians to permit rebellion against, or even disagreement with, patrician objectives in business and politics. A touch of bad conscience lingered perhaps, and there were uneasy feelings about splendid churches and proud institutions resting on a foundation of *turpe lucrum*. Nuremberg's chronicler, Sigismund Meisterlin, surely reflected an old-fashioned uneasiness over the ethics of a business society when he wrote his account of the origins of trade in the city. "Three motives," he thought, "led burghers to engage in respectable commerce: first, the desire to provide their sons with experience by sending them into the world; second, to provide adequately for our city (for Nuremberg can raise little on her poor, infertile soil); third, to find steady occupation, for leisure is irksome to our young men." The real story was a bit different, though even by contemporary standards not dishonorable.

Meisterlin was right at least to the extent that Nuremberg merchants stayed clear of the more speculative types of enterprise on which their Augsburg competitors, the Fugger and

Baumgartner, and Höchstetter, rose to power and notoriety. In this respect too, the ingrained conservatism of Nuremberg's ruling class acted as a brake on what elsewhere was called progress. Nuremberg merchants tended to regard the rampant capitalism of Augsburg entrepreneurs with much suspicion and not a little disdain. No Nuremberger ever amassed the staggering wealth and influence of a Fugger; on the other hand, none ever perished an outcast in debtor's prison, as did Ambrosius Höchstetter in 1565. Nurembergers were satisfied with reasonable objectives, limiting their aims to what could be attained without sacrificing the purpose of their calling to the means of achieving it.

But the fact that Nuremberg stood first, at least until about the middle of the fifteenth century, among the south German mercantile cities is due to nothing other than the energy and acumen of her leading merchant families. Backed by the growing might of their city state, they built for themselves and for their community a widespread system of trade connections. These men acted in a dual capacity: first, as merchants driven by the expectation of profits and second, as city fathers anxious to supply their town with its needs and sell abroad the products of native skills in order to maintain full employment and assure a fair distribution of gains. Between these two roles they made no distinction, nor between themselves and the commonwealth as beneficiaries of their activities. The partnership worked to mutual advantage. Not unlike the pioneers of nineteenth century imperialism, Nuremberg merchants felt confident in the knowledge that their state's diplomatic, financial, and, occasionally, military might stood behind them in their far-flung negotiations. At the same time, the awareness that their city's life depended on the continued success of their operations must have imbued them with that cautious, responsible sense of moderation on which their renown and that of their city came to rest.

As early as the fourteenth century Nuremberg occupied the center of an imposing trading area. Twelve major trade routes converged upon Nuremberg, two or three bringing traffic to and from each of her main gates. Reciprocal customs treaties had been concluded with dozens of important cities: Worms, Cologne, Strassburg; Eger and Prague; Munich; also Brussels and Antwerp, Louvain, Lübeck, Arles, Bern, Solothurn, Neuchâtel, and many others.[11] On the Danube, Nuremberg goods passed toll-free from Regensburg to Passau. By 1500 the map of Nuremberg's business connections reached from Spain to Poland and from the Baltic shore to the Adriatic. From Germany to Spain went tin and wine and metal products, down the Rhone and then by sea route through Port-de-Bouc and to Barcelona, or by land to Geneva and along the Rhone to Lyon, thence across the Pyrenees over the Col de la Perche or the Col de Canfranc. Returning ships and wagons carried bales of cotton and bundles of skins. The Imhof and Tucher maintained a regular traffic with southern France. Their carts (large wooden vehicles with boat-shaped bodies and canvas roofs stretched over hoops, huge rear wheels to bear the load and negotiate deep ruts) lumbered on the great road through Ulm, Constance, and Zurich to Geneva and from there to Nantua or along the right bank of the Rhone to Lyon. In Lyon, branch offices of Nuremberg firms controlled commerce with Arles, Marseilles, Tarascon, Toulouse, and Narbonne.* A Nuremberg factor in Lisbon managed the growing African trade for his countrymen. To Italy the roads led either through the valley of the Grisons into Lombardy or through Tirol and the Brenner to Venice. There, and in Genoa, Milan, and Aquilea, the Nuremberg branch of the Welser maintained agencies for the purchase of Levantine goods. The great Main-Rhine artery drained Nuremberg of the metal wares for which her craftsmen were famous and brought in return English and Flemish cloth and saltwater fish.† Nuremberg's location midway between Main and Danube made her a natural point of transit, from Würzburg or Bamberg on the Main to Donauwörth or Ingolstadt or Regensburg on the Danube. With Poland, Nuremberg had maintained commercial relations since the fourteenth century, and Nurembergers were active in Lodz, Cracow, Warsaw, and Lublin. In Hungary, Nuremberg supplied many of the

---

* One of these merchants, Willibald Imhof, kept a *Memoriabuch* from 1533 recording his travels and enterprises. It is in manuscript in the Stadtbibliothek, Nuremberg.

† The importance of Flemish and English cloth may be seen from the earliest of Nuremberg's commercial records, the account book of the Nuremberg cloth merchant firm of Holzschuher, which dates from 1304 to 1307. Cf. *Das Handlungsbuch der Holzschuher in Nürnberg* (ed. Anton Chroust and Hans Proesler), Erlangen, 1934.

manufactured articles required by a country without any industry of its own and in turn extracted copper ore and procured grain and cattle. In eastern and northern Germany, the great market cities of Erfurt, Leipzig, Frankfurt on the Oder, and Breslau served as points of exchange for trade with the Hanse towns.[12]

In order to exploit this growing commerce, Nuremberg merchants developed a characteristic form of mercantile organization. Unlike the north German trader who liked to act the lone entrepreneur and offered investors no more than a silent partnership, the southern merchant tended to establish permanent and solidly endowed associations (Gesellschaften) composed largely of blood relatives who not only invested in the firm but worked in it as well. The Fugger of Augsburg are the most familiar example of this type of kinship corporation.[13] In Nuremberg there were dozens of such firms, nearly all enjoying enviable stability and a reputation for soundness. The latter was due, no doubt, to their avoidance of any suggestion of recklessness in their affairs. Nuremberg businesses were not organized to make huge or quick profits but to assure the gradual increase of the whole family's financial substance. Partnership agreements often placed limits on the amount of money that might be invested or lent at interest. There were exceptions to this; the Nuremberg Welser, for example, practiced an adventurous finance capitalism, and the Haller remained individualist entrepreneurs in the northern style. But in general the merchants of Nuremberg were cautious. They preferred to deal in safe commodities, those not subject to wide and unpredictable fluctuations of supply and price. They also liked to specialize in certain products in the expert handling of which they could claim long experience. Thus the Behaim and Ebner concentrated on the spice trade, and though they later diversified their activities, luxury spices remained the foundation of their fortunes. The Tetzel sold cloth to eastern Europe, the Landauer bought and sold copper, the Halbach remained wine merchants, and so on. Most avoided the slippery world of high finance, unwilling to risk their solvency on loans to princes of uncertain credit or on chancy deals on the Antwerp or Lyon exchanges. We do find a number of Nuremberg merchants among the early investors in the Indian and New World trade. One Jakob Cromberger, who had gone to Seville as a printer, and

his son Hans and his son-in-law Lazarus Nürnberger were among
the first to put their money into Caribbean voyages when the
America trade was opened to non-Castilians in the 1520's. They
sent tools and hoseshoes and nails to Santo Domingo and Mexico,
and imported sugar, pearls, jewels, and gold. They acted as factors for several other German merchants, and they themselves
maintained factors in Santo Domingo. They also did a flourishing
business in slaves, whom they bought in the Cape Verde Islands
and transported to America. But Cromberger and Nürnberger
had few competitors among their compatriots, most of whom
found these activities too adventurous.

Nor did Nuremberg merchants aspire to act as financial
agents to any ruler, secular or spiritual. For a time, when the
French king was in league with the Protestant estates in Germany, some merchants did make loans to him. But their unhappy
experience (Henry II stopped all payments in 1557) did not in-
vite emulation. Neither had they any plans for upsetting the
existing relations between workers and owners by experimenting
with the putting-out system, which elsewhere was beginning to
accumulate high profits. Nuremberg provided no foothold for
free-wheeling entrepreneurship. Council decrees would quickly
have put an end to such activities had they gotten started, which
in itself was unlikely because the very conditions that suggested
the putting-out system in other cities did not exist in Nuremberg,
where the Council's tight regulation of apprenticeship prevented
the accumulation of unemployed journeymen and day laborers.
In the metal trades where outlays for heavy equipment and large
facilities required considerable capital, a kind of entrepreneur-
ial system did arise. There the merchant acted as financier
(Verleger), advancing to the smelting master either the crude
material or the money to buy it in return for a portion of the
profit. Sometimes he also assumed responsibility for selling the
product. But so far as we know from the records, the practice
never led to exploitation, and the smelter preserved his essential
independence. Generally speaking, Nuremberg businessmen remained throughout the sixteenth century what they had always
been, namely, merchants in import and export traffic. As a result, the very names of Nuremberg businessmen had throughout
Germany the ring of solid respectability: Tucher, Imhof, Ebner,

Nützel, Schürstab, Volckamer, Kress, Behaim, Hirschvogel, Bräu-
tigam, Halbwachs, Landauer, Meissner, Penniger, Teufel, Top-
ler, Wirth, Zeringer, and many more.

These were, of course, also the families who controlled the
city, the most ancient and prosperous in the inner sanctum of the
Little Council, the rest as *Genannte* of the Large Council. Commerce and politics could hardly be separated in an age when
a merchant's goods might pass a dozen boundaries from ware-
house to market, when regalian prerogatives compelled merchants to use routes favorable to a territorial lord (*Strassen-
zwang*) and in certain circumstances offer their goods for sale
while in transit (*Stapelzwang*), when antiquated feudal customs
permitted a lord to confiscate the entire load if a wagon wheel
broke and the axle touched ground, and when international law
and custom had as yet set few limits to the wilfulness of a territorial potentate. Most of the major gains of Nuremberg's commerce had been won by means of negotiations in which delegates
spoke as diplomatic agents of their city no less than as proprietors
of merchant firms.[14]

This had always been so. As early as the fourteenth century
the city had embarked on an active commercial diplomacy. Trading privileges had been won from Duke Johann II of Lorraine
and Brabant, which opened Louvain, Brussels, and Antwerp to
Nuremberg goods on a basis equal to that of the Hanse cities;
in addition from Duke Louis III of Flanders free entry was won
for grain, wine, and textiles into Ghent, Bruges, and Ypres,
which included reduced scale and storage fees, favorable exchange rates, and low river-shipping costs. In Flanders, Nuremberg merchants traveled under their own laws except for capital
crimes, and even in such a case, should it arise, their goods and
properties were safe from confiscation. Other guarantees had
been won from Emperor Ludwig the Bavarian for free toll in
southern and eastern German cities, from the kings of Hungary
for unimpeded traffic across his crown lands, from Charles IV
for trading rights in his dynastic lands equal to those enjoyed by
his own subjects, and from the dukes of Bavaria and Austria for
compensation in case of losses due to unsafe conditions.

Most agreements stipulated that roads were to be kept in
good repair and safety was to be assured by means of armed es-

cort. But this traditional prerogative of territorial lordship, called *Conductus* or *Geleit*, was so often and so flagrantly abused that here again the city had to step in and determine matters by negotiation. Nuremberg had escort arrangements with perhaps a hundred governments. Some of these agreements were favorable, others over-priced relative to what was being offered, though they at least made routings predictable for the merchant, an important consideration, since transport often accounted for the major part of an article's cost. Escort arrangements were specific and binding. Except in a very few regions merchants could not choose their own way to their destination or try alternate roads. Routes were exactly described in the Nuremberg *Geleitbuch*, the *Escort Manual*. Here it was stated how many days were to be spent passing through a given domain, at what point a river was to be crossed, how to transfer from one border to another, and so on. For example, the journey from Nuremberg to Frankfurt, a distance of less than 150 miles, took six days and crossed six territorial jurisdictions, changing escorts four times: the margrave of Brandenburg, the bishop of Würzburg, the counts of Wertheim, the elector of Mainz, and finally the city of Frankfurt. On the road to the Erfurt fair, Nuremberg carters traveled in the successive custodies of the margrave, the bishops of Bamberg and Würzburg, the duke of Saxony, and at last the city of Erfurt. Often the points of exchange were in dispute, sometimes the route itself was the bone of violent contention among several lords. Occasionally double escort fees had to be paid out and double lodging money to rival bands of troops. That sort of obstacle could not be surmounted by the individual merchant, and it was left to the city's diplomacy to find a solution.[15]

The records of Council deliberations reveal how often the government had to deal with these and similar matters. Throughout the fifteenth and sixteenth centuries the management of the city's commercial undertakings reveals the presence of rational and informed direction at the center of affairs. Where it could, the Council acted alone; where not, it joined other cities for concerted bargaining. With Genoa and Milan, for example, it procured with the aid of other members of the Swabian League of cities the *Conventiones Alemannorum*, which contained a number of important favorable concessions. Moreover, Nuremberg revealed herself most intelligent in her liberal treatment of foreign merchants resident in, or passing through, Nuremberg, quite in contrast to more narrow-minded restrictions operating elsewhere. In Nuremberg an alien businessman could obtain a residence permit, he could even own a house. Regulations affecting foreign merchants and merchandise were written with an eye to the corresponding position of native men abroad. Laws to compel the display of goods in transit, for example, were not devised for the sake of short-term gains from taxation but in relation to the favors Nuremberg hoped herself to enjoy in other places. In its customs policy, too, Nuremberg was wisely generous, partly in order to attract the lucrative transit trade, partly to encourage the importation of needed raw materials as cheaply as possible, especially iron, lead, copper, flax, and woad and other dies. Only at the end of the fifteenth century did the Council place a burdensome toll on a few products like lamb's wool, dies, and plumes, and then the object was not so much to restrict trade as to discourage a trend toward indulgence that had begun to worry city fathers. The Customs Order of 1465 placed a moderate duty on spices, silk, precious metals, and such, but gross or inexpensive items—herrings, wood, skins, wax—bore small surcharges. Cities with which Nuremberg enjoyed reciprocal import privileges were exempted even from these, though everyone, foreigner and native alike, had to pay a small road and bridge maintenance tax levied on wagon loads by the customs officer stationed at the city gates.*

Such liberality was of great benefit to the city, not only because it yielded reciprocal privileges elsewhere, but because it led to a diversification of the design and execution of native products. Nuremberg artisans had the materials of the whole world at their disposal, and they fashioned their objects for a universal market. To this diversity native workers responded with the inventiveness and the patient skill for which Nuremberg and Nuremberg products were to be famous in all Europe.

Every small town had its bakers, butchers, tailors, cobblers, masons, and brick layers, but only a very large city could support the sprawling proliferation of skills on which international com-

---

* The tax was 2 heller per wagon, 1 heller per cart. Only grain and malt were exempted from this duty.

merce depended. Unlike small town artisans, who worked almost entirely for the satisfaction of local wants and were willing to tackle any job for which they had the tools, big city craftsmen were specialists, highly and exclusively trained, and kept by statutes from meddling with the alloted tasks of other crafts. They were employed predominantly to support the city's export trade. The small town artisan was never altogether cut off from the land. He had his field and his garden plot to raise enough turnips and cabbages to leave him independent of market trends and merchants' luck. In Frankfurt, Strassburg, Augsburg, and Nuremberg, on the other hand, the worker was a city dweller, with at most a small kitchen garden to remind him of his former state of self-sufficiency. By training and by law he was limited to the pursuit of one highly specialized calling. He produced for a market over which he and his kind had no control. He did, of course, supply the indigenous demand too, taking orders from local citizens and seeking to attract custom and please purchasers by trying his hand at new designs. But experimentation had to be done within rules laid down by guild masters or, as in Nuremberg, by the city government. By and large, in 1500 artisans worked year in and year out on the same patterns, materials, colors, and techniques. New designs and imaginative departures were likely to come from members of free crafts such as painters and glaziers or from eminent masters like the goldsmith Wenzel Jamnitzer. Most artisans, however, never departed from traditional procedures. Durability, sound functional design, and above all respectability were the paramount concerns.* Artisans took pride in the perfection of techniques. Once they had attained it they tended to persevere, varying neither method nor speed of production. Only those few men who managed to cross the vague boundary separating craft from art professed a more autonomous approach to their work.

The development of Nuremberg's commerce is documented in the increasingly varied and specialized skills listed in the city's craft records. As far back as the thirteenth century there had

---

* The great number of artisans handling secondhand merchandise testifies to the quality and workmanship of what was produced. There could hardly have been so many shoe restorers (*Altschuster*) and tailors specializing in altering used clothes if articles had been made for quick replacement.

been goldsmiths, cutlers, furriers, belt makers, various kinds of wool cloth makers, armorers and swordsmiths, scythesmiths, pewterers, and mirror makers. Dyers appear in 1300; in the following two or three decades we begin to hear of paper' makers, wiresmiths, bottle makers, brass smiths, parchment makers, and bell makers. By the middle of the fourteenth century Nuremberg had several kinds of armorers, tinkers, nail makers, rope makers, needle makers, gunsmiths and powder makers, glaziers, dice makers, saddle makers, carpenters, and makers of gut strings for viols. Most of these were sworn crafts; only the painters and sculptors and wood carvers, who prepared the way for Nuremberg's renowned school of creative artists, belonged to the unorganized, or free, crafts. But goldsmiths and silversmiths, from whose ranks many of Germany's finest artists were to come, were old established artisans and had long been organized in Nuremberg. In 1400 the records of the Council and the registers of the *Rugsamt* reveal the existence of no fewer than 141 separate crafts, among them wooden shoe makers, comb makers, playing card illuminators, honey cake makers, makers of brass bowls, rosary bead makers, ribbon makers, polishers, spursmiths, scale makers, spigot makers—to mention only a few of the more interesting trades. Even at the time there seemed to be great curiosity about techniques and tools, and an occasional artist took pleasure in portraying the craftsmen at their jobs. In the second half of the sixteenth cenutry Jost Amman and Hans Sachs collaborated on a collection of woodcuts and verses that showed artisans surrounded by the tools and gadgets of their trade: tracing spectacle lenses with a compass, filing the notches of a lock, shaping pin heads with delicate blows of a tiny hammer.[16] To the modern reader this array of instruments and equipment has, of course, a special fascination, mixed with the inevitable nostalgia for the golden age of handiwork. In Amman's day too the sight of a workman turning out finely wrought objects with the greatest precision and economy of motion must have been encouraging in its communication of a solid and enduring skill.

To take an example: the production of metal wares, a handicraft in which Nuremberg was undisputably preeminent in her time. Nowhere else were metal products so highly diversified or so beautifully made. Because Nuremberg, unlike many other cities, did not find her main markets in her immediate vicinity, her products had to be designed to suit international taste and demands; hence the enormous variety. In Nuremberg one could buy bells in all sizes—from thimble bells to huge church bells whose sonorous peals were heard for miles—candelabra, table lamps, lanterns, mortars, flat irons, Jew's harps, spigots, thimbles, scale weights, hinges, doorknobs, locks, buttons and buckles, trumpets and horns, curtain rods, nails and screws, warming pans, scissors, tools of every description, scales and scientific instruments, body armor from common mail shirts to jousting plate, weapons from pistols to the heaviest siege cannons, swords and poignards, and many, many more items.

The beauty of some of these objects has to be seen to be believed. Anyone who likes tools will gaze with envy at the display of pliers, saws, drills, hammers, vises in the glass cases of the Germanische Nationalmuseum in Nuremberg. They are graceful in design, often embossed, inlaid, or engraved with lovely decorations; but their beauty impairs neither solidity nor usefulness. Suits of armor bear elaborate designs executed by a special class of etching artists of whom Nuremberg had some notable practitioners. Equally attractive in their way are beautifully shaped trumpets, slide trombones, and post horns. These were made in all sizes and registers, but large, low-voiced instruments were a specialty, gracefully drawn and splendidly decorated. For patrician banquet tables there were elaborately moulded serving cutlery and intricate centerpieces of gilded silver that were partly chased and partly cast. The list of examples could be extended almost without limit. In the metal crafts specialization reached its most highly developed form. There was, of course, specialization according to materials: goldsmiths and silversmiths, coppersmiths, brass and bronze workers, workers in iron, and so on. But specialization was also carried to products, down to thimble makers and needle makers. The Council had long ago decreed the strictest separation of tasks. Precise definitions listed the articles each craft could make: bladesmiths were limited to two-edged swords, that is to say they might not try their hands at knives nor rapiers, because those were the monopoly of the cutlers. The latter, in turn, were forbidden to produce pocket knives, nor might any of the blade craftsmen make their own sheaths. Veit Stoss, the sculptor, had no end of trouble obtaining the Council's permission to cast one of his statues in bronze. That was not his trade, and there had been complaints from the brass smiths. In the end he got his approval but only because his patron in this case was Emperor Maximilian.

Though similar regulations also bound members of other crafts, laws were much more pervasive for the metal trades because the Council realized that much of Nuremberg's international reputation as an exporting city rested on that industry. Fineness of gold and silver was established by decree so that buyers of rings or chains or goblets knew what they were getting without having to subject their purchases to irksome tests. Silver alone might be gilded, except where the Council gave express permission for copper gilding, and then a spot the shape of a penny must be left ungilded to reveal the base material. Extraordinary steps were taken to keep the products of irregular workers from reaching the export market "so that good, honest, solid work may raise the fame of our city and its masters, and the ancient reputation of our gilding craft will not be impaired," to quote from a decree concerning gilded objects. Nothing could be publicly sold without prior inspection (Schau) by one or two, sometimes three sworn masters. Articles involving the city's reputation for integrity, such items for example as weights, guns, scythes, brass trumpets, and scientific instruments, had to be stamped with the "N" or the Nuremberg eagle, which signified inspection by a municipal officer. Every article had to also bear the stamp of its maker. Each Nuremberg metal master had his own mark, a letter or a device of some kind recorded in double registers, one kept by the sworn masters the other by the Rugs-amt. A heavy fine or even suspension awaited a craftsman who forged the mark of a more famous colleague. Staudenmeister, improperly qualified workmen operating from shops outside the city walls, were not allowed to imprint a personal device but had to identify their work with a telltale punch mark. The right to sell was, in any case, restricted to licensed masters. Piece workers (Stückwerker) who were craftsmen without workshops, acting as contractors and using tools and materials not their own, could sell nothing by themselves.

The purchase of metal ore and its refinement was a business in the hands of patricians. Individuals and firms combined to invest in the opening of ore mines and to finance metal purchases in Saxony or Bohemia or on the lead market in Antwerp; then they sold the crude material to the owners of liquation works for copper and lead melting and to forging works for the treatment of iron ore. The latter were large and expensive blast furnaces with water-driven bellows and hammers, housed in wooden sheds (Hütten) to protect machines and workers from the elements and make year-round production possible. They were built to satisfy a rapidly growing need for raw material. Most artisans still used the small traditional hand or treadle blowers, but mass production methods for purification of crude material were beginning to take over, as were factory procedures for turning out wire, sheet iron, silver leaf, copper roofing, and steel. The age of power and of mass production however was not yet a threat to the city's craftsmen and their carefully nurtured style of work. Most of the anxieties that clouded the serenity of the sixteenth-century workshop had to do with maintaining the flow of business from abroad, with ridding the market of cheapjack imitations of Nuremberg articles (the "N" and the eagle mark were much copied by towns of lesser reputation), and with keeping ecomonic peace in the city by spreading the work and assuring to all a fair share of the profits.

Most of Nuremberg's master artisans are known to us by name. We can identify their handiwork not only by the maker's mark but also by those subtle touches in execution that distinguish the creative artisan. We can trace their names through municipal records, deeds, and registers from baptism through marriage and the purchase of a house to the papers of the Rugsamt and, for an occasional reprimand, the police court. The more famous among them even had their biographers.[17] Those who are clearly "artists" in the sense in which we now distinguish a Veit Stoss from his more modestly gifted craftmates in carving wood and stone, or an Albrecht Dürer from a host of lesser masters of portraits and altarpieces, will be taken up in a later chapter. There are enough of the others to fill a whole book, but even a sampling will suggest the rich and varied talent at work.

Among the metal workers we hear of the coppersmith Sebastian Lindenast, renowned for his vessels and effigies; of Dürer's father-in-law, Hans Frey, who cast and chased statues for ornamental fountains; of Hans Lambrecht, a scale maker, specializing in tiny goldsmith's balances of uncanny accuracy; Hans Weinmann whose brass and copper weights were respected in all Germany for their reliability; Hans Lobsinger, a versatile tool maker, of whom it was said that he could make anything out of anything, who designed and built stamping and saw mills, polishing machines with foot treadle action, hydraulic fountains, and also a lathe on which he turned decorative objects of wood and bone. Evidently Lobsinger found it difficult to turn his ingenious devices to money, for in 1550 he addressed a petition to the Council asking for tangible recognition of his talents and appended a catalogue of ninety-eight categories of artistry he had perfected in metal and woodwork, organ and fountain building, silversmithing and alchemy.

The brothers Hans and Leonhard Donner made huge jacks and other lifting devices. Georg Weber designed and built counter-weight mechanisms for draw bridges and cast toothed and notched wheels for lumber mills. Hans Bullmann made articulated metal figures for clocks; he was famous in his day for his *androids,* mechanical men and women who walked about, beat drums and clashed cymbals, and danced with striking versimilitude. Though entirely self-taught in astronomy, Bullmann also turned out an animated model of the solar system operated by springs and balance weights.

Clocks, of course, were one of the specialties of the Nuremberg metal trade. Peter Henlein has gone down in history as perhaps the inventor, certainly the first extensive producer of pocket watches (called "Nuremberg living eggs" after their action and shape); he owed the success of his venture to his skill in turning out tiny but perfectly true steel wheels. Among the surviving specimens of his and his colleagues' workshops are travel clocks for hanging in coaches, necklace watches, pocket watches in oval and octagonal shapes and in the form of a book, elaborate table clocks, and alarm clocks with spring-operated flint locks to light a candle.[18] No less respected than clock makers were the locksmiths of whom one deserves special mention: Hans Ehemann, who perfected a keyless lock activated by a mechanism consisting of concentric rings that had to be brought into proper alignment for the lock to open or shut.

It was a mere step from such devices to scientific instruments. Nuremberg was renowned for the versatility and excellence of her instrument makers, and a number of men of science were attracted to the city for this reason, among them Regiomontanus, who came in 1471 and stayed four years, mainly to take advantage, as he said, of Nuremberg's excellent facilities for obtaining astronomical instruments. Best known of all the metal artisans was the amazing Wenzel Jamnitzer, a man interested in every aspect of art and science, and a genius for translating ideas into practical designs. As the city's leading goldsmith, he was, for many years, Nuremberg's official *Münzmeister*. He designed the coins, supervised die cutters, even bought gold and silver for the treasury. Jamnitzer was famous for his carved gems and seals, for his chased work and enameling, and for his sumptuous reliquaries, but even greater in demand were his scientific instruments, his scales and compasses and quadrants, his gilt levels and rulers and spheres. Tiny silver imitations of flowers and insects fascinated him, but he also liked to design ornate gold and silver table fountains. In middle age he turned to the exploration of perspective and composed a curious treatise on the subject called *perspectiva corporum regularium*, in which, by analogy of the five regular polyhedrons and the four elements, he laid out the design of the entire cosmos for his readers. Jamnitzer also made astronomical clocks to indicate time, date, and the positions of the planets. He was so famous a representative of Nuremberg's craftsmanship (Charles V and Ferdinand I both appointed him court goldsmith) that he attained the greatest distinction available to one of his birth. Already a sworn master of his craft and member of the Larger Council, he was designated late in his life artisan member of the Little Council.

Many exemplars of this great age of instrument making have survived. The Germanische Nationalmuseum in Nuremberg has splendid examples of globes and armillary spheres, astrolabes, pace counters, compasses, sun dials (including travel dials no larger than decks of playing cards), elaborate instruments for directing the drilling of mine shafts and for calculating trajectories. Musical instruments are no less exciting as illustrations of Nuremberg craftsmanship. The city had some splendid makers of brasses and pipes and a few reputable viol makers too. These men were also practicing musicians and were frequently called on to perform on their instruments. Organ builders were represented by one Master Burckhard who had constructed the organ in St. Sebald, also by Konrad Rotenburger and Georg Voll, the latter no less known for his pipe constructions for water works.

While the metal trades tended to the most refined specialization, there were always some artisans who refused to limit themselves and were so successful at their various skills that no attempt was made to restrict them. Thus Sebald Behaim was famous as both a bell caster and a cannon maker; indeed his biggest gun gained some notoriety as one of the heaviest pieces ever cast. Nuremberg gunsmiths seem to have done pioneering work in developing improved boring techniques; one of them, August Kutter, is said to have invented rifled barrels, and another may have developed the fire lock. Georg Hartwig, who was also vicar of St. Sebald, invented the caliber system based on the relation of diameter of bore at the mouth of the barrel to the weight of the shot. In this profession, too, it is hard to separate craft and artistry. Gun barrels were often beautifully engraved, carriages ornately chiseled, and pistol stocks elaborately inlaid with designs of contrasting kinds of wood and mother of pearl.

Space is lacking to continue this recital of artisans, but it would not be difficult to fill page after page with the names of cabinet makers and pewterers, of makers of iron money boxes with ingenious locking mechanisms, of chest-benches, tables, goblets and beakers in all shapes and materials, spice mills, biscuit tins, stove tiles, dolls and doll furniture of wood and alabaster, decorative fruit and plants in painted wax, and so on and on. It is not hard to imagine what the scene was like at the three annual Nuremberg fairs held at New Year's, Easter, and St. Egidius (September 1), each one lasting three weeks. Buyers and sellers came to these from all over Germany, and the stalls and booths in front of the houses must have displayed the full range of Nuremberg skills, the market square thick with people and the streets congested with carts and horses.*

Where no evidence of skills has survived, we can turn to the specifications for masterpiece requirements for an appreciation of the talents required to become a recognized craftsman in Nuremberg. Aspiring master masons were asked to prove their ability to erect a building on any kind of soil and to design an elongated groin vault. They also had to gauge from a distance the precise height of a tower and calculate from its height the thickness of its walls. Clock makers (who did not form a sworn craft until 1565) had to give two proofs of their mastery; first, they had to make a standing clock that sounded the quarters and the hours with distinct peals and showed on one side the sun and moon traversing the sky "in such a way that the two bodies always indicate the quarter, half hour, and hour, and, on the other side, calendar date, length of day, and positions of the planets"; second, they had to make a watch for wearing round the neck capable of sounding alarm at the waking hour. Carpenters made a doweled window frame with six panes and six shutters and also a tall wardrobe inlaid in different veneers and supported by carved columns in the Doric, Ionic, or Corinthian orders. Goldsmiths, according to the Council's Goldsmith Statutes of 1515, had to fashion a silver goblet in the shape of a columbine, a gold ring with mounted stone, and either a carved seal or an ornate belt buckle. All items must accord with specifications prepared by the sworn masters. Regulations also required that approved masterpieces remain in the town hall for display and instruction, but this could not always have been done, at least not with the larger objects.

Certain kinds of master artisans, whose skills were frequently needed for public work, were kept on part-time employment by the city. Most of them were in the building trades—masons, stone cutters, bricklayers, carpenters, plasterers, whitewashers, street pavers, roofers, also glaziers, rope makers, locksmiths,

---

* These three were international fairs. In addition, there were periodic market days for the local sale of products and produce. For example, the wine market was held every Thursday on the square of that name and attracted hundreds of carts from the grape regions of Franconia, the Neckar, Tauber, and Rhine.

chimney sweeps, carters, and so on. Though free to take on private work, these men were obliged to hold themselves available for municipal jobs, in return for which they received from the public treasury the so-called *Wartegeld* (stand-by money) in addition to pay for work done. The city also ágreed to give them preferential employment. Thus the government could enter the labor market directly if and when it chose. With their journeymen assistants and their apprentices, these municipal masters constituted a sizable work force, augmented by a small army of day laborers for unskilled work. The latter constituted the lowest economic group in the city, living from hand to mouth, a fact recognized by the municipal architect's habit of paying them their weekly wage on Saturday morning rather than just before quitting time in the evening so that their wives had some money for the weekend marketing.

Municipal employees were under the direct supervision of the municipal architect *(der Stadt Baumeister)*, a political official and member of Council, about whose office we know a good deal from the description given of it by one of its most distinguished incumbents, Endres Tucher, who was architect from 1464 to 1475.[19] The architect did not merely contract with the municipal masters for work to be done for the city, while leaving them free to organize and direct their own work force; but true to Nuremberg's centralized administrative practices, the architect himself employed all workers down to the privy cleaners and the apprentice locksmiths who cleaned and oiled all the locks ·in the city before the onset of winter cold each year. He supervised them at their jobs, inspected finished work, walked about the city "every day and all day, going from one job to another to make sure that they start work on time and have all the materials they need and, if not, he must send it to them." At the end of the week he paid them out of the city treasury.

Nonmunicipal masters were, of course, self-employed, though, as we have seen, prices and wages were a matter of public policy and subject to Council decisions. This does not mean that such legislation was necessarily bureaucratic in objective and implementation. Councillors not only associated with the city's artisans as cocitizens, but they were even more intimately involved with them as fellow members of a closely integrated economic order. Thus artisans could be sure that informed and understanding attitudes prevailed in Council, though, needless to say, the Council's responsibility for balancing the often divergent concerns of a variegated economy, a complex political organization, and a precarious position in international affairs sometimes produced dissatisfaction in certain groups. But not even a critic could deny that patrician councillors cared deeply for the economic well-being of the city's artisans and handed down decisions meant to preserve their favorable position.

The official testing by municipal inspectors of almost every finished article was therefore looked upon without resentment as a legitimate extension of the government's concern with the general welfare and the commerical reputation of the city. Inspection gave force to production regulations and assured compliance. It ascertained, for example, that ebony or boxwood were the only materials used for compass boxes. Comb makers were forbidden to utilize claws or goat horn, and inspection made sure that only the prescribed bull horn was used. Inspection began before an article left its maker's bench, for the sworn masters went round to the workshops and examined work in progress, entering their findings in a production record, the *Umgangsbuch*. When the completed item reached the market, public inspection took over. Every single flint lock was tried to make sure that it worked. Finished artillery pieces were fired twice on each of three successive days, and after every pair of shots the gun barrel was dismantled and the bore examined. Armor plate was submitted to inspection before as well as after polishing; the latter had to be done with emory, not sand. Export pewter could contain no more than one part in ten of lead, though work to be sold within the city might be of a softer mixture. Defective or otherwise unsatisfactory articles were immediately destroyed without compensation to the maker. The same procedures kept inferior imports from reaching the home market; inspection of foreign articles was fully as rigorous as of domestic ones. Moreover, no imported manufactures could enter except under conditions determined by the Council, either in its reciprocal trade agreements or in its protective legislation. Quality control aside, the Council never permitted the market to become flooded. In fact economic policies and political objectives coincide at almost every point, and the thousands of individual regulations relate to each other to form a comprehensive web of social legislation. Statutes that seem petty or even appear to violate sound reason when considered by themselves (such as the ban on street hawking on Sundays and holidays while permitting sales to customers who entered a shop uninvited) make sense when considered as part of a coherent view of society and its functions.[20]

Economically, the aim was to make the city as self-dependent as possible. Thus cattle dealers were instructed to supply the demands of local butchers before selling animals abroad, and butchers had to sell skins first to local tanners, and tanners supplied leather to local cobblers and saddlers before looking for customers elsewhere. Wealth-gathering and profit-making were not recognized as the final cause of economic activities. Far from seeing society as a mere aggregate of competitive producing and consuming groups, the ruling patriciate considered their city as an extended family engaged in a common civic pursuit and held together by mutual political duties and social responsibilities. A separation between the latter and the aims of business would have seemed arbitrary and unnatural. In Nuremberg the attempt to adjust economic objectives to social and ethical ends went particularly far, a fact that may well have contributed to the rapid rise from about 1500 on of the more ruthless Augsburg to Nuremberg's former place as the first among southern German cities. Augsburg's better geographic location had much to do with this shift, of course. So did her more flexible government and far less exclusive class structure, which encouraged the ascent of new men from the ranks of artisans to positions of real economic and political influence.* But an important factor seems to have been the laissez-faire attitude of Augsburg's government toward monopolies, profiteering, and the accumulation of great fortunes. In Nuremberg these enterprises were subjected to searching supervision and rigorous control. Wealth and moneyed power were not objectionable when held in accustomed and

---

* Augsburg's Little Council was considerably larger than Nuremberg's (69 members as against 42), allowing much wider representation.

trustworthy hands. But unproven and unpredictable elements must not be permitted to disarray the carefully contrived economic and social order. Money-making at the expense of fellow citizens was frowned upon not only for its intrinsically unworthy motives but also for the social decay it was bound to bring.

Speculative buying *(Fürkauf* or *Vorkauf)* was particularly suspect as a form of exploitation and a socially unproductive pursuit. Ordinarily it was outlawed, or, where middle men were deemed necessary, controlled by making them sworn agents of the Council. Especially in the food trade did the would-be *Fürkäufer* find himself blocked by the full force of the law. No one, citizen and noncitizen alike, could buy cattle for the purpose of profitable resale, and this injunction included informal agreements as well as fixed terms of sale. Butchers were forbidden to intercept approaching herds and arrange their purchases on the road. Statute after statute condemns this "riding out" as a wicked transgression, but the very repetition of the ban shows that it must have been difficult to abolish a deep-rooted practice. Fruit vendors could not sell their produce to middle men until they had displayed it three consecutive days in the fruit market. Similar rules governed profiteering in craft materials. It was considered *Fürkauf* if an artisan master bought more leather or copper or tin than he and his journeymen helpers and his one allotted apprentice could use. If in some way a craftsman came upon an unusually advantageous supply of raw material, he was required to notify his colleagues of his luck and, if asked, to share it with them. In some trades individual purchase was altogether forbidden; spectacle makers, for example, bought collectively and then divided. A fine of ten gulden awaited the master who struck out on his own. Such restrictions applied to every one of the crafts. Where *Fürkauf* was licit, in the purchase of grain and hay and also cattle during the years of meat shortage in the 1550's and 1560's, the Council kept its eyes on it.

To what extent collectivism was preferred to uncontrolled individual enterprise may be seen from a brief and unsuccessful experiment with profit sharing tried by the city's cloth shearers in 1556. As established by the Council on request of the eleven Nuremberg masters of this craft, the procedure called for deposit of all money taken in and its distribution to the members at the end of each work week. To quote the statute:

All work done in each of the eleven workshops is to be brought to the house of the Sworn Master, there to be marked with a badge. And all money collected in each workshop for work done there by the master and his helpers is to be placed in a locked chest kept by the Sworn Master. Every Saturday the sum is to be divided among the eleven workshops in such a way that the highest producer and the lowest producer get each an appropriate share [*ein gepurender teil*], no matter whether he has done much work or little. And this will be of great help not only to the old and tired masters, but also to the reputation of this craft, for daily inspection of the finished cloth will encourage superior workmanship.

Six months later the statute was rescinded and the practice abolished following complaints to the Council by dyers, tailors, and other workers in the cloth trade. There is no evidence that it was ever tried by any of the other crafts in the city, though many of them must occasionally have faced the same problems as the cloth shearers, namely, a large number of aged and semi-retired masters and, perhaps, masters' widows. The point is that there was nothing in the suggestion to frighten the Council. Indeed the Council often admonished the more successful masters to share their work with less occupied colleagues. On the other hand, moves to break through established practices in the opposite direction, toward economic individualism, met with determined resistance.

By the 1550's, to be sure, Nuremberg had seen her best days as a leading manufacturing and mercantile city. Though she was able to maintain her eminence for another century or so and her political independence until 1806, the later sixteenth century saw the beginning of her gradual demise as a center of power and influence.[21] The reasons for this decline are both political and economic and the latter, again, both indigenous and relative to general developments in German and European economics. As we have seen, the voyages of discovery had brought about a gradual shift of the bulk of world trade from the Mediterranean and Adriatic basins to the Atlantic, with Lisbon and Antwerp usurping the positions formerly held by Venice and Genoa. Ger-

man merchants had adjusted to this development by intensifying their ancient connections with these centers of European
traffic. For about half a century after 1500 the new commerce
quickened the international trade of Nuremberg and Augsburg
and other cities, and it more than compensated for the rapid
decline of the transalpine carrying trade on which they had
formerly depended.

But south German business firms were so far from the ocean
and so alien to the problems of a large-scale maritime trade,
that none could rise to a position of eminence in Atlantic Europe.
In the late 1550's a change became apparent. The disastrous
effect of the reigns of Charles V and Philip II and of Francis I
on the economies of Spain and France was brought down upon
several German commercial houses when Philip II and Henry II
stopped all payments in 1557.[22] Restrictive and protectionist
policies in many national and territorial states looked to the ex-
clusion of foreign merchants as a desirable step toward economic
independence. Charles IX of France imposed a heavy tax on
German merchants. Increased territorial tariffs in Bavaria, Silesia,
Bohemia, Austria, and Hungary threatened to make trade there
unprofitable for Nuremberg. Worst of all for German merchants
was the interruption of commerce with the Netherlands due to
the Spanish war and to Philip's stringent tariff policy, by which
an export duty of one tenth of value was laid on all products. In
the late 1560's German ships traveling upstream on the Rhine
were stopped and searched by Spanish troops and all Spanish
and Italian goods confiscated. At the same time, the Duke of
Alba began to impose Philip's tolls and tariffs in Nijmwegen,
Arnheim, Duisburg, and Dordrecht. In late November of 1576
came the plundering of Antwerp by the Spaniards. Twenty
houses belonging to Nuremberg firms were damaged in the pil-
lage, but far more profound in its adverse effects was the consequent decline of Antwerp and the rise of Amsterdam as a commercial and financial center. In Amsterdam, German merchants
had no position from which to recoup their western losses. Thus
the great commercial houses of Germany were gradually eliminated from the most lucrative of commercial operations. Politics
and war combined to endanger, sometimes to destroy, trade.
Charles V, locked in his long conflict with France, sought to in-

terdict German trade with the enemy and to keep Frenchmen
and French money from moving about the Empire. He did not
succeed, but his attempts were hardly conducive to good commercial relations. As a result, Nuremberg lost many of her long-
standing trading privileges in France and the Netherlands.

To make things worse, a simultaneous shift in Nuremberg's
mercantile relations with Italian firms raised the threat of competition from another quarter. Until the middle of the sixteenth
century, a formal agreement had kept south German and Italian
merchants from intruding on each others' spheres of economic
influence. Italians were to avoid German soil north of Trent and
leave the traffic from Italian ports to the northern countries in
German hands, while Germans agreed not to meddle in the
Levant trade and recognize Venetian monopoly in the Mediterranean. The Germans, for their part, had managed to live up to
the agreement, though we hear of an occasional Nuremberg
merchant being prosecuted by the Council, and in one case even
exiled, for illicit attempts at direct trade with the East. The Italians, too, generally stuck to the bargain. But this was in the
fifteenth century. In the later part of the sixteenth century the
arrangement no longer served Italian purposes. The flight of
shipping from the Mediterranean and the Turkish encroachment
sent Venetians and others looking for new sources of income.
Their agents began to appear in south German cities, founding
depots and establishing offices and acquiring houses, especially
in Nuremberg where the Council's customary liberality toward
foreign traders had encouraged them to be bold. By 1574 Nuremberg had resident representatives of eighteen Italian firms,
the Torrigiani from Florence, the Arconati from Milan, the
Franchi and Maranelli from Verona, the Lumaga, Beccaria,
Crolalanza, and Vertema from Piuro, the Butti and Perez from
Lucca, and so on. They had taken over much of the commerce in
spices, velvet, silk, and other luxuries and had made inroads on
what remained of the Netherlands' trade. Frequent protests to
the Council reflect the bitterness of native merchants over the
presence of these foreigners who could so effectively undersell
them because their purchases at home were not subject to the
many taxes and restrictions under which German merchants had
to buy in Italy.[23]

In short, the shrinking of her commercial horizons and increased competition for the economic opportunities that remained meant for Nuremberg, and for many other cities, an end to that long period of gratifying economic and political expansion which makes so remarkable a chapter in the history of the late Middle Ages in Germany. Not that prosperity was changed to penury or that burgher fortunes dwindled. The astounding career of Bartholomäus Viatis alone would disprove that suspicion. Viatis, one of the resident Italians just mentioned, was a self-made man from Venice who entered Nuremberg as a poor boy in 1550, built up an enormous trade in leather, plumes, dye stuffs and cloth, and died 74 years later, an honored citizen worth more than 100,000 gulden.[24] Fortunes could still be made in the late sixteenth century and new companies founded, like Paul Pfinzing's reorganization of the old family firm in 1595.[25] But for the community as a whole, growth had come to an end.

Diplomatic and military involvements compounded Nuremberg's difficulties. From 1552 to 1554 the city fought a bitter war with the Margrave Albrecht Alcibiades, which left her with a public debt of over four and a half million gulden on her books and interrupted her commerce disastrously. The civil war in Germany also took its toll of prosperity. Although Nuremberg never joined the Schmalkaldic League of Protestant powers, she was compelled to subscribe to its war fund to the tune of 80,000 gulden. When the wars were over, in 1555, defenses had to be strengthened and new towers built. Meanwhile the city had to meet constant demands for contributions to the defense of the Empire against the Turks. Seventy Roman months* were prescribed between 1566 and 1570 alone, and Nuremberg's assessments, reflecting her acknowledged wealth and position, were among the heaviest in the Empire. Diplomatic representation, litigation in territorial and royal courts, military preparations—these had to be paid for. Nuremberg began to realize that autonomy could be a heavy burden, as the means to secure her political independence swallowed an ever larger portion of her income.

---

* The "Roman month" was originally a monthly contribution to help defray the expenses of the emperor's trip to Rome to be crowned. In the reign of Maximilian this became a tax for military operations.

Until the middle of the century, the city's end-of-year accounting had regularly shown a surplus.* Not long thereafter the
books reveal an annual deficit of from 50,000 to 70,000 gulden.[26]
What was to be done? The tax on beer was doubled, territorial
property revenues increased, and domestic servants were forced
to pay a small tax, but these were palliatives and offered little
relief. A more radical solution was proposed by Endres Imhof, the
first *Losunger*, in 1566. If adopted, the proposal would have
decreed a compulsory public loan for ten years of one tenth of
the fortune of every citizen worth over 1000 gulden. But the
Elders turned against this project because they were frightened
of the effect of such a desperate expedient on the city's credit,
and they suspected that some among the wealthy would prefer
emigration to forced public lending. Instead a consortium of
wealthy patricians lent their city a sum of 110,000 gulden at 12
per cent interest. But it was not enough. More palliatives followed, higher taxes on wine and beer, increased tolls and duties
on transit goods. After long hesitation, the Council even adopted
a grain consumption tax, but this was dropped three years later
following an alarming rise in grain prices. All other prices rose
too, and during the rest of the sixteenth century and the first
decades of the next, Nuremberg's time of rising prosperity seemed
to have come to an end.

It is possible that a less rigid social order, bringing more
adaptable minds into Council deliberations, might have found
a way out. Augsburg, for example, did not shut its government's
political ears to advice from below and from outside. By the
1570's economic and political forces were at work in Europe and
Germany for which tradition-bound urban patricians had little
understanding and no sympathy. The fact was that even in the
Holy Roman Empire, with its fragmented authority and its cen-
trifugal jurisdictions, the independent city state had become an
anomaly. Its self-contained system of political and social values
and its parochial orientation inward upon itself were soon to
make it a museum piece. By the beginning of the seventeenth
century the free city had become a small enclave in the midst of
great territorial states organized and governed as political and

---

* In 1550, for example, income was approximately 168,000 gulden,
expenditures about 147,000 gulden.

economic units by their Habsburg, Hohenzollern, Wettin, and Wittelsbach rulers. There was simply not enough power available to city governments to continue to play the role to which the history of the previous three and a half centuries had accustomed them. But this was the only role their patrician statesmen had learned. As long as general external situations permitted, they guided their community ably and successfully. When changing circumstances proceeded to erode the political and economic world in which the imperial city had grown to maturity, a more sophisticated political wisdom than theirs was called for to resist the threats or to adapt to them.

But while the old medieval world lasted—the age not yet committed to the imperative logic of centralized and aggressively militarized power states—Nuremberg's particularistic isolationism served her well. Her system remained viable as long as she could maintain her freedom of action and keep intact her internal political structure, and this in turn was assured as long as citizens had no cause to question the purpose of urban communalism. Stray doubts and scattered criticism were stilled with brisk references to general prosperity and international prestige. And this was not mere political propaganda. For approximately a hundred years, from the middle of the fifteenth century to the decade following the Second Margrave's War, Nuremberg was in that rare condition where a society operates not only as well as it can be expected to manage but as well as its ambitions and principles encourage it to hope. During that century Nuremberg's statesmen achieved the objectives they held essential, and this they did without having to resort to means unworthy of the ends in view. From the vantage point of present-day principles of democracy and individual self-determination, the system is vulnerable on many points. It was paternalistic, high-handed, and, in a way, totalitarian. Its authority and competence reached into every corner of a man's life. No claims to privacy of action, speech, nor judgment counted against the demands of the social body as these were interpreted by its leading members. The words about the *utilitas publica* absorbing and extinguishing *privata utilitas* when the two were in conflict were no empty phrase. Thousands of laws brought them into the daily life of every resident, and the most determined assault from the eight-

eenth-century arsenal of arguments for individual autonomy
would have failed against them.

Nor would the rival claim advanced by some strong man with
a vaulting ambition to dominate have been taken more seriously,
namely, that men could be governed effectively by the arbitrary
power of a single will. In the absence of an indigenous spokesman
for the political doctrine of the independent city state, we may
appropriate Machiavelli's words at the opening of the fourth
book of his *Florentine History*. Wherever laws and institutions
are not well planned, Machiavelli writes, city republics fluctuate
between crises of oppression and chaos. Only where laws and law
enforcement keep the whims of would-be tyrants and the folly
of the multitude in check does good government prevail. "Such
a state may truly be called free, and its government pronounced
strong and stable, for, resting on good laws and ordinances, it,
unlike other states, has no need to be supported by the ability
and good fortune of any one man." Nuremberg qualified for
Machiavelli's designation as a *vivere libero*. Her governing magnates knew it, and her citizens accepted it on the evidence of
the blessings brought by success. Just as Renaissance Venice had
attained, in her self-estimation as well as in the boundless admiration her polity drew from the rest of Europe, a kind of suspended point of political stability, Nuremberg in 1500 had
reached what her leaders considered a safe haven from the natural momentum of political and social change. Their goal from
then on was to preserve what they had. Problems and challenges
were faced with that principal objective in mind.

FOUR

Ecclesiastical Affairs And Religion;
The Reformation

Church and State in Nuremberg—Churches and Monasteries
—The Council's Supervision of Religious Matters—Clerical
Abuses and Corruption—The Nuremberg Reform Circle—
Staupitz, Linck, Spengler—The Ninety-Five Theses—Spread of
the Lutheran Doctrines—The Edict of Worms and the Council
—Public Understanding of the Lutheran Creed—The Religious
Disputation of 1525—Organizational and Liturgical Changes—
Dissolution of the Monasteries—The Brandenburg-Nuremberg
Church Organization—Nuremberg's Position in the German
Civil War—The Second Margrave's War—Nuremberg in 1555.

Very little has been said in these pages of relations between
Church and State in the affairs of Nuremberg. But the very omis-
sion of this subject so far must have suggested that these relations
did not there take the form of those bitter and vindictive clashes
that marked Church-State connections elsewhere. In Nuremberg
piety and devotional exercises had always been considered aspects of civic conduct and as such not so very different from
selling shoes or guarding moats and walls. Churches and monasteries were property-owning and income-producing institutions.
Preachers and confessors influenced the conduct of citizens. Even
the metaphysical speculations of theologians bore on the functioning of secular society. A political system that regarded nothing as irrelevant to the public purpose and immune from administrative direction was not likely to exclude the religious establish-

ment from its competence. This had been the principle governing the coexistence of Church and State for a century or more.

Throughout most of her history Nuremberg's ties to her ecclesiastical overlord had been extremely loose, almost nominal. None of the bishops of Bamberg had been able to offer more than token opposition to the city's steadily growing autonomy in matters of church administration. Nor did much resistance come from clerics within the city. Considering her territorial extent and the size of her population, Nuremberg did not have an excessively large ecclesiastical establishment. The census of 1449 enumerated only 446 clerics out of a population of over 20,000, and the 446 included clerical retainers and household servants as well.[1] That is not much more than two per cent of the inhabitants. In the villages and hamlets of Nuremberg's territory the proportion was probably much higher (we lack precise information on this point), and real estate and properties were grasped more firmly there in church and monastic hands. But within the city, the clergy, secular and regular, played only those roles alloted to it by the government.

From the earliest days of Nuremberg's recognition as a parish, the Council had usually managed to have its way in vital questions of church management. Late in the fourteenth century, the first of her parish churches, St. Sebald, gained a kind of supremacy over the neighboring village church of Poppenreuth, to which it had formerly been *ecclesia filialis;* thenceforth tithes and annates and other moneys flowed into the city. A papal bull stipulated that the priests of Sts. Sebald and Lorenz must reside in their parishes and that no part of the income of the two churches might be spent outside the city. It was the Council's diplomacy at the courts of Urban VI and Boniface IX in Rome that had won these rights. (This was in the late 1380's, and rival lines of popes officiated in Avignon and Rome—a propitious time to gain concessions.) From then on the Council claimed a voice in the selection of priests to the chief parish churches. Needless to say, the bishop did not always cooperate. Habitual obstinacy in the face of Council-sponsored candidates safeguarded his rightful prerogative of appointment. But here, as everywhere, real power lay with money. Successfully claiming the right to manage the endowments donated by pious citizens, the Council used this legal tool to bestow or withhold financial largesse and thus control the selection as well as the conduct of the clergy. Indeed, the Council persuaded donors to draw up their deeds in such a way as to bring supervision of the benefice into its hands. In order to leave nothing to chance or to less determined heads, the Council began early in the fourteenth century to appoint some of its members to be superintendents over churches, convents, monasteries, and charitable institutions in the city. Called *Kirchenpfleger* or *Gotteshauspfleger*, these men, backed by the authority of the entire Council and wielding the prestige of their own standing in the city, were in charge of all aspects of church management involving property, land, and money. The legal ground on which the Council entered this venture in the gradual establishment of a state church was its constitutional right to make all decisions concerning construction and the utilization of real estate in the city. From these to the supervision of revenue and the management of ecclesiastical business affairs was but a small step. Priests were effectively excluded from all such responsibilities, and the Council's authority did not always halt at the border between secular and spiritual matters.

In 1474 Sixtus IV granted the Council the right of presentation, that is, of suggesting suitable candidates for the staffing of the two parish churches, these men to be formally confirmed by the pope. At first this right affected only the "papal months." (These were the odd months of the year: January, March, May, and so on when, in the event of an incumbent's death, the pope was by tradition empowered to name a successor; the even months were "episcopal months.") But in 1513 an agreement with the bishop and the Cathedral Chapter of Bamberg stretched the Council's authority over episcopal months as well. It cost the city 1000 gulden cash to win this prerogative from the bishop, plus an annuity of 100 gulden to compensate him for the financial loss entailed by this transfer of appointive power. But the money was well spent, considering the importance of the prerogative gained. Finally, in 1514, Pope Leo X granted the Council the full rights of patronage over the two parish churches.

Although the relatively small number of clerics might suggest the opposite, Nuremberg was in fact generously supplied with houses of worship and monastic settlements. In addition to

the two large parish churches, Nuremberg had (in order of antiquity and mentioning only the important ones) the churches of
St. Aegedius, originally the chapel of a twelfth-century Benedictine
abbey but much enlarged in the early fifteenth century; the
church of St. Jacob, belonging to the Knights of St. John; the
Hospital Church (*Spitalkirche*), part of an institution built in
the 1330's by Konrad Gross as a refuge for old people without
means; the church of St. Martha, also a hospital church; and the
Church of Our Lady on the market square, erected, as we have
seen, in the middle of the fourteenth century on the site of the
razed synagogue. As for monasteries and convents, there were
eight of them; the oldest was the Benedictine house of St.
Aegidius, founded in 1140, the youngest that of the Carthusians,
built on the outskirts of the city in 1380 but soon enclosed by the
expanding walls. Also represented were the Minorite friars in
their house on the southern bank of the Pegnitz; the Dominicans,
who had come to the city about 1250 and built a compound on
donated ground north of the river on the slope leading to the
castle; the Carmelites located in the Lorenz parish, also on donated soil; and the Augustinians, who had established themselves
in the city in 1265 from an earlier location beyond the walls and
who gained a quick popularity as preachers, particularly among
the educated. Johann Staupitz frequently spoke in the Augustinian church of St. Vitus, as we have seen, and in 1517 and 1518
a close friend of Luther's, Wenzeslas Linck, was preacher there.
Luther himself stopped at the house in 1518 on his way to and
from Augsburg. The Order of the Knights of St. John had been
in Nuremberg since about 1200, originally outside the walls with
the Order's hospital, St. Elisabeth (usually called the Old Hospital to distinguish it from the New Hospital of the Holy Ghost
founded in 1331 by Konrad Gross). The Johannites were the
leading hospital order in Germany and a well-endowed and influential organization in Nuremberg no less than elsewhere.

There were also two convents, St. Clara's and St. Catherine's.
The former had been the Convent of Mary Magdalen but was
assigned to the Clares in the late thirteenth century, when the
original order was abolished by Gregory X. The Clares were the
female equivalent of the Franciscans, and St. Clara's in Nuremberg, having adopted the rule of St. Francis, became a highly

respected order of well-born and high-minded ladies. Its last and most distinguished abbesses were two sisters of Willibald Pirckheimer, Charitas and Clara, and his daughter, Catherine. The Convent of St. Catherine had at one time been a lay association of women devoted to nursing the indigent; their house had been endowed as a hospital by a wealthy citizen. But later they reorganized themselves under the Dominican rule and were placed under the spiritual supervision of the Order of Preachers in Nuremberg, a connection which lasted until the time of the Reformation. This too was a domicile for the well born, a fact that did much to determine the fortunes of these groups after 1525. The Order's last prioress was Felicitas Tucher, a member of the most distinguished family in the city.

All of these monastic establishments were governed by Council directives of varying stringency. The Carthusians, for instance, were limited to twelve brothers and six novices headed by one prior. No one personally unacceptable to the Council was admitted to the group, of which the Council itself acted as protector, appointing an official (called *Schaffer,* the usual title for an administrative officer) to keep the government informed of affairs in the house. Nothing in secular matters could be undertaken without the *Schaffer's* approval. Peasants working on monastery lands were placed under the jurisdiction of municipal courts. All this was agreed upon and drawn up in 1380, when the Carthusians settled in Nuremberg following their endowment there by the patrician Marquard Mendel. Other orders were bound by similar agreements. Where reform was advisable, the Council did not hesitate to intervene. At St. Catherine's, for example, the Council insisted on introducing a stricter order of obedience as a consequence of complaints and a threat by one of the inmates to transfer herself and, what was worse, her fortune from Nuremberg to a reformed convent elsewhere. A number of Council members accompanied the Dominican prior to the house—this was in 1428, following an earlier, unsuccessful, attempt to introduce observantist rules—and their influence was decisive in persuading the sisters to place themselves under a new prioress summoned from a reformed convent nearby. Kinship helped, of course, in this case; St. Catherine's was a refuge for unmarried and widowed members of Nuremberg's patrician families. Half a century later the Council obtained a bull from Pope Sixtus IV limiting membership to native Nurembergers and to as many as could be properly supported by the house's income. But the Council was no less successful in its supervision of every other monastic establishment in the city.

Most likely all this sounds more impressively authoritarian than it really was. Complaints of and agitation over clerical malfeasance were as prevalent in Nuremberg as everywhere else at the time. Corruption and immorality also existed and occasionally came into the open as scandals. As this sort of thing was all but unknown among the civic officials directly appointed by and solely responsible to the Council, it is reasonable to suspect that the control of clergy at the opening of the sixteenth century had not proceeded very far in Nuremberg. Numerous entries in the Council minutes reveal the annoyance that these abuses of trust and office caused in the Council chamber. In the very years when Martin Luther's name began to give a new urgency to the familiar call for reform, Council books record appeals from nearby villages concerning the unsatisfactory performance of their priests; rumors about the vicar of St. Sebald who was said to be having improper relations with a number of married women; incidents of accused murderers obtaining sanctuary in monastery churches to escape trial; widespread annoyance in commercial quarters over the citation of burghers before the papal court in Rome; complaints of absenteeism by beneficed priests* and of incompetent and indifferent hireling substitutes, and so on.[2] These were the usual grievances heard everywhere in Germany at this time. They do not amount to very much really—human failings compounded the slovenliness of an aged and deeply entrenched bureaucracy. But an occasional crisis provided better cause for resentment than petty annoyances. To cite one: not long after the Council had paid the last installment of the large sum owed Leo X for his confirmation of the Council's patronage right over the two parish churches, Leo's successor, Hadrian VI, refused to recognize the agreement as binding and demanded fresh payments. There were other incidents of this kind, and

---

* The prior of St. Sebald, for example, Melchior Pfinzing, was also the city's procurator at the court of the Emperor Maximilian. (The priors of Nuremberg's two parish churches were always professional jurists.)

each added fuel to the smouldering fire of anticlericalism. Events were soon to show the virulence of latent popular antipathy toward the clergy and how quickly it could boil to the surface. The Reformation in Nuremberg, in large part, was a response to this resentment and a decision to eradicate the last refuge from the Council's authority and the last enclaves of independence from civic responsibility.

Not that this reformation was conceived as a solution to purely administrative problems. For some time there had been in existence in Nuremberg a group of important men who were receptive and well acquainted with Luther's theological ideas. They were important men not only for the role they were about to play in the reformation of their city but because of their high standing in Nuremberg's social and political elite. The fact that such men were drawn to the Wittenberg cause determined events in Nuremberg even before Lutheranism became a matter of controversy in the early 1520's.

We have heard, in other connections, of the numerous visits made by Johann Staupitz to Nuremberg. In his capacity as vicar general of Augustinian observantists in Germany, Staupitz often passed through the city on his visitation trips and occasionally stayed on for several days' preaching in Nuremberg's Augustinian church where he was a most welcome speaker. In 1516, as we have seen, he preached the Advent sermons on the subject of the inefficacy of human works. Staupitz was a powerful orator and a moving personality. A group of friends gathered round him during his visits, to draw him out while he was there and discuss his sermons and the issues they raised after his departure. These meetings became a forum for exploring serious matters beyond the cares of day-to-day commercial and political affairs. The city's two *Losunger* of the time were members, Anton Tucher and Hieronymus Ebner, also Kasper Nützel and Hieronymus Holzschuher, both belonging to first patrician families, also Sigmund and Christoph Fürer, Christoph Scheurl the jurist, Lazarus Spengler the secretary to the Council, Albrecht Dürer, the prior of St. Lorenz Georg Behaim, and several others. They met in rooms in the Augustinian monastery and called themselves, after their mentor, the *Sodalitas Staupitziana*.

In the spring of 1517 they were joined by a man who was to

form a direct connection between Nuremberg and the Wittenberg reformers, Wenzeslas Linck, formerly prior of Augustinians in Wittenberg and, as professor of theology at the university there, a colleague of Luther's. Staupitz had sent him as preacher to the Augustinians in Nuremberg. News of Brother Martin and of his stirring lectures on Paul's *Epistle to the Romans* thus got to Nuremberg months before the *Ninety-five Theses* made his name a national cause. Christoph Scheurl, whose letters are our best source for the group's activities, had written to Luther in January 1517 asking for his friendship.[3] But Luther replied evasively, rejecting the praise lavished on him in Scheurl's humanist hyperbole and warning the jurist that he, a miserable sinner, was unworthy of the notice of so learned a man.[4] The correspondence continued nevertheless. In September Luther sent the ninety-seven theses he had written for the baccalaureate disputation of his student Franz Günther on certain questions of justification, grace, and free will. They were much acclaimed in the Nuremberg circle.* It is Scheurl's next letter to Luther that opens with the challenging words "*Christi theologiam restaurare et in illius lege ambulare.*" When the *Ninety-five Theses* on indulgences were published in November, Scheurl got hold of a copy at once and circulated it in the city. His letters tell us that he and his friends studied them carefully and discussed them. Kaspar Nützel translated them into German to spread their message among the people. Nützel's interest in the subject and his eagerness to publicize Luther's vigorous rejection not only of the abuses of indulgence sales but of the very principle of pardons was not altogether academic. The Council had already refused to permit the sale of the indulgences for the building of St. Peter's, and it was Nützel who was conducting the correspondence about this with the authorities in Bamberg and Rome. Administrative and intellectual concerns once again coincided to give impetus to thought and action in influential circles.

Luther himself came to Nuremberg, briefly, in October 1518 on his way to and from Augsburg where he had his inconclusive interview with Cardinal Cajetan. He stayed in the Augustinian monastery and met briefly with the *Sodalitas*. He made a fine

---

* Though not in more professional centers of learning like Erfurt, where their aggressive anti-Aristotelianism was condemned as objectionable.

impression. Not long afterwards, however, some of his admirers began to have second thoughts. It was especially his rash and apparently unguarded pronouncements during the Leipzig debate with Johann Eck, a brilliant scholar also much admired by members of the *Sodalitas*, that served to alienate some of those who had first acclaimed him. Scheurl began to lose interest now, but another member of the Nuremberg group came forward to seize the leadership of the Lutheran cause in what was to become the Nuremberg reform circle: Lazarus Spengler. Spengler had read, and was to read, everything that came from Wittenberg, not only Luther's sermons and tracts and pamphlets but also Melanchthon's first attempt at a systematic exposition of the new doctrines, the *Loci Communes*. He himself tried his hand at apologetic and expository writings in German to put the Lutheran creed before the public and defend it against its assailants in the city and abroad. The first of his booklets appeared in 1519, titled *Defense and Christian Reply of a Lover of Divine Truth as Contained in Sacred Scripture, Against Several Opponents*, originally written for the members of the the the *Sodalitas* but soon printed. Luther's teachings, Spengler wrote, accord perfectly with the Gospel, with Paul, and with the prophets. Whether or not they also agree with the opinion of theologians and churchmen is a small matter. They offer us not only peace and consolation but also a practical guide to regulating our lives. They make us strong and purposeful and independent of those ritual observances urged on us by a corrupt and self-seeking priesthood.

Much the same sort of message could be heard at the Augustinian chapel, where in 1518 Linck was preaching his thirty Advent sermons on the Beatitudes, Matthew 5, 3–11. They too breathed the spirit of Luther's creed. Rely on God alone and on God's word, which is the only instruction you will ever need on the proper preparation of heart, mind, and body as the soil in which God can do his work. "Be humble, gentle, and good," Linck concluded, "if you would be in God's grace, on earth and in the hereafter. Be merciful, pure at heart, and peaceful. Above all, be in all things ready to suffer, for suffering is the way of salvation."[5]

One of the "several opponents" Spengler had in mind was, of course, Johann Eck, Luther's able opponent at Leipzig and writer of a critical commentary on the *Ninety-five Theses*. For his trouble, Spengler saw his name appended to Luther's on the bull of excommunication brought by Eck from Rome in the fall of 1520. For good measure Eck had also included another prominent Nuremberger, Willibald Pirckheimer, whom he suspected of being the author of a scabrous satire on him that was making the rounds of all who could read Latin. For Nuremberg's government this public branding of two distinguished citizens was exceedingly embarrassing. Months of delicate and, for the two men involved, humiliating negotiations passed before Eck agreed to grant them absolution, as he was empowered to do. Even so, the two names appeared on the bull along with Luther's when it was finally published in January 1521, which did not, however, prevent Spengler from representing Nuremberg at the meeting of the Estates at Worms that year. This was the first confrontation of German notables with their newly crowned Emperor Charles V. For Nuremberg the political decisions reached by the Diet of Worms had far-reaching significance. In voting to revitalize the languishing Governing Council and Chamber Court as agencies of central government, to locate them both in Nuremberg, and in deciding to hold the next meeting of the Estates there as well, Diet and emperor made of Nuremberg something like the capital of the Empire. Late in 1522 the Governing Council began its sessions, and the Court took up residence, carting along the dossiers of more than three thousand pending cases. The City Council deputized two of its members to act as liaison men with these organs of the realm's central government. Thus for two critical years in the history of the Reformation, national and local concerns happened to coincide in Nuremberg.

All this made it rather awkward for the Council that the opinions of some of its leading members and most trusted advisers, and the evident sentiment of the masses, were resolutely opposed to the enforcement of the Diet's decree of proscription against Luther and his followers. The Worms Edict had been obediently posted at the town hall, in September 1521, but no action was being taken on its provisions for collecting Lutheran books and prosecuting Luther's followers. Because Luther's overt supporters in Nuremberg included some of the most prestigious men in the city, the posting of the Edict must have suggested a touch of irony. But the Council went further than mere inaction in showing that it did not consider itself bound by the Edict. When new priors had to be chosen for the city's two parish churches, Wittenberg men were named in both cases. Hektor Bömer, who went to St. Lorenz, was still a student at Wittenberg at the time of his election. Georg Pessler, named to St. Sebald, had also studied there. When a preacher's position opened at St. Sebald late in 1521, the Council asked Luther to suggest a candidate and appointed the man recommended, Dominicus Schleupner. At about the same time Andreas Osiander was named preacher at St. Lorenz, also a former Wittenberg student and, before his election to the new post, teacher of Hebrew at the Augustinian monastery and member of the *Sodalitas Staupitziana*. When Osiander began almost at once to preach in an unmistakably Lutheran manner and to speak aggressively against papal and Church doctrines, the Council got worried. But it did nothing to silence him nor any of the other preachers, for example the new man in the Hospital Church, Thomas Gechauf called Venatorius, who got this post in 1522 on the recommendation of Willibald Pirckheimer. He too preached the Gospel according to Luther.

The dilemma in which the Council thus found itself was real enough, and in the matter of the obligations imposed by the Worms Edict it was embarrassing.[6] The authority of the imperial government was placed in clear conflict with widespread inclinations and practices in the very city in which the national government was meeting. There was little doubt in 1522 that popular sentiment, as well as the opinion of the intellectuals, was swinging to the Lutheran side of the controversy. Nuremberg was not unique in the speed and thoroughness with which the Wittenberg creed took root among the masses of citizens; this happened in nearly all the imperial cities. Not only were they the first political bodies to turn to the Reformation, but of the independent cities more than fifty either became Protestant or harbored large Protestant congregations.[7] Two general explanations of these facts offer themselves. First, even where city governments were not themselves persuaded by Luther's views, they could not but be more responsive to citizen demands for changes than the territorial sovereigns, who neither knew their subjects nor cared much for their spiritual welfare. Second, and more important, it was in the cities that the fervent and persuasive preaching by Lutheran and other Protestant ministers had the most powerfully concentrated effect. This was the case in Nuremberg where the Council itself was responsible for the choice of those preachers who aroused popular zeal. The Council recognized the force of the momentum being released. Traditional political principles dictated that control of events remain in Council hands. Meanwhile, the imperial government, was calling for repressive action. It was a difficult position for the council to be in.

Under the circumstances the only thing the Council could do was to temporize, and this it did successfully. Pleas and threats by the papal nuncio and the Archduke Ferdinand to remove the pro-Lutheran preachers went unheeded, though the Council called the preachers to the *Rathaus* and admonished them to speak moderately and avoid controversial subjects. Council members went to the various churches to see that this was done. Firm measures were taken against public baiting of monks and priests. An artisan who had caused an incident by taunting a Franciscan who was preaching against Luther was exiled from the city for three years (though pardoned a few days later). Booksellers and printers were cautioned not to produce or sell Luther's and Lutheran books, but Chieregati, the nuncio, reported to Rome that such books were in fact sold openly. An ex-monk was expelled from the city when it became known that he had married a former nun. Penalties were applied against all who were seen eating flesh on fast days; sick people in need of meat for nourishment were told to apply to the Council for permission. When in March 1523 the priors of St. Sebald and St. Lorenz asked for instructions on offering the cup to their parishioners, which, they said, is a thing clearly according to Scripture but, on the other hand, might be unwise in the present circumstances, the Council agreed that it was indeed unwise. For the present, it told the officials, keep things as they are. Later on we will see what can be done.

Thus the city's emissaries to the Emperor and Archduke Ferdinand could claim without hypocrisy that while the Council had tried hard to obey the Worms decree and to hold the line on innovations, it could not do so indefinitely against the public clamor for reform. It was only a question of time before concessions would have to be made. Indeed feelings ran high already. When in January 1523 the nuncio moved to have the Worms decree actively enforced in the Empire, and to make a beginning of it in Nuremberg by arresting the preachers who were defying it openly, there was shouting in the streets, an emergency session in the town hall, and a decision to protect the city's freedom of action by force of arms, if that should become necessary. It did not become necessary but the Council must have seen clearly at that time that the Wittenberg cause had taken too firm a root in Nuremberg to permit turning back.

This is one of the most puzzling aspects of the entire history of the Reformation: the extent to which men had been moved by, and had accepted, the Lutheran teachings about human depravity and the undeserved grace of God, freely bestowed according to God's unfathomable purpose without any merit of man's will and deeds. That these teachings were accepted and understood is certain. Luther's own struggle must have struck a deeply responsive chord in the souls of thousands who read his sermons and treatises and found there a message of liberation and comfort, and also by the tens of thousands who heard these texts expounded by a devoted and zealous band of preachers. By 1523 Luther's popular following in the German cities was secure. In Nuremberg in the summer of that year Hans Sachs published his long paean to the Reformer, *The Wittenberg Nightingale*.[8] Awake, Do you hear the nightingale's dulcet call? The night is ending, day dawns, the sun has arisen and the moon, whose deceiving glow has lured the flock from its shepherd, is fading. The nightingale, Sachs explains, is Martin Luther, whose song rouses us from the long sleep induced by the moon, which stands for the teachings of sophists whose appeals to reason lured us away from the Gospel. Sachs proceeds from this introduction to a long and vituperative diatribe against priests, monks, bishops and the rest of the clergy. But now their evil rule is at an end. Luther has revealed the true meaning of the Scripture, plainly and in German, and it has been printed for everyone to read:

> First Luther tells us that we all
> Inherit sin from Adam's fall,
> In evil lust and foul intent
> And avid pride our lives are spent;
> Our hearts are black and unrefined,
> Our wills to horrid sins inclined,
> And God, who judges soul and mind
> Has cursed and damned all human kind.
> In our hearts we know this state,
> Feel burdened with a dreadful weight
> Of anguish, fear, bewilderment
> That we should be so impotent.
> Sure of man's inability
> We change pride to humility
> And then, and only then, we see
> The Gospel, sent to make us free,
> For in it we find Christ, God's son
> Who for us men has so much done,
> Fulfilled the law, wiped clean the stain
> And won God's grace for us again.

Christ speaks of the Lamb of God, which takes upon itself all mankind's sins. He is come, Christ says, not for the just and pious but for the sake of the sinners. Whoever believes in Him shall have everlasting life.

> So Jesus speaks. All who have heard
> His comforting, consoling word,
> Who trust him without doubt or scorn,
> Such men, we say, are newly born.
> Quit of all fear, no longer prone
> To sin, they live God's word alone.
> In total love they turn to God,
> Submit themselves in deed and thought,
> Accept his judgment and decree
> In sorrow and adversity,
> Trust and revere Him, come what may,

"God gives, God takes" is what they say,
Because they know, God's on their side
Through Christ, His Son, the crucified.
Whom God grants such a faith, he is
Already saved, he lives in bliss;
His deeds are good, his efforts right
His works find favor in God's sight.

Sachs continues through hundreds of lines, chronicling events of recent memory: Pope Leo and his dismay over the disruption of his profitable indulgence trade, the Leipzig debate, and the meeting at Worms. What is remarkable is not so much the unrestrained invective and acid ridicule of clergy and Rome (these were common enough) but the poem's extraordinary length. Like most other works of Sachs, the *Wittenberg Nightingale* was written to please a popular demand and conform to public taste. We must assume that there was enormous interest in Luther and the Lutheran cause in Nuremberg in 1523. No deep immersion in the Reformer's writings was needed to produce Sachs' street ballad version of the new creed (though, in fact, Sachs did possess copies of more than forty of Luther's sermons and tracts in 1523). Sachs only put into easy doggerel what the preachers in most of the city's pulpits had been saying several times each week for at least a year.

It is pertinent, though perhaps not very fruitful, to ask how much all this meant to Sachs. Did he fully understand the call to submission and the challenge to a new kind of freedom through the acceptance of man's total sinfulness? And if he did understand these things, did he draw the right theological conclusions from their acceptance? Sachs was a comfortably-off artisan in a rich and strong community; he had a commodious house, good food (his poems tell us that), an honorable calling, and an absorbing avocation. He was a popular figure and widely respected. Life was good to him, and he must have enjoyed it. Why go on so about depravity and the enslavement of the will and the anguish of the unregenerate heart? Albrecht Dürer also spoke of this. Writing to Georg Spalatin in early 1520, Dürer avers his eagerness to meet and portray Luther, "the Christian man who has helped me emerge from such terrible fear." The fear certainly was the fear of death and damnation, and the message of hope to dissolve that fear was the Gospel of the once sacrificed Christ, not a new Gospel, but one presently declared with fresh fervor and in vivid, colloquial, picturesque language. For plain folk of no particular intellectual pretensions the message had the virtue of utter simplicity. Men are weak and irresolute, the victims of forces and circumstances they cannot understand, much less control. This much is obvious, and men must accept it in a total acceptance presented as an act of courage. In the full consciousness of their helplessness let them turn to the greatest power imaginable, without a vestige of pretense and without demands. This is the turning point. From this moment of conversion, man becomes an instrument of God, his efforts are meritorious, his works blessed.

The doctrine, if believed, does indeed resolve doubts of the kind that plague every man of conscience. Self-confessions of sinfulness and imbecility, and the condition of despair engendered by them, are a phase in the attainment of certainty, a phase which is transcended on the evidence of Christ's sacrifice. Beyond lie confidence in righteousness and God's divine omnipotence and magnanimity to guarantee it. In a way, this doctrine was not so very different from what the burgher's society assumed and occasionally said about man and what it asked of man as a citizen: curtailment of the self-seeking drives of his natural instincts and submission to a larger purpose and greater strength than his own. Neither in religion nor in politics could the natural man attain salvation. The fatherly and essentially rational call to citizenship could not, of course, reach the existential depths where confidence impels and fears impede. To these regions the new religious message appealed, and there it was received as a gospel of hope, sanctioning all that a faithful man did, endowing his life and work with meaning not only in the transitory world of the city of man but in the eternal scheme of the City of God.

Stating the case for Lutheranism this way, in purely religious terms, can be defended by the absence of any demonstrable social motives for the spread of Lutheran ideas in Nuremberg. Elsewhere, in Regensburg, Goslar, Schweinfurt, and Mühlhausen, for example, social resentments and economic strains played their part in making Luther's creed seem attractive, its

meaning somewhat twisted from Luther's own unworldly interpretation of the Gospel. But not in Nuremberg. If there had been
social agitation along with religious protest, the records would
show it. What the records do show is that people responded
whole-heartedly to the religious promise held out in the sermons.
What they wanted, and what they got, was not a social gospel
announcing better conditions but a gospel of faith and confidence, promising a meaningful and saving place for the individual in his own society and that of God. "There is nothing good
in us except it become good in Christ," wrote Albrecht Dürer.
"Whoever therefore will altogether justify himself is unjust. If we
will what is good, Christ wills it in us."

What of more sophisticated men with minds too subtle to accept the Lutheran creed as a simple promise of divine support?
Lazarus Spengler is an example of a learned and pious man who
sought the deeper meaning of the religious issue raised by Luther,
and his writings during the 1520's record his struggle to make this
meaning his own.[9] He had read all Luther's works, he tells us,
some of them twice through, and he had drawn his conclusions.
Luther's creed was true because it is in flawless harmony with
Scripture, specifically with the Gospel, St. Paul, and the prophets.
No other criteria are needed, not St. Thomas and not the
other scholastics. Pious men have long known this, but none
until Luther has had the courage to discard the rubbish of scholastic obfuscation. Now at last we are free to rediscover the divine
truth in its pristine clarity. Everyone can, must do this. The
truth is openly revealed; all may find it in Scripture. The very
plainness of Luther's doctrine is evidence of its truth, for God does
not conceal His word from men whose eyes He had opened to it.
This openness of religious truth and its doctrinal simplicity are
major points with Spengler, moved as he was by a genuine concern for the spiritual peace of his fellow men. Every Christian,
he held, has a duty to help his brothers to the truth. How easy,
how pleasant this now is, with truth openly before us at last.

For Spengler, no less than for Sachs, the quest for certainty
and for the removal of doubt must have been the fundamental
impulse toward the acceptance of Luther's creed. This is what
the Reformer held out: a plainly revealed truth, firmly believed
and acted upon after a purgative experience in which all re-

servations were rejected. Knowledge of this truth rendered man independent of the contradictions of human opinion and historical accident, immune to the vicissitudes of fortune, confident and strong. As Sachs' cunning, Bible-quoting cobbler puts it: "Christ instructs us in Matthew 6,31: 'Therefore take no thought saying, What shall we eat? or What shall we drink? or Wherewithal shall we be clothed? But seek ye first the kingdom of God, and his righteousness; and all these things shall be added unto you.' And I Peter 5, 7: 'Cast all your care upon the Lord, for he careth for you.' "[10] It was a faith that cleared a man's mind, lightened his conscience, and gave him strength to do his daily work with resolution and in a cheerful spirit.

While Spengler's fervent heart responded to the spiritual excitement of Luther's cause, others supported it for less exalted reasons as a timely struggle against traditional foes. Christoph Scheurl, though fascinated by the intellectual implications of the creed when it was discussed in the Staupitz circle, saw its emergence into the arena of public opinion and action mainly as an acceleration of a trend toward religious and ecclesiastical particularism, fed by traditional German resentment of curial exploitation. To Willibald Pirckheimer, on the other hand, Luther at first was another Reuchlin, struggling in the good cause of enlightenment against the unholy alliance of monkish meddling, curial greed, and scholastic obfuscation. Pirckheimer was one of the band of German humanists who had rallied to Reuchlin's side during the Dominican attacks on him a few years earlier, and he had spoken and written in Reuchlin's behalf. He blamed the monks not only for their ignorant and malicious assault on a fine scholar but also for much else that was wrong with religious and ecclesiastical conditions in Germany. When Hadrian VI became pope in 1522, Pirckheimer prepared to tell him this, and much more, in a memorandum on the corruption of the Church and the reforms needed to restore it. As for Eck, he regarded him as a vainglorious controversialist, bent on winning disputations, not on finding truth. Against these forces Luther had declared open war, and Pirckheimer was with him.

It is not known for certain whether Pirckheimer wrote the satire on Eck attributed to him.[11] If he did, it identifies the enemy against whom he saw Luther tilting his lance and de-

clares his partisanship. But the alliance did not last long. Pirckheimer—the offspring of a deeply cultured professional family
with ties and associations in many countries, himself widely
traveled, educated at Italian universities and groomed at the
Renaissance court of the Sforza dukes in Pavia, a trained lawyer
and an experienced diplomat and soldier, above all a refined man
of learning devoted to the great authors of the patristic and
classical past, many of whose works he had translated into fine
humanist Latin—Pirckheimer was not a man to find Luther's
fundamentalist creed convincing or attractive. As with Erasmus,
it was Luther's rejection of free will that forced Pirckheimer to
take a stand. That was in 1524. His letter to Erasmus in September of that year indicated the break with Luther. He remained
in the traditional faith, not altogether happily, but unwilling to
forsake it.

Pirckheimer's disillusionment left him as bitter toward the
Protestants as he had earlier been toward the old religion. "Originally," he was to write, "I was a good Lutheran, and so was
my friend Albrecht [Dürer] of blessed memory, for we hoped
that the roguery of Rome and the knavery of monks and priests
would be bettered. But instead of that, things have so gone from
bad to worse that the Protestants make the Popish look pious by
contrast." It may well be that personal reasons contributed to his
refusal to go along with the majority of his city. Pirckheimer was
a mercurial and irascible man, forever engaged in private rows
with members of the Council and others. In addition, seven of his
sisters and three of his daughters were highly placed nuns in
Nuremberg and elsewhere. However that may be, his initial acclaim of Luther and the early support he gave him sprang from
the impression that the new learning was finding a new champion
in German lands and the discredited obscurantism of the school-
men another assailant.

As for the Council, its individual members may have felt attracted or repelled by Luther or indifferent to him, but as a corporation it pursued only one aim in its religious policy, the en-
hancement of the city's freedom of action. The question of
conscience must have presented itself essentially as a problem of
civic responsibility. Long accustomed to acting on complaints
of clerical mismanagement, the Council was responsive to any

voice that seemed to infuse with new vigor the religion its people believed and practiced, the more if the voice spoke with such obvious conviction, and especially if it spoke in German. The Council's sympathy with the popular desire for a simple creed, plainly taught and easily and totally grasped, must have blended with the vision, also held out by Luther, of a municipal and territorial religious organization immediate to the needs of its government. Luther had suggested this possibility in 1520, in his general call to reform and renovation under the aegis of secular authorities. Such action, it was said, accorded with Scripture and with good sense. Supervision of churches and religious conduct was a natural extension of the government's parental concern with its people's condition. It was a responsibility that the Council, like governmental bodies elsewhere, had always claimed to possess. Luther's cause now offered argument and occasion to incorporate the last functions of city life not yet totally in harmony with the Council's objectives.

Taking this step was not, as a modern observer will be quick to label it, a blunt grasp for power and money. The Council would not have embarked on its road to secularization if that had not seemed the right thing to do. Luther's voice and the echoing voices of the Lutheran preachers sounded convincing. Judged by the text of the Bible, Rome and its organization had been shown base and wicked. Too long had their false teachings been tolerated. Now the long anticipated time of renewal—the *Renovatio* prophesied by wise and holy men through the centuries—had dawned. As Spengler put it: "The fundamental question is, Shall we be Christians, or not?" Christ and his Gospel, that is what the struggle was about, not politics or taxes or Luther himself. The Council clearly identified this as the basis on which it planned to act:

It has always been the Council's thought and opinion to conduct itself as pious Christians and obedient members and subjects of the Christian Church and the Holy Empire, to follow neither Luther's nor any other man's teachings or to allow such teachings to deflect it from Christian obedience, but only to remain true to the Holy Gospel and the word of God on which alone our faith, our consolation, our salvation depend. In this we will remain resolute until death.[12]

The Easter season of 1524 was a time of great agitation in Nuremberg. Diet and Governing Council were meeting in the city, Archduke Ferdinand and the papal legate called for decisive measures against the spreading heresy, and the City Council was still marking time. Here is how an eyewitness, an unfriendly one, described conditions in Nuremberg as Pope Clement's legate, Campeggio, made his entrance in mid-March:

In this city the sincere faith in Christ is utterly abolished. No respect is paid either to the Virgin Mary or to the saints. They ridicule the papal rites and call the relics of the saints bones of men who have been hanged. In Lent they eat meat openly. Confession is neglected, as they say it should be made only to God. They generally communicate under both forms. They make a laughing stock of Pope and Cardinals by circulating drawings and caricatures. In short, they consider Martin their enlightener, and think that until now they have been in darkness.

The description seems exaggerated, but there is no doubt that the new creed had made deep inroads on the old dispensation. Thousands of citizens, we hear, took communion under both forms during Easter, openly if not defiantly. Monks, particularly Dominicans, were set upon in the streets and greeted with scurrilous rhymes and ribald sayings. Caricatures of the Pope, his legate, and even of Ferdinand circulated from house to house. Tempers cooled a bit in May when the Diet adjourned, but the situation could not continue unresolved for long.

Early in 1525 an altercation in the Carthusian monastery furnished an occasion to bring matters to a head. The prior, Blasius Stöckl, was accused of heresy by several of his brothers and demanded a debate on the points in dispute. The fracas involved the Council in its role of protector of the monastery, and it seized on the idea of a disputation as a public airing of the controversial issues. In Feburary the city's preachers were summoned to the town hall. Each was told to prepare a list of articles he held essential to religious belief and practice. All of them complied except that the anti-Lutherans preferred to submit a single list of articles. Among these anti-Lutherans were the preachers of the Dominican, Franciscan, and Carmelite monasteries and the convents of St. Clara and St. Catherine. (The

Carthusians had been sent an Augustinian preacher following the quarrel over Stöckl.) As for the Lutherans, or crypto-Lutherans, they represented the city's two parish churches, also the Hospital Church, the Benedictines, Johannites, and, of course, the Augustinians. Meanwhile the Council examined the lists of articles and reduced them to twelve main questions. On these twelve questions the preachers were to debate at a meeting set for March 3, 1525.

But when the arrangements became known, it was only too apparent to the opposition that the whole affair was rigged. Presiding were the priors of St. Sebald and St. Lorenz, also the abbot of St. Aegidius Friedrich Pistorius, a man known to be sympathetic to Wittenberg, and a preacher from Würzburg, Johann Graumann called Poliander, a well-known Lutheran enthusiast. Proceedings were to be public, the audience to include not only the Council and the Great Council but also as many burghers as could be squeezed into the Great Hall of the *Rathaus*. All speeches were to be in German and a record was to be kept.[13] Announcement of the debate had excited the city, and a large and predictably anticlerical crowd was expected to gather outside the building. Under the circumstances, anticipating an outcome already assured, the monks refused to appear. We are asked to take part in a religious disputation, they said, and religious disputations are forbidden by imperial decree. But the Council insisted. The meeting should not be classified as a disputation; it was meant to be a friendly discussion to prepare the ground for agreement and reconciliation. This was true. The record of the Council's deliberations and the opinions of its legal advisers show that the councillors did hope to open the priests' eyes to the rightness of Luther's theology and persuade them to preach it in unison with the Wittenberg men. It was the preaching that mattered. To permit two discordant creeds to be taught from the city's pulpits was unthinkable. That was what the conflict was about. As usual, the Council had its way. From March 3 to March 14 the preachers debated, argued, and exhorted each other on points involving fundamental theological questions as "What is justification?" "What is the Sacrament of the Altar and what is its effect in us?" "Do good works lead to justification, or does justification produce good works?" "What is original sin, and

what its penalty?" "How is the old Adam to be killed?" More
practical questions concerning political authority were also
raised. ("What powers has divinely instituted secular authority,
and to what extent do men owe it obedience?") Osiander spoke
last, summarizing the Lutheran position on the articles and rejecting one and all Catholic contentions. At the end of his speech
he turned to the assembled mayors. Do not wait for a national
Council to determine what shall be done, he told them. Enough
time has been lost in procrastination. Act now. Institute the
service of God on the basis of Scripture. We have proven our
case. There is no reason to wait any longer.

The consensus of those present clearly supported Osiander
in his call to immediate action. Three days later the Council had
made up its mind. The most vocal of the opposing monks were
expelled. (Their spokesman, Andreas Stoss, Carmelite prior and
son of Nuremberg's most renowned sculptor, Veit Stoss, was
given three days to leave the city.) Dominicans, Franciscans, and
Carmelites were ordered to stop preaching and hearing confessions. The divine service as conducted at St. Sebald was made a
model for all other churches to follow, and a committee of Council members set up to assure compliance. The Roman Mass was
declared offensive and outlawed in public churches. From now
on the sacrament of the altar must accord with a manual written
by the chaplain of the Hospital Church, *The Evangelical Mass as
It Is Celebrated in the New Hospital in Nuremberg.* Several
traditional customs had already been abolished, the Good Friday
passion play, private Masses, and the Corpus Christi procession.
Now the veneration of saints was declared unbiblical and most
of the feast days were canceled. Only the days of the apostles
and the day of St. John the Baptist (midsummer) were retained.
Religious holidays were limited to Sundays, Christmas, Easter,
Ascension, Pentecost, and three festivals associated with the Virgin: Annunciation, Candlemas, and Visitation. As the Council
had, in effect, now assumed direction of Nuremberg's territorial
church, major organizational changes were quick to follow. Clerical appointments in city and territory were taken over. A school
was established to train ministers, and Philip Melanchthon himself
was brought down from Wittenberg to plan its curriculum. A
generous sum of 1000 gulden annually was set aside for the

operation of the new Gymnasium. Charity disbursement was centralized, and the City Court was given power over marital cases, formerly an episcopal prerogative. Organized crafts were ordered to admit only Lutheran apprentices and employ no Catholic journeymen.

As for the monasteries, their long and distinguished history in Nuremberg was about to draw to an end. Dissolution followed reformation in Nuremberg no less swiftly than elsewhere. The Augustinians led the way even before it became necessary. ("The Augustinians were the beginning of all our misfortunes," wrote Charitas Pirckheimer in her memoirs.) In December 1524 they volunteered to transfer their possessions to the city. These included agricultural and pastoral land, real estate and buildings, and rent payments in money and kind. All income and the moneys realized from the sale of property went to the common chest. The city became the legal heir of all secularized clerical properties; occasional attempts by private persons to repossess what they or their ancestors had donated were defeated. The only condition the monks asked was a promise from the Council to clothe and feed the remaining brothers to the end of their lives. On March 22, 1525, a week after the disputation, the formal deed of surrender was signed by both sides. A few monks chose to settle for annuities, the rest took up new careers as Lutheran ministers.

The Dominicans had read the portents too. In December 1524 they had offered the Council everything they owned in exchange for annuities. After the disputation, the Council sent some of its members to consult each monk privately concerning his intentions. Several wanted to leave the Order, others wished to convert, still others, including the prior, asked to be allowed to transfer. In the end nothing was done; the few monks who stayed on were left unmolested, except that the Council made use of the spacious buildings for various purposes, a school at one time, the town library at another. In 1543 the last five brothers moved out in exchange for pensions of 52 gulden a year. Good use was also found for the empty Carthusian buildings, which had been handed over in the autumn of 1525. The monks had accompanied this act with a declaration that they had been persuaded by the "clear and pure word of God" to give up their lives as "self-seeking Carthusians avid for nothing more than bodily comfort and full bellies." The monastery garden made way for a block of new houses, and the vacant cells became homes for the widows of ministers and schoolmasters. Really determined resistance to secularization came only from the two convents, particularly from St. Clara's, and there it was due mainly to the resourceful actions of the abbess Charitas Pirckheimer (who has left us an extraordinary record of the many chicaneries and indignities to which she and her charges were subjected).[14] Rather than incur ridicule by using strong arm methods against helpless women, the Council wisely refrained from insisting on dissolution, satisfying itself with banning new admissions, encouraging citizens to remove their daughters (which not many did), and assigning reliable preachers to the rest. Thus deprived of new life, but otherwise left in peace, the two convents survived to the end of the century, when the last of the sisters died.

To draw the sum of the changes: As far as the city was concerned, clerics had now taken their places in the ranks of citizens. No longer the first estate, in fact no longer set apart by any distinction not arising from their functions as citizens, they obeyed the laws, paid taxes, took their litigation to municipal courts, were loyal to the city's government, and served the city's aims. Luther had provided the theological justification of this leveling of the estates, but the political principle of civic equality was at least as convincing. To be sure, the integration of ecclesiastical and political functions never proceeded as far in Nuremberg as it did in those cities (largely in southwestern Germany) where the Reformation was carried on according to the ideas of Zwingli and Bucer. In Strassburg, Esslingen, Augsburg, Constance, Ravensburg, and the Protestant cities of the Swiss Confederation, lay participation in church affairs was extensive.[15] In Nuremberg governing patricians were too frightened of the effects of diffused authority to experiment with a presbyterian system. The year 1525 made no real difference in this respect in Nuremberg. Ordinary citizens had little or nothing to say about their ministers and their religion.

Politically, however, the barrier between clergy and laymen had fallen. For the clerical establishment, this signified the abandonment of a centuries-long struggle for preëminence and the assumption of an auxiliary role in the governance of men. Of course no one saw it that way in the sixteenth century, not the government, so keen on using its newly acquired *jus episcopale* to do the right thing by faith and people, and not the clergy, so eager to commence its new mission of spiritual and moral regeneration. Preachers took an active part in the affairs of the city. Their leaders met with the college of legal advisers whenever a question of religious or moral import was up for discussion, and they had a great deal to say. But their role was subordinate. We can see the contradiction now, and crassly, because we have learned to anticipate the extension of political power and because we think of political adminstration as a self-sufficient and ultimate end in itself. But in Nuremberg in 1525 neither the Council nor its political advisers separated the demands of politics from the claims of God and faith. The actions taken during the 1520's constituted, as they saw it, a wholesome return to conditions both normal and right.

The events of 1525 and their immediate consequences did not conclude the Reformation in Nuremberg. The decision to separate from Rome and the diocese involved the city in a flurry of litigation and diplomatic moves and counter moves. As expected, the bishop initiated complaint actions with the Swabian League: Nuremberg had rebelled against his rightful competence; she was withholding tithes and other payments due him. In 1526 it was not clear where the bishop would find allies in his efforts to regain his prerogatives, but in 1529 the situation changed, and the Catholic majority at the second Diet of Speier that year seemed confident of its ability to rescind "innovations" and compensate deprived prelates. Similarly, the Johannites complained to the Swabian League about the Council's high-handed manner of taking over the Order's buildings and grounds. A huge correspondence ensued between the Council and the executive organs of the League. Meanwhile a new church organization had to be established to replace the old institutions. It was always possible (and it did happen elsewhere) for the Church to rebound from its defeat and regain control for Rome.

Counterrevolution was not, however, the most imminent danger. A much more acute peril to ecclesiastical institutions as

well as to the political system of which they were a part arose
from the activities of men not content to regard reform in
Nuremberg as fully accomplished. Soon after 1525, Nuremberg,
like most other communities, saw the first of her spiritualists, Anabaptists, *Schwärmer*, and various other representatives of the sec-
tarian wing of Protestantism. Hans Denk himself resided in Nuremberg for a year and a half after 1523 as Latin teacher and
rector of the school of St. Sebald and as advocate of his mystic
views of the inner light and the inner word. Zwingli's religious
and political doctrines, both in deep conflict with dominant ideas
in Nuremberg, were spread by a handful of vociferous preachers,
as were Karlstadt's. Late in 1525 three students of Albrecht
Dürer—among them Georg Penz, one of the most prolific of
Nuremberg artists—were reported to the Council for some loose
talk about the Bible meaning nothing to them and the Incarna-
tion being nothing more than a legend. An inquisition brought
out disturbing, if rather confused, opinions:

George Penz replies to the questionnaire as follows: Does he believe
in God? Yes, he feels that there is a God, but what he should take to
be this God he cannot say. What does he think of Christ? He thinks
nothing of Christ. Does he believe in Holy Scripture as the word of
God? He does not believe in Scripture. What is his opinion of the
Sacrament of the Altar? He has no use for it. Of baptism? He has no
use for baptism. Does he believe in worldly authority and does he
recognize the Council of Nuremberg as lord over his body, his goods,
and all that is material? He recognizes no lord but God alone.

Even if the Council had been able to stomach the religious devia-
tionism of the first answers, it would have been moved to quick
action by the political heresy of the last reply. Penz and his as-
sociates were summarily expelled. As the Council saw it, the danger of all this talk lay not merely in the relative radicalism of
the ideas but in their multiplicity. Few men in that time of fierce
confessional competition knew that truth has many faces and
speaks with many tongues. Truth to most was not only single, it
was exclusive as well. Adhering to accustomed principles, therefore, the councillors acted swiftly to nip rival movements before
they could gain a toehold. City preachers were ordered to use
the pulpit against the sacramentarians; disputations in public

places were forbidden; Zwingli's writings were banned. Hans Denk was invited to submit a defense of his views to Osiander; when it was rejected, Denk was given until nightfall to leave the city. Anabaptists if caught were despatched to Osiander and Linck who tried to convert them; if they failed (as they usually did) the heretics were expelled, though not as in other places physically injured or stripped of their property. In 1528 the Council published a *Basic Instruction on How Pastors and Preachers Are to Admonish and Teach the People Concerning the Perverting and Corrupting Doctrines of the Anabaptists.* The booklet was issued to all clerics as a guide in their efforts to keep the faith pure and society safe.

Thus Nuremberg returned from her brief flirtation with innovation to an accustomed and comfortable conservatism. There remained only the need to work out the details of a permanent ecclesiastical organization. In conjunction with Margrave Georg of Brandenburg-Ansbach, an enthusiastic Lutheran whose lands touched Nuremberg's in the west, the Council inaugurated a thorough church visitation, then, with the information thus gathered, issued a general *Kirchenordnung* in 1533 to establish a clerical bureaucracy and reliable procedures: uniform services, equitable social positions for clerics, appointment of Superintendents to direct the clergy and be responsible for their performance, and the formation of a central standing commission of Council members and representatives of the ministry to make ecclesiastical and religious policy. The Brandenburg-Nuremberg Church Organization of 1533 is a case study in the impact of the Reformation on the progress of administrative unification in Germany. While the Roman Church had preserved, in fact had encouraged, diffused and overlapping and vaguely adumbrated authorities, the new dispensation established, at least in clerical matters, those clear cut and decisive procedures which advocates of centralization have always regarded as indispensable to good government.

In internal religious matters, then, Nuremberg held to her objective of autonomy justified by good government. But could the same independence and effectiveness be achieved in managing her external relations, confessional, diplomatic, and military? In the 1530's this was not an academic question. The intransigent position taken by the Emperor at the second Diet of Speier in 1529 and the protestation of non-Catholic princes and cities against the reimposition of the Worms Edict, made it more than likely that all Germany would soon split into militant factions. With war perhaps not far away, the Protestant princes pressed for a grand alliance of territories and cities opposed to Rome and the Emperor. Would Nuremberg join and contribute both her wealth and the prestige of her leading place among south German cities to the cause? The question was raised at a meeting of Protestant estates (excluding Ulm, Strassburg, and the Swiss cities loyal to Zwingli) held in Nuremberg in 1530, and the pressure on the Council was intense. But Nuremberg resisted not only the blandishments and threats of her would-be allies but also the admonitions of her own preachers. She would not enter an alliance that might compel her to raise arms against the supreme and sacred sovereign of the Empire. This was the consensus of legal and diplomatic experts consulted, and it was the decision taken after prolonged discussions by the Council, not on religious grounds of passive obedience (a position from which even Martin Luther was soon to deviate) but on the arguments of political obligation and constitutional duty.

This lapse into neutrality in the impending war cost Nuremberg her role as spokesman for the southern cities and brought her the disdain of all the committed Protestant powers. On a purely ideological consideration of the issues it would indeed be difficult to justify this withdrawal from her natural allies. After all, Protestantism was fighting for its life in the 1530's and 1540's, and it would seem that Nuremberg's support ought to have gone to her coreligionists. But it did not (except for a reluctant contribution to the Schmalkaldic League's treasury), nor did her sympathies. Ideology was not a habit of thought with Nuremberg councillors, and arguments for religious solidarity were defeated by weightier considerations. Once again Nuremberg acted in her own best interests as her government calculated these and in accordance with her traditional political principles as it understood them.

The fact was that Nuremberg's very existence as an autonomous city, as well as her continued well-being as a commercial center, were inextricably linked with the fate of the Empire.[16]

And it was the Empire which would be, as the councillors read the signs, the ultimate victim of the militant Protestant princes. What else could come of a victory by a league of territorial lords, each sovereign in his realm and striving to sever the last historical and legal ties connecting him to the other constituent parts of the Empire? Large territorial states could, perhaps, exist on their own, like sovereign kingdoms, but not the free cities, not even one with so large a landed domain as Nuremberg's. At least this is how the problem appeared to the councillors. Their insistent backward look into their city's history persuaded them that since the Empire had created the preconditions for her rise to constitutional, political, and commercial eminence, so only the continued existence of the Empire could guarantee her survival in the face of domestic and foreign predators. This is the reasoning which sent Nuremberg's diplomats to all forums where the reform of imperial institutions was being discussed. It also explains Nuremberg's leadership of the southern Protestant cities in their patient effort to persuade Charles V to accept the permanence of their separation from the Church of Rome. In 1526, at the first Diet of Speier, this effort seemed to bear fruit, as religious and ecclesiastical changes already consummated were acknowledged, at least for the time being. But three years later everything changed, and Charles, fresh from his triumphs in the campaigns against France and the pope, seemed bent on destroying what in 1526 had been approved.

This was the moment of decision for every Protestant government. Most joined the anti-imperial coalition; but Nuremberg held back. Two possible outcomes could be anticipated, both undesirable. If the Emperor should win out, his vengeance on a rebellion combining heretical and insurrectionary motives was not difficult to predict. (The pitiless treatment received by Augsburg at the hands of Charles V in 1548 proves the validity of this fear.) On the other hand, should the Protestant League triumph, the often-predicted demise of the Empire would be at hand. Of course, staying out of the conflict was not likely to prevent either calamity. But in the light of her traditions and her carefully weighed political advantages, there was really nothing else that Nuremberg, acting on her principle of intelligent self-interest, could do. Perhaps she went a bit too far in her eagerness to propitiate the Emperor, joining at one time a temporary "Imperial League" of cities and territories, accepting Charles' Interim after his initial victory over the League, even reintroducing the Catholic liturgy for a time, including the Mass. These steps only prove that what mattered most with the Council was the preservation of the city's security and internal autonomy. The policy was delicate and occasionally unpopular, but in the end it worked. The line Nuremberg took was not, as was so often charged at the time, a timid course of vacillation. It was a perfectly logical extension of her wonted political attitudes.

This is how it happened that Nuremberg never joined the Schmalkaldic League of Protestant powers and escaped the trying experiences of the civil wars. But that did not mean that she survived the turmoil of the midcentury unscathed. In fact, the early 1550's embroiled the city in the most agonizing and by far the costliest of the many assaults on her position, the so-called Second Margrave's War, a two-year bout with a notoriously lawless and self-seeking princeling. Margrave Albrecht Alcibiades of Brandenburg-Kulmbach.

Son of Margrave Kasimir and nephew of Margrave Georg with whom the city had collaborated in reorganizing its ecclesiastical establishment, Albrecht had received the counties of Bayreuth and Kulmbach upon coming of age in 1540. It was far too small a domain to satisfy his ambitions and his taste for action. The religious conflict served him perfectly as pretext and occasion. First on the Emperor's side in the 1540's, when Charles seemed invincible, he switched camps in 1552 and joined the League of Princes arrayed against the Emperor. Nuremberg's stubborn neutrality in the last phase of the conflict suggested the kind of predatory war he liked best. Nuremberg must side with the princes he demanded, and support them with the wealth of her merchants. To lend force to the ultimatum, he occupied a strip of Nuremberg territory and razed a village. In the city frantic war preparations were in progress. Defenses were strengthened, powder makers worked over-time, the inventory of the armory was checked,[17] buildings and fences in a circumference of 300 paces from the wall were leveled, and peasants were organized into troop units.

In May 1552 Albrecht struck.[18] For two months he ravaged

the countryside, plundering what he could lay his hands on, destroying what had to be left behind. Those lucky enough to escape from his armed bands fled to the city to tell stories of abominable atrocities. As the city held out, the Margrave built fortified gun positions and sent a hail of cannon balls flying over the walls. He also threatened to burn down the whole forest, and his reputation did not leave room for much doubt that he meant what he said. Nuremberg preferred to give in. Only during the negotiations for settlement, however, did it become clear what Albrecht really wanted: He demanded "reparations" in the amount of 200,000 gulden and restoration of a long list of feudal prerogatives won by the city from his forbears. The most the city could salvage for itself was a provision that matters in dispute be submitted to a committee of princes for adjudication. In June 1552 the humiliating treaty was signed, and Nurembergers could open their gates, survey the wreckage, and begin rebuilding.

But less than a year later it started all over again. Once more the Margrave and his army appeared before the city. He had switched to the Emperor's side again, had dropped his demand for Nuremberg's participation in the civil war, but was no less eager than before for conquest and booty. Nuremberg levied troops, allied herself with the neighboring bishops of Bamberg and Würzburg, and faced the renewed onslaught. Whatever had not been sacked and burned in 1552 was ruined in this second campaign. Altdorf and Lauf were laid in ashes, the small imperial city of Schweinfurt conquered. In the bishoprics the destruction was no less fearful. But at long last help arrived. Against so distasteful a marauder even the creaky defensive machinery of the Empire could be mobilized. Proscribed by the Imperial Chamber Court and declared under the ban of the Empire, Albrecht now faced a relief army furnished by a number of princes and cities. The end came for him in June of 1554 when his troops were defeated in a battle near Schweinfurt and his residence, the Plassenburg, destroyed a week later. He lived a few years longer in exile in France, but his power was broken.

For Nuremberg the consequences of this nasty war were profound. Huge debts incurred during the struggle, the need for a substantial improvement of her defenses to discourage future raiders, and the job of rebuilding the razed countryside—all these put a stupendous burden on her economy, the effects of which we have already discussed. Compounded by the curtailment of her economic opportunities in the second half of the sixteenth century, they were to bring on a gradual decline in Nuremberg's economic and financial position.

In the autumn of 1554, however, less pessimistic thoughts are likely to have prevailed. The city's strength had just proved itself adequate to the most ferocious frontal assault in her history, while her passage through the decade's religious conflicts had left her new ecclesiastical organization standing, her constitution intact, and her autonomy unimpaired. If to the historian 1555 appears to mark the end of an era in Nuremberg's history, to the participant of those tumultuous years, it must have seemed a time of respite.

FIVE

Daily Life And Work

The Quarters—Fire Fighting—Police and Security—The Streets
—Rubbish Disposal—Plagues and Diseases—Bathing—Physici-
ans and Midwives—Hospitals—Lepers—Poor Relief and Public
Welfare—Begging—Private Houses—Eating Habits and Food
Preparation—The Cost of Living—Money and Its Purchasing
Value—Wages and Incomes—The Poor and the Very Rich—
Working Hours—Entertainments in Summer and Winter—St.
John Capistrano and Other Preachers—Prostitution—Display
of Imperial Regalia—Public Executions—Carnival Plays and
the Theater—Hans Sachs—Law and Legal Process—Influence
of Roman Law—The Nuremberg "Reformation" of 1479—The
Role of Lawyers—Civil and Criminal Cases—Torture—Sum-
mary: Rewards and Punishments in Urban Life.

"A city is an assembly of men brought together to live happily."
Thus said Giovanni Botero in 1588 in his treatise on the place of
cities in European society.[1] Botero's definition really illustrates
the shift of perspective away from the self-governing commune
toward the all-powerful state, which had taken place by the late
sixteenth century. To Botero a city was a place where population
and money proliferated, where industrial power was gathered,
and where a country's economic, social, and cultural resources
were concentrated. ("And greatness of a city", he continues, "is
termed not the spaciousness of situation or the compass of walls,
but the multitude of inhabitants and their power.") There is nothing in Botero's book to suggest that a city should or could have a
purpose distinctly its own, different from, perhaps at odds with,

the objectives of the territorial state. But for the independent city this is just what the struggle of the past three-and-a-half centuries had been about. A municipal polity and a civic ethic had been created and maintained against king, prince, and baron. Botero did not understand this. He and his book speak for the nascent age of absolutism and mercantilism. A citizen of Nuremberg reading *The Greatness of Cities* in the last decade of the sixteenth century must have put it down with an uneasy apprehension of how times were changing.

Still, there is nothing wrong with the statement that men are gathered in cities "to live happily." As an empirical observation of the rewards of civic life it is unobjectionable. By and large, urban life was pleasant, and urban institutions were designed to make it so. No one has ever invented a device for measuring happiness, but where the material conditions were never less than adequate, where society provided not only security but purpose and direction as well, and where work and pleasure coincided, there was bound to be at least contentment. But let us go behind the generalizations and test Botero's statement by trying to find out what it was like to live and work in Nuremberg in the sixteenth century.

For administrative purposes the city was divided into quarters but not, as the name might suggest, into four quarters. Nuremberg had five quarters in the fourteenth century, six in 1400, and from 1449 on, eight: four each in the Sebald and Lorenz parishes. Originally the quarter organization had served military purposes, and the two quartermasters *(Viertelmeister)* of each of the sections were directly responsible to the three captains general of the city. Their most important duty had always been the mobilization of the residents of their district in the event of siege or attack. But the quarters were used for other civic purposes as well: taxing, census taking, fire fighting, enrolling men for forced labor duty. Quartermasters were helped by street captains, each taking charge of a block of houses. The citizen swore an oath of obedience to his street captain and furnished him with lists of possessions useful to the city in case of emergencies and liable to requisition: arms and ammunition, grain reserves, carts and horses, lanterns, ladders, spare rooms, and so on. The quartermaster coordinated these lists, thus providing the Council with an up-to-date inventory of men and material available when the need arose.

The most dreaded emergency and the most disruptive of civic affairs was, of course, a sudden predatory strike by some rural war lord or a protracted siege by a hostile prince, though Nuremberg's splendid defenses and her reputation for wealth and diplomatic skill discouraged most of the kinds of capricious assaults suffered by lesser cities. But one had to be prepared and Nuremberg was. However, the most frequent use to which the quarter organization was put was not mobilization but fire fighting. News of fires turns up monotonously in the chronicles of the city. Sometimes a single house burned down, often a whole block was reduced to cinders. To the medieval town these fires were anything but ordinary. Every city had its great conflagrations when whole sections of the town were destroyed, with incalculable loss of property and income. In Nuremberg the great fire of 1340 was still remembered after two centuries; starting in the kitchen of a widow's home, it had quickly spread to nearby structures, and two days and nights later more than 400 houses lay in ashes. Next to the dreaded plague, the worst catastrophe that could hit a medieval community was a fire burning out of control. Its destructiveness often remained evident for decades, for, without insurance, few people could put their hands on enough money to rebuild a razed home and workshop. This fact explains the prevalence of clear spaces and garden spots in medieval towns. Houses had once occupied many of these, but fire had gutted them, and the ground had come into the hands of neighbors who preferred to keep it open.

By the fourteenth century most governments had learned to meet the dangers of fire with statutes concerning building materials and space utilization. But little could be done in a country where lumber was cheap and customary and where every householder liked to store his own supplies of wood in his shed and grain under his roof. Not many residences were really well built, and the annals make frequent mention of houses collapsing of their own weight or falling apart when an adjacent structure was damaged. The only practical precaution was to have an effective fire fighting organization. In Nuremberg the quarter administration enabled authorities to call out a large number of men within minutes of the alarm, each prepared to do an assigned job and familiar with the equipment. The public baths were required to keep large vats filled with water mounted on carts ready to go, and every quarter had two hand pumps with adjustable brass nozzles. Fire hooks, leatherbuckets, ladders and axes were mounted on designated houses in each block. Fitted boards to dam up the *Fischbach*, which ran through the center of the city, were in readiness for creating a reservoir from which to deploy bucket brigades. Rewards went to the four carters first to bring water to the scene and to the first three men up the fire ladders. Everything was precisely regulated: responsibility for refilling the vats and cleaning the pumps, guarding the charred site for twenty-four hours, repairing damaged ladders, and so on.[2] The system worked so well in Nuremberg that none of the innumerable isolated fires of which we read became a major conflagration.

The same can be said of security arrangements to control nighttime horseplay and hooliganism. Though these measures were not foolproof, and the courts were kept busy enough sentencing nocturnal brawlers, the worst of the trouble makers were probably discouraged by the precautions taken against them. Once the curfew bell had rung two hours after sunset, everyone was expected to be off the streets unless he had valid business. Patricians were permitted in their *Herrentrinkstube* after dark, and they could also play cards and dice there, but only until the hour before midnight. If legitimately abroad, a man must carry a lighted torch (the streets themselves were dark); failing to do so he was liable to arrest by the city's men at arms who patrolled the streets at night. If upon questioning a person was able to make himself known, he was let go after payment of a fine. "But any citizen, resident, or visitor who cannot establish his identity or provide a credible sponsor will be taken to prison." After midnight the fines doubled, and knives or other weapons found on the suspect, even a lute if he had been out serenading, were confiscated.

Inns closed at sundown, and a traveller lodging for a night could get nothing to drink once the curfew had sounded. If for any reason a tumult got under way, the government was prepared for it. Lanterns and torches were mounted on designated houses, and residents instructed to light them when they heard noise or sensed trouble. Most streets could be blocked off with iron chains drawn across the road from house to house; main thoroughfares were guarded by sets of double or triple chains. Ordinarily these chains were wound on drums enclosed in locked cases, but when trouble began and a crowd gathered, the street captains drew the chains out, making a clatter frightening enough to dishearten at least some of the ruffians. Endres Tucher, the city architect in the 1460's and 1470's (whose description of his office has been mentioned before) lists the location of all these chains. There were 420 of them in 1475. Like all other public property, the chains were maintained in good working order, oiled regularly, locks tested, and the drums inspected. No doubt the idea for this system occurred to the Council in the unhappy days of the Rebellion of 1349. It became a standard security device soon after that, always kept in readiness.

The streets themselves were in good condition, well surfaced, and, by and large, clean. This may be a difficult fact for the modern reader to accept, irreconcilable as it is with the commonly held image of mud, filth, and debris in medieval towns. But the evidence to the contrary is conclusive. Nuremberg's unpleasantly wet climate (every visitor complained of the frequent downpours and the ankle-deep mud on country roads) makes it easy to imagine what the city would have looked like had its streets not been properly surfaced. Stone paving was therefore introduced as early as the middle of the fourteenth century and from 1368 on proceeded systematically. The city architect had charge of this work, which was carried on by several paving masters, assisted by journeymen and apprentices and a detachment of day laborers. Streets were paved at public expense to within four feet of the doorstep of a private house. The remaining distance was paved at the home owner's expense. Work was governed by exact regulations. Size and quality of paving stones were determined by the architect, as was the minimum number of blows each stone had to receive from the pounder. The architect noted defective surfaces on his daily tours about the city and ordered immediate repairs.

More difficult was the problem of keeping streets free of trash and refuse, and the most determined measures were required to induce householders to surrender their time-honored right to allow pigs to forage freely on the streets—a practice not only unsightly in itself but also bound to encourage the dumping of garbage onto the streets to feed the scavengers. In 1475 the Council forbade the free circulation of pigs, confining them to sties in front of or behind houses. Once a day they could be driven to the Pegnitz to drink, but their droppings had to be swept up at once and thrown into the river.

The Pegnitz provided a ready receptacle for anything unwanted, from wilted cabbage leaves to cattle carcasses, but here also the Council was determined to prevent the worst of abuses. It ordered the *Fischbach* kept entirely free of refuse, but the very repetition of warnings, threats, and exemplary penalties issuing from the Council Chamber are sad evidence of the inveterate habit of discarding rubbish where most convenient. In the Pegnitz, dumping was permitted only at certain places downstream, set aside for the disposal of the foulest matter, including the contents of the fifty or so public privies located about the city. (Privy cleaning was a job in the hands of skilled technicians called *Nachtmeister* and their helpers, supervised and inspected by the city architect and confined to certain times in the year when the Pegnitz was sufficiently high and swift.) Industrial waste, sweepings from the workshops, and harmful chemicals used by tinsmiths and etchers and others were to be taken to the same spot, and care was urged on apprentices to see that nothing was dropped or spilled on the way. Householders were instructed to keep servants from emptying slops into the street and were held liable for infractions. Carcasses had to be taken to a field beyond the gates and buried there. Building sites were to be tidied as soon as construction had come to an end to keep loose soil and mortar from running into the streets. No great accumulation of trash was permitted in front of houses "so that the rains may not wash it into the streets." Small compost heaps were permitted, but these had to be renewed once a week.

The very punctiliousness of these laws and their constant reiteration suggest that citizens tended to take the Council's warnings lightly. There must certainly have been more dirt around than the regulations allowed.[3] Only in plague years did the citizens seem really to have heeded the Council's admonition that cleanliness was a good precaution against disease. Plague epidemics struck the city frequently in the fifteenth and sixteenth centuries, particularly bad outbreaks occurring in 1462, 1474, 1494, 1505, and 1522. Syphillis too made its appearance around 1496, and from the very first it seems to have assumed epidemic proportions. Afflicted persons (*elende Frantzöser,* "wretched Frenchmen," as they were called) were banned from the public baths and told to shun company. In 1505 the Council decided to forbid all interments within the walls during plague years, which is why so many distinguished sixteenth-century Nurembergers, including Dürer, Spengler, Pirckheimer, and Hans Sachs, lie buried in the cemetery of St. John outside the gates. While no one was quite sure just what dead bodies and poor ventilation had to do with the progress of the disease, it seemed evident that "poisoned air" was a major factor in bringing on outbreaks. Experience had convinced the doctors that the plague was rampant where infected men and women lived at close quarters. They therefore insisted that victims and their homes be shunned, that crowds be avoided, and public bathing curtailed. Few people seem to have heeded this sensible advice. None of the many treatises on the plague (plague tracts were written in each town upon every visitation of the disease) fails to complain of popular resistance to sound preventive measures. Thus government regulation became necessary, and the Council forbade large concentrations of people and told priests to keep their sermons short to disperse congregations quickly. Clothing of deceased persons was ordered destroyed, bedding was to be thoroughly washed, and fires had to be lit in sick rooms to fumigate the atmosphere. Various means of purifying the air were recommended because stenches were held to disseminate the disease, while pleasant smells promoted good health. Open fires, especially of juniper wood, were always helpful. Fumigating powders could be made cheaply of pulverized juniper berries, chopped bay leaves, and thyme, but costly preparations compounded of imported substances were much better. For going out of doors, doctors prescribed an apple stuffed with herbs and spices and held close to the nose. Or, they said, breathe through a sponge soaked in rose water. Daub nostrils and tongue several times a day with aromatic tinctures. Avoid overeating and stay away from excitement, especially anger. Keep house and kitchen spotless. Cleanse your body thoroughly by means of sweating. If the disease should strike, call a doctor at once for the administration of enemas and for blood letting.

Even in healthy times personal cleanliness was highly prized. Indeed, one gets the impression that bathing and grooming were favored pursuits of all classes of society. The invitation to the weekly bath in Jost Amman's description of crafts sounds attractive:

> Come to the bath house, rich and poor,
> The water is hot, you may be sure,
> With fragrant soap we wash your skin,
> Then put you in the sweating bin;
> And when you've had a healthful sweat,
> Your hair is cut, your blood is let,
> And then, to finish, a good rub
> And a pleasant soak in a soothing tub.

"Bathing money" constituted a regular part of a man's salary, paid weekly, usually on Saturdays. Municipal building workers left work one hour early once a week to go bathing. Like every other profession, the bathing masters had their official *Ordnung*, periodically revised and augmented by Council decrees. Professional bath attendants were trained in the technique of sanitary and medicinal bathing, also in hair cutting and depilation and in simple medical operations, notably blood letting with suction cups. It took three years of apprenticeship to become a journeyman in the craft and seven more years of journeyman's work around the country before one could qualify as a master. During the sixteenth century, Nuremberg had fourteen licensed baths, all located on or near the Pegnitz and the *Fischbach,* whence the water was drawn by means of wooden pipes, then heated over wood fires. Prices of admission to the baths were kept low by Council order so that very nearly every person in the city could go. (Children were admitted free if accompanied by parents.) The usual Council-appointed inspectors went from bath to bath to ensure cleanliness and expert performance. If one paid for the full treatment one was in for an elaborate ritual. It opened with a trumpet or bell signal to indicate that the water was hot and the bath was open. Once inside and stripped of one's clothes, one began with foot washing, then the body was scoured and slapped with a sheaf of twigs, next steam bathing and rubbing to induce perspiration, swatting the skin with wet rags, scratching (for the pleasure of it; bathing masters and employees were obligated to provide this service), hair washing and cutting, combing, lavendering, blood letting, and finally a nap to recuperate from the exertion.[4]

As for medical services, Nurembergers were professionally attended by at least half a dozen doctors, a team of midwives, and several apothecaries. Municipal physicians had practiced in the city since before 1400; they were paid by the Council for the treatment of poor folk, but charged fees for visiting the rich. In the late sixteenth century the medical doctors organized themselves into a *collegium medicum* to suppress quacks and regulate fees; one gulden was charged for the first housecall, a quarter gulden for each subsequent visit, with higher fees for the treatment of infectious diseases. Even in a time of inflation these were high prices, and some kind of free or low-cost medical care was obviously needed. Midwives were salaried, and their activities supervised by several matrons of good family who had a charitable concern for pregnant women, helping out where assistance was called for. Apothecaries were bound by oath to fill prescriptions faithfully. Periodic inspection by two Council members and one or two doctors ascertained that everything was done properly and the scales were accurate.

For the seriously and incurably sick and the very poor, there existed a number of free hospitals, all of them charitable foundations dating back hundreds of years: St. Elisabeth's built by the Johannite Order just outside the walls, near the gate named for it; the so-called "New Hospital" of the Holy Ghost, originally a refuge for the poor but turned into a place for the sick in the 1480's; the Hospital of the Holy Cross in the western part of the city, set aside for syphillitics at the end of the fifteenth century, St. Sebastian's for plague patients and St. John's, St. Leonards, and St. Jobst's for sufferers from infectious and loathsome diseases. The Hospital of Sts. Peter and Paul accommodated foreign lepers. Persons judged to be mentally ill were incarcerated along with prisoners of war and common criminals in a tower in the *Burg*.

It is impossible to discover just how much actual healing went on in these institutions. Probably not very much. Most of them had been established and were being operated as good works and pious gestures of humility by men who craved to do this service for the sake of their own souls or the souls of others, thus illustrating both the good and the bad aspects of medieval charity. The spirit of this conception of charity is revealed at its most compelling in the annual ministration to lepers which, beginning in 1401, occupied nearly the whole city on the Tuesday of Holy Week each year. On the afternoon of that day the gates were opened to lepers of whatever station and origins. Hundreds, sometimes thousands, had been gathering outside in anticipation of the feast. They were given a medical examination, then taken over by the priests who heard confessions, spoke words of consolation, and offered Communion. Following this they were served food and drink by honorable citizens, given warm cloaks and other apparel, and offered lodging. These acts were repeated until dinner time on Good Friday, when the gates closed on them again.

The money for all this food and clothing came from an endowment set up about 1400 by three patrician women. It was a substantial sum, as we know from the expenditures for 1462, where we happen to have some figures. No fewer than six hundred lepers answered the invitation that year. Kunz Has, the mastersinger, described the scene[5] and thought it not only illustrative of the generosity of Nurembergers but also a useful reminder to one and all that good health and a snug home were gifts of God, and but for His grace we too might spend our lives as intinerant lepers. The many charitable foundations which Nuremberg boasted were evidence of her citizens' eagerness to return at least some of their good fortune to God by devoting it to the care of these wretches whom God had afflicted and, perhaps, sent to warn the lucky ones of the instability of fortune. Charity thus served to make amends, to propitiate an unpredictable deity, and to teach a social lesson. A good deal of it was perfunctory—even the handsome treatment of lepers once a year was vitiated by stringent provisions to keep them away from the city at all other times. But no matter what the motive, the result bestowed a good deal of social benefit on the community. There was never cause, before the Reformation transferred all these endowed operations permanently to the government, to supplement privately funded charity with municipal welfare.

In fact, there was hardly an ill fortune not mitigated by some sort of charitable establishment. Unwanted children found a refuge in privately endowed, but publicly supervised, foundling homes. Nuremberg had one for girls and another for boys. They apparently were decent places. A visitor to the girls' home in 1537 described "a large room wherein I saw forty-six foundling girls, the foundling father and mother, and a few servants. On the walls were racks for drying laundry in winter. Adjacent, a chamber with beds for the children, another for the master and mistress, also a kitchen, a place for firewood, a bath outside, and stables." The children were taught to read and write and kept busy with simple work.

Grown to adolescence, poor children had recourse to several sources of help. Honest girls of poor families could apply to one of a number of foundations for sums up to twenty gulden to buy a trousseau. Serving maids with years of household service behind them might procure a dowry from Andreas Oertel's Marriage Endowment. Older women who had neither prospects of marriage nor sufficient means to enter one of the better convents found a haven in the *Seelhaus* (founded by a well-to-do merchant to speed the salvation of a soul in purgatory). Rehabilitated prostitutes were accommodated in homes maintained, until the Reformation, by the two convents. Other funds provided help for women after childbirth, granted scholarships to poor boys to study at home or abroad, helped men who had met misfortune in business or fallen into debt because of illness. One of the handsomest foundations in the city offered free lodging and board to twelve retired master artisans who had not been able to save enough for a dignified life in their declining years.* And for the really poor there was the so-called Rich Alm, an endowment

---

* This was Konrad Mendel's *Zwölfbrüderstiftung*, founded in 1388. It was remarkable for its *Memorial Book* containing portraits of nearly all the members through the centuries, showing each at his craft or trade.

established privately in 1388, the interest from which bought every Sunday enough bread, meat, flour, herrings, and seasonal vegetables to feed the city's needy during the week. This charity was directly administered by the Council, whose agents compiled fresh lists of the poor and indigent every three months, to make sure that, on the one hand, no one undeserving got on the list and, on the other, no needy person had to do without these basic means to a civilized life.

Occasionally a single case reveals the quality of the Council's concern for its cocitizens. In 1555 the goldsmith Niklas Sailer, despondent over ill health and poor business, made a half hearted attempt at suicide, but failed. The incident was brought to the Council's attention and investigated. Convinced that the man was at the end of his wits through no moral fault of his own, the Council granted him a weekly subsidy of one gulden, and in order not to humiliate him with this handout, it was arranged that a third person would receive the gulden and turn it over to Sailer without naming the source. The case illustrates the combination of administrative efficiency and personal solicitude characteristic of Nuremberg's government. A similar concern was reflected in the new beggars' regulation of 1522, where special provisions were made for "poor people who feel ashamed to beg and wear the beggar's badge, either because they think it a disgrace to their parents or a dishonor to their craft."

When most of the manifold private charitable activities were unified and brought under the Council's direction during the Reformation, they were expanded and made even less selective in their application. The principle at work was the desire to ease, if possible, every social want and meet every reasonable need. Once the Council had convinced itself that there was need of a bank to lend small sums of money without enslaving the borrower to an enormous rate of interest (this was after the expulsion of the Jews in 1498), an institution was set up, modeled on the Italian *Monte della Pietà* and the Augsburg *Leihhaus*. The bank functioned under a patrician director and a member of Council as supervisor. It charged only such interest as it needed in order to operate without loss. And it reduced no one to beggary by exerting inhuman pressure on delinquent debtors. Begging, incidentally, though it was always in evidence, was efficiently controlled by means of regulations and a staff of overseers to enforce them. Only people with physical disabilities could beg and not before they had registered with the *Bettelmeister* and received a badge of authorization. Beggars were not allowed to molest people, could not make a display of their deformities or sores ("for these might do great harm to pregnant women seeing them") and unless blind or crippled had to keep busy with needlework or wood carving or some such task.

Few of these services could have been carried on by a community less wealthy than Nuremberg. Hospitals and orphanages and generous alms provisions cost a lot of money, and they reflect the growing economic prosperity of the city and its burghers. Indeed prosperity was so pervasive in the whole social body, and Nurembergers of all economic strata lived so comfortably and ate so well, that neither individual charity nor public welfare burdened their resources unduly. Squalid hovels and ragged beggars on the streets would have been a sight gravely embarrassing to Nurembergers, as men of conscience and as citizens. The good burgher of the medieval commune felt neither callous disregard nor self-righteous censure toward his less successful fellow man. He grieved for him and invited him to share at least a morsel of his own good fortune.

A few observations may illustrate the conditions of material life as enjoyed in Nuremberg at the beginning of the sixteenth century. Almost every family, from patrician to journeyman, had its own house. Statistics from the middle of the fifteenth century show that the largest number of buildings in the city accommodated no more than three or four persons plus a servant girl or two and an apprentice. In time of war, especially when the city was under siege, the picture changed, of course. Rural residents, territorial officials, and even peasants whose farms had been destroyed or occupied sought refuge in the city and were quartered in burgher houses. In fact this need for occasional quartering is one reason for the lack of crowding in normal times: the Council liked to know that space was available for the accommodation of territorial subjects if the need should arise.

Dwellings were places of work as well as of residence. Ground floor rooms never accommodated living quarters but provided space for workshops, storage, and such. During working hours and unless the weather was inclement, work spilled over into the street; in fact, fire regulations obliged all activities causing sparks or fumes to be carried on outside. Upstairs, even the least pretentious house had enough bedrooms to separate children from parents and servants from their employers. It is interesting to note from the available statistics that the proportion of residents and households to buildings increased as the centuries advanced toward the industrial age.[6] In 1500 few families were crowded close on one another. Tenements did not exist. Even factory workers, the surviving information suggests, were housed in comfortable quarters. To give an example of this: there was a combined copper and iron hammer and flour mill on the bank of the Pegnitz just outside the city. It turned out wire, brass, and metal foil, as well as flour for bread. Workers' residences were attached to the factory, the whole establishment forming a closed rectangle of buildings and sheds. The residences, two rows of attached one-story houses, consisted, each, of a living room, one or two bedrooms, and a kitchen. A small stable for a goat or two and a sty for the inevitable pig were adjacent. All this was provided rent free. Every spring the houses were whitewashed, and stoves and other equipment were maintained at the factory-owner's expense. Workers' widows moved to smaller houses in the colony but could live rent free until their deaths. For the children there was a schoolhouse with a salaried master. Probably not all the workers employed in the city's hammer and paper mills lived quite so nicely. But in general the description accords with local expectations of acceptable conditions of work and residence.

This was true also of the amount and variety of food consumed by Nurembergers. All available information, and there is an enormous lot of it for all periods and for all segments of society, indicates that people ate well and abundantly—superabundantly, if one is to believe the many sermons and verses that portrayed Germans as uncontrollable gluttons and guzzlers. Rich and poor ate differently, of course, then as now, not only because of differences in purchasing power but because each estate had its inherited tastes and preferences and its own occasions for eating. Hans Sachs' professional cook, whose services were for hire at private parties and public festivities, assumes these social culinary differences in announcing his repertoire:

> I am a cook, I do my best
> To satisfy the noble guest
> With rice and pepper, fish and meat,
> Aspics and sauces, sour and sweet.
> For artisan and peasant taste
> I cook up oat and barley paste
> Peas, beans, and lentils, beets and cabbage,
> Blood pudding, sausages, and pottage.

One meat dish daily, except on fast days, was standard fare, but two were by no means exceptional. Soldiers, municipal employees, even prisoners got their "morning soup" of meal, bread, cheese, and beer; then at noon at least half a pound of meat, often augmented by a slice of roast or boiled beef or pork purchased privately, taken with bread, meal, and beer. In the evening the food was light, usually bread with lard, some cheese, and beer again. Beer was the ordinary man's drink, and enormous quantities of it were consumed, for nourishment as well as for pleasure because this was a rich brew of good ingredients. Since 1471, beer was brewed municipally in Nuremberg, but each of the monasteries made its own beer, and there were private brewers too, all under governmental supervision, of course. In order to raise a big thirst, people ate salted bread or, if they had them, *Pfefferkuchen*, highly peppered and spiced little cakes. Wine cost much more than beer, even local wine, and artisans took it only on special occasions. But for the well-to-do, wine was the everyday beverage. Brandy was held to be harmful, and its sale was restricted. No one, of course, drank water, and milk was used only in soups and pottages.

Most dishes were highly seasoned—not, as the old notion has it, because meats were always on the verge of putrefaction (the laws against offering any but freshly killed meat for sale in the market were strict, as we have seen) but because people liked their food spicy, and medical authorities attested to its wholesome effect on liver, bile, blood, and the digestive process. Hotly peppered pork sausages were special favorites with all classes of society. Cabbage, the cheapest of the available vegetables, was turned into a delicacy by steeping it in pungent sweet and sour marinades. Everything we hear suggests that food was prepared with care and consumed not only for sustenance but also for the delight of eating it. Imaginative combinations of flavors were especially enjoyed, some of them rather weird for our taste. We hear of an aspic made of mustard, honey, and figs; of chicken with fish in a ginger sauce; of sweet cakes filled with minced pork and crab meat; of trout served with a sauce of milk and crumbled honey cakes. Certainly it was not dull fare. The available varieties of meat, fowl, fish, and cereals assured almost everyone of a varied diet, and when vegetables and fruit were in season there were plenty of these. Every housewife knew that fresh fruit would keep if it was bedded in layers of moist straw. Only the well-to-do could afford dried fruits in winter, but even for the poor there were nuts and raisins and plenty of beets and turnips and carrots stored in the cellar.

Extraordinary care was taken to see that fast days did not cheat stomachs of their accustomed comforts. The city maintained a splendid system of spring-fed ponds and dammed-up lakes within easy walking distance of the gates and stocked them and the brooks connecting them with an enormous variety of fish: pike, carp, roach, trout, barbel, nerfling, burbot, dace and tench, and many more. Crabs and crayfish were also much liked on meatless days and were used as fillings for pasties and pies. Even the commonest type of fish could be made delectable by sprinkling it with ginger and bread crumbs, stuffing it with grapes and figs, roasting it on a spit or baking it in batter, or serving it cold in aspic. Recipes for such preparations were available in cookbooks, some passed from generation to generation in manuscript, others printed. Fishing, incidentally, was permitted in public waters, subject to the usual very specific regulations (a season for each kind of fish, no nets, no congregating in groups of more than two).

Nuremberg's extensive territory guaranteed abundant supplies of nearly all that could be raised; everything else considered necessary—beef, for example—was procured abroad, and the Council made sure that enough was available. Thus the market itself tended to keep the cost of living reasonable. When it did not the Council stepped in and sold grain from its stores or lowered market prices. It is probable that the lowliest workers, laborers digging foundations or doing odd jobs around town, spent almost three quarters of the pittance they received on food for themselves and their families. But even they ate adequately, tongue and tripe and sheep's head and calves' feet and decent cuts of two-day old meat bought at reduced prices. Salt herrings were cheap enough for everyone to eat his fill and so were sausages. In addition, every house had at least a small patch for raising a few cabbages and turnips.

This brings us to the difficult problem of determining real income and gauging living standards. Though here, as in most other aspects of the daily lives of Nurembergers, we have abundant evidence, it is not always easy to interpret it. Prices of necessities, though subject to all kinds of control and manipulation intending to keep them stable, rarely remained stationary very long, usually rising in the wake of wars or other disturbances and responding to variations in the supply of the essential products.[7] Wages and fees stayed not far behind, after the usual lag, when adjustment of income to expenses became indispensable.[8] The Council's social solicitude never countenanced penury very long if it could be helped; still there must have been times when a low-paid wage worker's Saturday morning pay was insufficient to see his family through the next week.

The basic monetary unit in Nuremberg was the *Pfennig (denarius, d)*. It was a silver coin, its silver content determined by a monetary agreement concluded between the city and the neighboring margraves of Brandenburg in 1457 and remaining more or less unchanged after that. For daily purchases, a still smaller coin, the *Heller* (*hl* originally *Haller* from Hall in Württemberg, where these pieces were first minted in the thirteenth century) circulated widely; two of the *Heller* made up one *d*. Twelve *hl*, or six *d*, came to one *Schilling (solidus, s)*. The *s* actually circulated as a coin but was useful principally as a standard of value or coin of account, as were the two summary units of the silver system, which did not exist as coins at all, the "old" pound *(lb* containing 5*s*, or 30*d*, or 60*hl*, and the "new" pound, more convenient for reckoning large sums, comprising four "old" *lbs*. The simplest way of displaying the silver system is the following table:

$$1 \text{ "new" } lb = 4 \text{ old } lb = 20 \, s = 120 \, d = 240 \, hl$$
$$1 \text{ old } lb = 5 \, s = 30 \, d = 60 \, hl$$
$$1 \, s = 6 \, d = 12 \, hl$$
$$1 \, d = 2 \, hl$$

These were all indigenous coins and values, minted in the city. But foreign pieces circulated also, either because the Council recognized their merit and incorporated them in the local system (like the *Groschen*, a Bohemian silver piece much liked in the German cities, and worth $1\frac{1}{4}$ *s* or 15*hl*) or because nothing could be done about it, as in the case of the *Kreuzer* and the *Batzen*. As for the gold system, *Gulden* (*fl*, *Florin*, because the first gold coins to gain wide currency in Germany were made in Florence in the 1350's) has been minted in Nuremberg since the early fifteenth century. The *Gulden* was, of course, the coin of the wealthy. Officially the equivalent of 8 old *lbs*, 12 *d* of silver, it became worth more and more as silver coins deteriorated in the course of the sixteenth century.[9] Merchants and others with enough money to collect it in chests piled up large hoards of *Gulden* and their silver equivalents, the *Guldengroschen*, despite Council decrees interdicting the practice. They also collected Hungarian gulden, ducats, and other international gold coins of reliable merit. It was not unusual to see a dozen or more denominations of bagged and boxed coins listed in testamentary inventories and other legal documents.[10]

For the ordinary man, of course, the crucial question was how much will my money buy for me? Perhaps the following items will convey an idea of the cost of living around 1500. First, the cost of basic food stuffs. A pound of pork sausages (four sausages of standard size and content) cost 4 *d*. Beef was also 4 *d* a pound, lamb and pork 5 *d*. This was a considerable increase from the earlier part of the fifteenth century, when beef had been 2 *d* and lamb and pork just a bit more. Lard in 1500 cost 8 *d* a pound, and eggs were 2 *d* for three, which made them luxuries, as were chickens at almost 20 *d* each. A salt herring on the other hand, cost only 2 or 3 *hl*. Milk was 2 *d* per measure (about a pint and a half). Beer, depending on its quality, cost from 3 *hl* to 2 *d* per quart. Bread was cheap, one or two *hl* per loaf of a pound's weight.

As for clothing, an ordinary cloth coat cost at least 3 *lbs* and a pair of shoes about 1 *lb* or more, depending on style and quality. The evidence is extremely confusing but not because there is any scarcity of it; on the contrary, we have a great number of account books, household budgets, lists of maximum prices, and so on. But the figures vary wildly, even within the same year. Apparently much depended on shopping habits, and bargaining also brought the price down. There is no doubt that the pauper could buy his cabbage and salt herring at a *Höker's** stand for less than the artisan's wife, who went to a more reputable retailer. It seems clear, however, that food, at least, was no problem except for those at the very bottom of the economic scale.

Some idea of wages and other income may be gained from the following.[11] Journeymen carpenters earned 28 *d* a day, plus bathing money. Masons got 22 *d* for ground level work and 26 *d* for dangerous jobs aloft. Ordinarily the employer was not obligated to furnish food and drink during the working day, but if a job was dangerous or unpleasant or had to be done quickly, he made a per diem payment in addition to regular wages. A roofer earned 24 *d* and his helper 16 *d*. A master whitewasher got 22 *d* and his assistant 18 *d*. Plain laborers got 16 to 18 *d*. Presuming steady work, that meant an annual income of about 200 *lbs*, though in view of the many holidays it probably came to rather less. Craftsmen selling their products by the piece did much better of course. At the end of the fifteenth century the city architect paid out the following sums for work done on walls and towers: for an oaken window frame, 2 *lbs* and for a smaller one made of pine, 12 *d*; for a wheelbarrow with an iron-hooped wheel, 4 *lbs*, 5 *d*; for a winch rope, 10 *d* per pound; for a hundred roofing nails, 1 *lb*, 20 *d*. Municipal privy cleaners were paid about 2 *lbs* per job, plus a few pennies for candles and bread and cheese and beer. At about the same time, an artist of no particular distinction got 12 *lbs* for a small picture of Jesus and a goldsmith four

---

* *Höker* is an old German word for pushcart vendors and such; from *hocken*, to sit hunched over, to squat.

gulden for a plain golden ring. Albrecht Dürer was paid 85 gulden in 1512 for portraits of Emperors Charles IV and Sigismund, and in 1526 the Council made him a gift of 100 gulden in exchange for his two paintings of the Apostles. A disciple of Dürer's, Georg Penz, received 80 gulden for a St. Jerome. Jörg Nöttelein, a free-lance astronomer and geographer got 21 gulden for an astrological prognostication of the events of the coming year.

Given these prices, an artisan, if he was well regarded and his work found favor, could live comfortably, and most did. Veit Stoss, the sculptor, could pay out 800 gulden to buy a house in 1499, but he probably got it at a bargain price because the house he bought was one of the buildings confiscated from the Jews when they were driven from the city the year before. In 1518 Stoss was paid 426 gulden for his "Angelic Greeting," commissioned by the patrician Anton Tucher for the Church of St. Lorenz. Fifty-five small hanging lamps surrounding and illuminating the carving brought their maker, the blacksmith Pülmann, 124 gulden. Salaried officials were paid on a widely differing scale, but most full-time civil servants did very well. The two Council secretaries (*Stadtschreiber*) got 200 gulden (more than eight times the income of an average journeyman worker). Jurists could earn as much as 300 gulden or even more. The warden of the municipal prison got 32 gulden a year, which counted as a very good salary. Members of Council, who were, of course, independently wealthy, drew complementary salaries for the various offices they held in the government. From one of these men, Christoph Kress, who kept a record of his earnings in the early years of the sixteenth century, we know that he received for Council membership a salary of 32 new *lbs* (i.e., 128 old *lbs*), and for his position as keeper of the seal he got an additional 104 new *lbs*. For being military captain (*Oberster Hauptmann*) he drew 78 new *lbs* and finally for his position as quartermaster, 16 new *lbs*.

With such enormous discrepancies in earning capacity, it is no wonder that dwellings, clothes, daily food directly reflected the differences in standing. Even the penalties set for transgression of Council statutes mirrored social conditions. The sort of thing an ordinary workman might perpetrate, parting his hair in a forbidden manner, for example, cost him a fine of 5 *lbs*, which was steep enough, of course. But breaking any of the numerous wedding injunctions decreed by the Council in order to counteract spendthrift habits by the wealthy meant a forfeiture of as much as 100 gulden. We cannot be sure how a moderately paid workingman distributed his income, how well clothed he was or whether his shoes were tight, though we know that the Council saw to it that at least bread was abundant (during the great inflation of 1482, for example, bakers were ordered to draw on the public grain supply to bake special four-pound loaves and sell them twice a week at a nominal price). On the other hand, we do have a great deal of information on how the rich lived, for even the big spenders in Nuremberg tended to keep careful account of all their purchases.

Willibald Imhof, for example, listed the following items in his expense book wherein he entered his disbursements from the middle of the sixteenth century on: for household costs: 13 gulden a month, or 156 gulden a year; for entertaining guests: 46 gulden annually; wine: 134 gulden, beer: 45 gulden; medical costs and drugs: 12 gulden; clothing for himself: 37 gulden; for his wife: 70 gulden, and for his children: 140 gulden. Up-keep of the house and garden required some 30 gulden during the year, but servants' wages came to little more than 3 gulden, including kitchen staff. Servants came from the country and worked mostly for room and board and occasional gifts at Christmas and other holidays. Imhof was a great collector of pictures and "antiquities," as he called them, and he was generous in allocating funds to himself for these, nearly 250 gulden in one year. The fact that his income could well support such expenses is attested by his entry of a *Losung* tax of nearly 400 gulden for the year (this was 1565) —one of the few occasions, incidentally, where we are informed about this vital item of public and private finance, treated with so much secrecy in Nuremberg.[12] As for the opposite end of the social scale, we know that a single man with no more means than it took to eke out a mere existence, could get by on something less than 20 *lbs* (about 2.5 gulden) a year. Not many in the city had as little as that; most had enough to live comfortably and in expectation of an easy old age. But only when the enormous economic discrepancy between the poor and the very rich is taken into consideration, can the financial power of the latter be appreciated.

Life was by no means unremitting toil. There were many holidays, even after the Reformation, for people to enjoy leisure, and enough free entertainment to give everyone something to do. But hard and dedicated work was a way of life for merchant and artisan alike, and it is clear that labor and achievement in one's calling came first in the scale of values. The working day varied in length according to the season, as is only natural where so much work is done outside and where artificial illumination is costly. Nuremberg, along with many south German cities, went by the so-called Great Clock, which counted the hours consecutively from sunrise to sunset: the first hour after daybreak was one hour of the day ("when the clock strikes one"), the first hour after sunset was one hour of the night, the second hour was two of the night, and so on. When the day was shortest it had eight hours, and the night sixteen; from the winter solstice on, the relation changed until it was reversed. Regiomontanus worked out the system scientifically for Nuremberg in 1488. Before that the days for changing the count had been determined by rule of thumb.

During the day, watchmen went about the city and rang the bells to indicate the hours of the clock. Working hours followed the length of the day, the working day being longer in summer than in winter. To quote from the regulations governing building workers:

When the clock strikes eight or nine hours in the day [i.e., when the day is eight or nine hours long] be at work when the last hour of the night is over. When it strikes three [i.e., 11 o'clock by the modern clock, the day having begun at 8 a.m.], go to have your midday meal, and return to work at four, until the last hour of the day is over. When the clock strikes fourteen hours in the day, be at work when the clock strikes one [6 a.m.], have your breakfast at three [8 a.m.], return to work at four, take your midday meal at seven [noon], return at eight, have your Vesper at ten [3 p.m.], return at eleven, and leave work for the night when it strikes one of the night [7 p.m.].

Thus the shortest work day was seven hours in length, not counting meal times, the longest thirteen. The elongation of the working day to correspond to daylight hours may explain the proliferation of holidays and half-holidays during the Middle Ages. Reformers disapproved of these, not only on theological grounds, but one wonders how the public responded to the cancellation of so many feasts when the change brought abolition of most of the days that could be spent at games or sports while the weather was good. Since so many people were paid by the day and since prices were always on the rise, the grief over missed shooting matches and rope pulls probably was mitigated by the expectation of more pay at the end of the week. But it gives us pause for thought today that a work week of six days and a work day in spring and summer of from twelve to sixteen hours, including mealtimes, left very little occasion for diversion and recreation.

In winter the problem was the reverse: what to do with all the dark hours before bedtime. Most likely people slept much longer in the winter season; there was little else they could do, since no one was expected to be about the streets after it had gotten fully dark. The inns closed down, most convivial occasions were confined to daytime hours, and theatrical plays were not performed in the evenings. Card playing was probably the great favorite for whiling away time; it had been forbidden for some years in the fourteenth century, along with other games of chance, but in the fifteenth, cards reappeared on a list of licit games that also included chess and other board games. Nuremberg had several well-known card makers, artisans who hand painted expensive playing cards and also turned out cheap decks of block-printed cards. Dice throwing was outlawed, as were other means of gambling ("games in which one wins or loses one's pennies" in the official language of the decree), but it is clear from the constant repetition of the ban that it was largely ignored, even though the law specifically included private homes in the injunction.[13]

For Sundays and holidays the available entertainment was abundant:

On the second day of Pentecost we had a bonfire in the market square, and the town pipers played from the gallery of the Church of Our

Lady, and the young men danced round the fire, and we also had an excellent conjurer.

Or:

We had an Italian juggler here, a professional swordsman. When he did tricks with his blade, he moved so fast that we could not follow him with our eyes. He also stood on top of a barrel, touched the points of two swords to his throat, and turned a somersault off the barrel without hurting himself. He also walked the tight rope wearing high wooden boots, forward and backward, and holding a long pole with a bucket of sand hanging from each end. One time a tile broke off the roof where the rope was tied, making it shake so violently up and down that he had to sit on the rope. The crowd grew alarmed, but he said, "Don't be frightened," and stood up again.

Almost every feast day provided such amusements. Not infrequently, at least before the Reformation, the arrival of a celebrated preacher brought another kind of diversion, and perhaps inspiration also:

In this year [1478] a Dominican monk came to Nuremberg, and he spoke excellent Hebrew and could read the Jews' books. And a tall speaker's stand was erected for him in front of the cemetery wall at the New Hospital, under a lime tree, and there he preached the first of his sermons, and the crush of people was so great that he would never speak on Sundays again. And he preached seven sermons, in Hebrew, right out of the Jews' own books, and translated them into German, and invited any of the Jews to dispute with him. But they said, "We will find a rabbi to interpret the Scripture better than you," and they sent to the most learned rabbi among the Jews, who was from Bohemia, and he came, but when he heard the preacher, he would not dispute. And the monk had a notarized letter made out to himself, attesting that no Jew would dispute with him.

Rarely did a year pass without the appearance of at least one such itinerant preacher. But the most sensational of them all was St. John Capistrano, who passed through Nuremberg in 1452 and stayed on to preach. The memory of Capistrano's penitential sermons lingered throughout the fifteenth century; they were still spoken of at the time of the Reformation. To quote from the Nuremberg annuals:

In the year of our Lord 1452, on the Monday after St. Margaret's day [17 July], between the eighth and the ninth hour, the Pious Father rode in at the Ladies' Gate, met by the entire Council bearing the holy imperial relics, and received by the priests and doctors with great solemnity, all of which well became him, for no such preacher had ever been seen or heard in our lands. He was a Franciscan, called Brother John of Capistrano, an Italian. Next day he said Mass in the market square before the Church of our Lady. A splendid stage had been erected there for him, like the one used to display the imperial Regalia. Standing there he said Mass every day and then preached for about an hour and a half in Latin and afterwards one of his friars translated what he said into German. These proceedings usually lasted about four hours. He did this every day while here, during four whole weeks. They had put up a railing across the middle of the square, and behind this sat all the men, and in front of it, the women. The Fish-market [adjacent] was fenced off to make an enclosure within which were placed sick and infirm people. Each day there were 1800 of them. The Pious Father went to these unfortunates, touched them with the venerable relic of Saint Bernardino and so fervently asked God to have mercy on them that blind men were made to see, deaf men to hear, and lame men to walk; and many other notable miracles occurred. And on Saint Lorenz' Day [August 10], having preached a three-hour sermon in Latin, he had a fire made on the square and burned 3,612 checkerboards, more than 20,000 dice, cards without number, and 72 painted sleds.

The Sunday after St. Lorenz' Day he said Mass and preached a fine sermon, and then he showed us the venerable relics of the most venerable St. Bernardino, first his beret, worn by the Saint on his own head in life and death, then some of his holy blood which on the twenty-first day after his death flowed from his holy nose; after that he showed a piece of the shift of our Lady, and a piece of the cloth in which Jesus was wound when placed in the tomb. Then the Pious Father admonished us to give the tithe regularly, took his mid-day meal, and rode out in the direction of Forchheim, the entire Council accompanying him. And he blessed them all, and departed.

The year 1525 wrote an end to such spectacles, and one cannot help wondering what cause henceforth engaged the enthusiasms and imagination formerly absorbed by these great public cathar-ses. Life must have become a good deal duller, even though there is no suggestion of puritanism in the Nuremberg Reformation. Houses of prostitution continued to flourish, under Council supervision, of course. Prostitution seems to have become generally more prevalent in the fifteenth and sixteenth centuries, probably because women were being squeezed out of crafts and occupations, and there was little a single female could do in medieval society. In Nuremberg the Council had organized the prostitutes into houses, each under a male keeper, and given them a code of statutes which affirmed their rights: not to be forced to consort with men against their will, free to leave the house at any time, a warm bath at least once a week provided free of charge. On the other hand, they were not permitted to solicit openly, and the Council made it plain that it frowned upon the public appearance of women "in their whores' clothing." In 1562 the houses were permanently closed, not for moral reasons but because they were a hazard to the citizen's health.

One victim of the break with Rome, and one whose abandonment cost the city a good deal of income, was the annual festival for the display of the imperial regalia, a lavish and sacramentally potent assemblage of relics and precious objects associated with the German emperors and their coronation ceremonies. Since 1424 this trove had been stored in Nuremberg, at first temporarily, to keep it safe from the advancing Hussite troops, then permanently, by favor of Emperor Sigismund. It was a gratifying privilege, raising Nuremberg almost to the importance of Frankfurt and Aachen in the pageantry of imperial coronations. When the treasures were brought to Nuremberg in March 1424, "everyone made a holiday of it, and the prisons and dungeons were opened and all prisoners released, and Sigmund Stromer and I rode behind the wagon [bearing the regalia] and the seven elders walked alongside, and the rest of the Council walked after the wagon, and the entire citizenry, men and women, behind them." (This is from the memoirs of Georg Pfinzing, who had been sent to Hungary with Stromer to receive the sacred objects.) They made up a fine collection: an imperial crown set with jewels and pearls, two gilded scepters, three orbs, two gilded swords (one of them said to have belonged to Charles the Great himself), various ceremonial garments and shoes, stirrups, clasps, and so on. Even more splendid was the rare selection of relics, which included the lance that had opened Christ's side, one of the nails by which the Savior was affixed to the Cross, a piece from the True Cross itself and five thorns from the Crown of Thorns, a piece from the tablecloth upon which the Last Supper was laid, a tooth from the mouth of St. John the Baptist, an arm bone belonging to St. Anne, a fragment from the cradle in which the Christ Child had lain, and several more. All these, by special permission of the emperor, Nuremberg was allowed to display publicly once a year on the feast day of the Sacred Lance.

For the first showing of the treasures in May 1424, and for every showing thereafter, the Council ordered a large structure, newly built each year, to be put up on the market square. It stood on tall stilts and had a canopy-covered platform above, on which stood festively attired priests holding out the sacred objects. Three times the priests descended and walked about the square in stately procession. Following this, one of the clerics announced the indulgences attached to the beholding of the relics. Colored drawings were made of the scene and sold to visitors who flocked to Nuremberg by the thousands to witness this occasion.[14] In fact, the crush was so great that elaborate security precautions were taken (described in detail in the *Architect's Book* of Endres Tucher, the city official responsible for the success of the festival), not only to protect the regalia, but also to assure the safety of spectators. Iron chains were drawn across the streets near the market so as to channel the crowd and keep it moving. Otherwise traffic would have become utterly blocked. When not being shown, the relics rested in a fine oak and silver shrine suspended by a golden chain from the choir loft of the Holy Ghost church. The imperial crowns and garments were stored in cupboards in the sacristy of the church. Naturally the theologians of the Reformation in Nuremberg objected to the public excitement occasioned by the display of these holy objects. The Council therefore reluctantly decided to abolish the annual festival. In 1523 the relics were shown for the last time, though even after that the shrine could be seen in its customary place in the Hospital Church.

Other public diversions were freely available on town meadows and in sections of the trench where sports and games were permitted. In the 1430's the Council had bought a large piece of property along the Pegnitz just west of the city walls, landscaped it with shade trees and fountains and decorated the bank attractively. The Haller meadow, as it was called, was set aside as a recreation area for all who wanted to use it. Games apt to lead to quarreling were discouraged, but ball playing, bowling, wrestling and jumping, crossbow shooting were promoted. Another large common was available on Schütt Island just inside the eastern walls, and shooting matches took place in several places where the trench was straight enough and covered with grass. On holidays these places were the scenes of noisy festivities involving energetic dancing, running competitions, and sausage eating. A less admirable but apparently highly popular form of entertainment was provided by attendance at public executions, which sometimes involved ghastly brutalities. Nuremberg annals give innumerable cases of individuals hanged, decapitated, broken at the wheel, pinched with red-hot tongs, and worse. A great spectacle was made of each of these occasions, partly no doubt to teach a lesson of the rewards of law-breaking. But that did not keep the spectators from enjoying the action and the holiday atmosphere.

More humane occasions for laughing at the misfortunes of one's neighbors were offered by the popular stage. Nuremberg had a lively theatrical tradition in the fifteenth and sixteenth centuries. Plays and skits had long been performed as part of the divine service, and plays also helped to celebrate the holiday outside the church. But it was in the fourteenth century that carnival and other festal plays became so extraordinarily popular. Shrovetide especially was a time for wild indulgence in otherwise forbidden conduct. Since the middle of the fourteenth century, Nurembergers had inaugurated the carnival with an indigenous festival, the so-called *Schembart* (an old word for a grotesque facial mask). According to the chronicles, the *Schembart* originated at the time of the 1348 rebellion when the butchers, in recognition of their exemplary loyalty to the Council, were awarded the right to "run and dance masked through the city" and also to perform pantomimes and little plays while in disguise. Soon the *Schembart* became an elaborate affair, involving not only the butchers and other craftsmen but members of the patriciate as well, who, clad in resplendent fancy dress, formed a sort of guard to the butchers, running and leaping rhythmically and tossing nuts and eggshells filled with rose water to the spectators. Clowns ran ahead of the dancers, and the rear was brought up by weirdly attired maskers representing wild men in shaggy coats, demons and blackamoors, outlandish animals. But the focal point of the procession was the so-called "Hell," a lavishly constructed float on wheels, representing a realistic scene: a castle stormed and burned by soldiers, a dragon killed by St. George, a ship of fools, a Turkish siege, an elephant and castle, hell itself going up in flames. The excitement occasioned by the *Schembart* was, of course, enormous, but it was not always harmless. At a time when everyone and everyone's business were officially known and observed, the mumming must have served as a welcome release from identity and duty. Occasionally the maskers got out of hand. In 1539, when they took it into their heads to lampoon the zealous Protestant reformer Dr. Osiander, who had been fulminating from the pulpit against the carnival as a relic of darkest Catholicism, the Council decided to forbid the whole *Schembart*, not just that year but forever.[15] Even so, Shrovetide masking continued thereafter, though much more stringently supervised.

Theatrical performances had their origins in these carnival observances and showed the marks of the excesses condoned then. In the old days, an occasional individual, a master artisan perhaps, used to gather a group of journeymen or apprentices and rehearse them in the performance of a rhymed skit of his own composition. Hans Rosenplüt, a Nuremberg coppersmith, seems to have been one of the first of these organizers of festival troupes; his men performed at inns and other places where artisans gathered. The plays themselves were crude, usually abusive, nearly always scatological in their blunt humor.[16] The fun came from holding one's fellow citizens up to ridicule, from malicious slander of clerics, peasants, and old women, from travesties on courtly manners and speech, from dirty jokes on such favorite subjects as constipation and unmarried pregnancy, and from idiotic medical diagnoses offered with professional gravity:

> *A peasant with a bottle of urine* :
> Listen, dear doctor, and examine this flagon,
> I've come a long way by horse and wagon

To bring this water for your inspection.
Can you tell me what illness or infection
Troubles the invalid who lies abed?
He has no money, but sends you these hens instead.

The Doctor, after peering at the urine:
My good man, your peasant is a lout,
There are worse diseases than his going about;
The sickness with which he is infested
Is only a sausage he hasn't digested.
Tell him to go to his compost pit
And empty his guts of two pounds of shit.

Another man with a bottle of urine:
Sir, will you please examine this water?
It was made by my gravely ill young daughter
Who lies on her bed all feeble and weak,
Eats nothing, drinks nothing, nor does she speak.
What is the plague that caused her affliction,
And what is her fate, by your prediction?

The Doctor:
Your daughter, it seems, is a serving maid;
The hired man is the cause of her state;
He broke into her lower story
And punched a hole there, deep and gory,
Which made her belly bulge and swell,
But in a few months she will be well.
It's a disease, I understand,
Widespread these days in our land.
It causes women to ache and vomit;
The holy nuns, too, suffer from it.

This was all right at carnival time, but even after they had
become separated from their original occasions, the plays retained the characteristics of their early association with the
season of abandon. There was no scenery, often not even a script,
and always room for direct response to the mood of the audience,
which could be counted on to participate actively in the spectacle.

Needless to say, the Council kept its eye on these goings on. No one could playact without having obtained official approval, not only for the performance itself but also for the script if there was one or the subject of the play if there was not. One Master Kunz, for example, was authorized to give a play in a certain inn but not to charge admission, though he might solicit contributions after the performance. Another was reprimanded for impersonating the pope in a cope borrowed from the sacristan of the Holy Ghost Church. The councillors always summarized the plot of the play in the decree authorizing performance, probably to allow them to punish deviations. During the troublesome years of the Reformation, the Council's cautious censorship became increasingly severe. Complete scripts had to be handed in for approval, and someone in the Council went over every line. By then the time for mounting plays had stretched from carnival week to a season spanning the New Year and Easter. More than a dozen troupes flourished in the city at that time, the most famous, of course, that of the shoemaker Hans Sachs, who was both the author of his plays and the chief actor in them. For all his popularity, Sachs was no freer of official censorship than his less admired colleagues, and to someone used to thinking of Sachs as the grave and wise patriarch portrayed in Richard Wagner's opera, it comes as a shock to read the abject petitions and apologies accompanying scripts of plays he wished to put on or clear of the Council's suspicion. Sachs' plays, and those of other writers, were staged at the Church of St. Martha, occasionally at the Dominican monastery now empty of monks, and not infrequently at one or the other of the city's pubs. Plots and situations were realistic, the language earthy, and characters liked to step out of their roles to address the audience or improvise. The humor was boisterous and often topical. If the performance was good—and it probably was, for these artisan-players had considerable stage experience—everyone must have gone home content.[17]

Taken all in all, then, the evidence suggests that life in the city was indeed pleasant. If the picture leaves out the inevitable exception, if it does less than justice to the huddle of men struggling for a marginal existence at the bottom of society, it is nonetheless fair in its view of society as a whole. If this were not so, one would find it difficult to explain the lack of pronounced social discontent on the one hand and, on the other, the absence of the kind of heavy-handed despotism that alone can keep a restive society in a state of quiescence. Conflicts arose, of course, probably more of them than the documents reveal, and friction existed between classes, callings, journeymen and masters, subjects and their government. And Nuremberg had her share of antisocial rebels, chronic objectors, delinquents, and misfits. But for the handling of such as these, and for the settlement of private disputes arising among citizens, the city provided an efficient system of laws and legal procedure that satisfied the claims of justice as well as the demands of peace and order.

This, too, was a function of government. Where social stability is so highly prized and the adjustment of internal conflicts so important, law and law courts are bound to play a major role in the relations of men. At the opening of the sixteenth century, Nuremberg had just been through an extensive revision of her judicial institutions. In part this had been done in belated acknowledgement of the many problems created by her salient commercial status, in part it was a response to the innovations appearing in other law courts throughout the Empire. The object was to make the law more uniform and more universal in its application, also to bring procedures in the city in line with practices established elsewhere. A modernization of Nuremberg's legal apparatus was, in any case, long overdue. The reforms of the 1480's and 1490's were therefore sweeping and thorough-going.

To make law was, of course, a sign of autonomy, and in Nuremberg the Council had made law since the thirteenth century: police regulations, market rules, decrees of all kinds. Most of this legislation was passed piecemeal as the occasion arose, without much reference to legal philosophy or judicial principles. If there was a theoretical basis it was the Germanic *Gewohnheitsrecht*, the law of custom and tradition, as written in the *Schwabenspiegel*, the thirteenth-century code from which most territories and cities in southern Germany derived their laws.[18] Even in the fourteenth century this procedure had sometimes been found inadequate. Specific laws not only proliferated, they often conflicted or overlapped. The men charged with their interpretation and application, the *Schöffen* or jurors (in Nuremberg, thirteen members of the City Council, it will be remembered), faced an unwieldy tangle of prescriptive statutes and judicial precedents that confused them and, worse, encouraged arbitrary judgment. Everything was informal and imprecise. Courts had no properly delimited competence with reference toward each other, and it was not even clear what authority, if any, outside tribunals (among them the notorious *Vehmgerichte* of the fourteenth and fifteenth centuries) enjoyed over citizens. The whole organization cried out for renovation, and as early as the fourteenth century some fumbling attempts were made to sift existing laws and produce a more rational code.

Into this fluid situation came the systematizing and, in some ways, alien influence of the Roman law. At first it did not clarify things at all. Some courts in Germany adopted the forms of the *corpus iuris civilis*, others did not. Thus multiple ways of thinking about law, of writing it and presenting it in court prevailed simultaneously in the Germany of the fifteenth century. But sooner or later the Roman way won out. Ecclesiastical courts had long been accustomed to the Roman style as adapted to the canon law, and the civil courts in ecclesiastical domains duly followed. From Italian universities came lawyers trained in the principles and methods of the Justinian code, and they proved persuasive advocates of the superiority of a unitary system of law based on rational precepts which were formulated in lucid phrases and which advanced from general legal categories to detailed and specific provisions. The old Germanic statutory law by contrast was ill organized and ambiguous, and the lawyers had little difficulty in presenting the Roman code as a superior version not of alien doctrines but of a basic and natural system of rights. Pressure also came from merchants demanding a modernization of commercial statutes. Jurists and diplomats responsible for presenting the city's case in territorial or episcopal or imperial courts argued for an adjustment of legal style to the more formal manner in use elsewhere. To such a chorus of insistent demands the authorities could not close their ears. In the late fifteenth century, therefore, much legal reform took place in Germany, in the cities first, a little later in the territories. Nuremberg was in the vanguard of this movement.

From the government's point of view, the incorporation of

the Roman law served another purpose. It represented a radical intrusion of governmental authority into a realm where it had once been only grudgingly tolerated. Every "reformation"—the usual name for a modernized code of law in Germany—promulgated by prince or city council aimed at more than rationalizing what had been clumsy in legislation and legal procedure. It also extended the law giver's powers into an increasingly broad range of private and local relations formerly immune from it: marriage, inheritance, agreements, working conditions, and so on. The Roman code was not just a body of law of universal application. It was also a set of principles reflecting and advancing authoritarian purposes. As such it was an ideal model for sovereigns bent on increasing their authority, and it usually served that objective, especially in the princely territories.

In Nuremberg the arduous process of sifting and codifying began in 1477 when a commission of council members, assisted by professional jurists, reviewed all existing statutes of the civil law and worked out a draft code to replace them.[19] This draft was then put before the entire Council, ratified, and promulgated in 1479. Priests were instructed to read it from the pulpits, and a printing was prepared. In substance, the law remained what it had been, at least where it was still appropriate and borne out by actual usage. But in matters of procedure the commission made thoroughgoing revisions. The model for these was the form of litigation used at the Imperial Chamber Court, the highest appeals court in the Empire, and at the episcopal court in the Bishopric of Eichstätt, which had recently undergone a legal reformation. Appeals there and to the Imperial Chamber Court had to be presented in writing and according to a prescribed style. Hearings and trials followed the form given in the *corpus iuris civilis* and the *corpus iuris canonici*. For some time past, Nuremberg's dealings with these courts had been carried on in the correct manner, and this was one reason for the employment of Italian-trained Roman lawyers by the city. Now the classical usage was brought into city courts as well.

This meant the introduction of many important changes. Plaintiff and defendant could now be represented by counsel in all actions, in fact they had to be, for proceedings became so technical that laymen could not follow them. Every step leading to, and during, trial required written documents, to be drawn up according to proper formulae. The law of evidence, of which older Germanic law had been almost entirely innocent, was brought in from the canon law and used extensively, as were laws governing the examination of witnesses, deposition, and so on. The readjustment was not easy, least of all for the amateur judges whom the city insisted on retaining. Where in the old days trials had been relaxed, informal, brief, the new style imposed a formal, rigid, prolix procedure, dominated by texts and experts. Many of the *Schöffen* must have thought that they were losing their grip on affairs, but the arguments of the doctors were insurmountable. The change was needed, and it had to come.

In 1484 Anton Koberger, the Nuremberg printer, published a fine edition of the revised civil code, *The Reformation of Statutes and Laws Undertaken by the Honorable Council of the City of Nuremberg in the Service of the Common Need and Cause*. It was the first publication, by printing, of a municipal law code in Germany and inevitably became a model for many subsequent codifications in other cities and princely territories. The object was to disseminate the code, "so that no one will be able to claim ignorance of what the law is." The *Reformation*, though it deals only with private law and with procedural matters, is a big volume of over 400 pages of laws and statutes, beginning with the rules for summoning the accused to trial and going on to such matters as registration of complaint, the position of women and minors in court, oaths, character references, examination of witnesses, evidence and exhibits, verdicts and appeals, and, of course, a wealth of substantive law relating to property, inheritance, contracts, debts, guardianship and trusts, torts, and so on. Revisions and fresh codifications followed in quick succession; a new commission was appointed in 1514, consisting of three councillors, three judges of the city court, and five jurists, and charged with adjusting the code to changed circumstances and fresh needs. The resulting code of 1522 in turn became the basis for further redactions in the 1540's and 1560's, each more comprehensive and logical than its predecessor in its arrangement and wording, and each giving still clearer evidence of the penetration of Roman principles into the substance and form of German law.

This process of Romanization was the work of the professional lawyers retained by the city. They were the experts, the men who knew the law, that is to say, the Justinian law, and from the 1470's on their role in law making and law administration was irreversible. This does not mean that lawyers made law. The old Germanic principle that in matters of politics the specialist should not exceed his advisory rank, that government and law were the province of the citizen, not of the professional—this principle remained inviolate. There was no lawyer in the Council and no jurist among the judges. Lawyers were advisors and assessors, but they had no access to the places where decisions were made.

There had been learned jurists in Nuremberg since the fourteenth century, men versed in the canon law who represented the city in her frequent legal encounters with ecclesiastical interests in the Nuremberg domain. Later on, when complicated litigation and diplomatic dealings with the emperor and princes occupied the councillors, they turned these over to the lawyers for skilled despatch. On the Imperial Chamber Court, at least half of the sixteen judges were professional lawyers, and this was the case also on the benches of many territorial and episcopal courts at the time. Cases put before such men had to be presented professionally, and only lawyers could do it. Since verdicts were now frequently being appealed—and the appeal itself represents an adoption from the Roman-canonic law to civil law—city courts were forced to employ procedures suitable for examination by the jurists of the higher tribunals. Thus the lawyer soon made himself indispensable around the city and, as in many modern types of government, became a person of great influence on the course of events.

Some of the lawyers were attached to the chancellery, but most acted as jurisconsults, available to the Council to give advice and to draft important documents and correspondence. The Council was cautious enough to limit their activities by frequent admonitions that "our doctors are advisors and not judges, nor shall they have a voice in deliberations, nor shall their opinion count when the vote is taken." Lawyers prepared written opinions on tricky questions of law or policy, often including citations from the *corpus iuris* to lend weight to their arguments. They regularly met as a group to discuss business put before them and formulate advice on action to be taken. The more far-reaching of these memoranda were collected for future reference, and these books, the *Ratschlagbücher*, contain a great deal of information about the sort of legal business Nuremberg was always involved in. Some of it was vital, as when the margrave refused to recognize the jurisdiction of Nuremberg's Forest Court, or when the bishop of Eichstätt claimed the right to ask services of Nuremberg citizens beneficed by him. But much of it was trivial: should vicars abandon their concubines before being granted citizenship? But such questions were argued with as much gusto and with as great a display of bookish learning as graver matters. Most cases were anything but academic, and the jurisconsults were expected to be familiar not only with Justinian law but with the city's statutes as well and with the charters and grants of privilege in the archives, for these were often called into question by the claims of Nuremberg's adversaries. Add to these documents the precedents established by Nuremberg's and other cities' past negotiations at foreign courts and chancelleries, and it will be seen that municipal lawyers had to carry a great store of fact and interpretation in their heads.

At the city court the lawyers functioned as assessors without votes to affect the verdict, but their presence was necessary to dissolve the tangle of formulations required for legal business. Amateur judges needed to know at every point what law was applicable, and what the law said. Of course, not all amateurs were ignorant of the law and how it worked. One did not have to be a scholar to possess at least a smattering of legal procedure, nor was it even necessary to read Latin, for there were many books written in the vernacular and in popular style intending, as the author of one of them said, to teach amateurs the rudiments of law "so that they will be versed in the duties of jurors, assessors, judges, counsellors, secretaries, prosecutors, defenders, witnesses, orators, or other positions in court and council chamber."[20] But this was never meant to eliminate the lawyers, and it did not. Some of Nuremberg's learned jurists were men of national fame, Gregor Heimburg, for example, a Padua doctor who joined the city in 1435 and helped handle some of the most important cases during Nuremberg's formative period as an autonomous city state.[21] Jurists like Heimburg were often called by prelates and secular rulers to represent them in legal matters, and Nuremberg consented to the loan, proud to have her jurists in such demand. It is not surprising therefore to learn that jurists ranked with the highest city officials in protocol. They could wear gold borders and lace on their garments if they chose and might even carry swords.

Private matters were usually taken before the city court, where complaints were received in writing, drawn up by one of the municipal attorneys available to citizens for a fee. In drawing up this complaint of the injured party, the attorney, being a city employe as well as a private counsellor, was expected to elicit all pertinent information and to administer the oath of truthfulness to the plaintiff. (He was also admonished not to be longwinded and to refrain from mixing Latin words with the German.) This document then went to one of the city court's legal consultants who studied it, wrote out his opinion in a lengthy formal relation, then handed it to a second consultant for a correlation. This procedure was followed no matter how petty the point at issue, and if relation and correlation produced no agreement, the matter went to a third legist for comment.* At the time of the trial the relations were read aloud and witnesses called if that seemed necessary. Then the jurors deliberated and voted on a verdict. The law cautioned them to reason independently and not follow slavishly the opinion of the lawyers, but in actuality they ordinarily did just that. This concluded the case, except that judgments could be appealed from the city court to the Council.

Criminal cases involved more formidable undertakings, excepting minor misdemeanors, which were handled summarily by a court of five councillors without the use of written briefs or legal advice. For serious crimes, however, a great display of judicial and ceremonial circumstance was marshalled to bring the culprit to justice and present his plight as a warning to the entire town. Nuremberg had no unified code for criminal law comparable to the "reformation" of the civil law in 1479, but

---

* "The moral tone of the middle ages scorned considerations of expediency, and always took right and wrong seriously, no matter how big or small the question at issue." Fritz Kern, *Kingship and Law in the Middle Ages* (Oxford, 1939), p. 169.

several collections of statutes existed, and after 1532 the pervasive influence of the new imperial criminal code promulgated by Charles V (the famous "Carolina") served to systematize these. Among serious transgressions were counted breach of peace, assault, housebreaking, theft and robbery, embezzlement, slander, rape, and, of course, murder and manslaughter. Any of these brought the criminal law into play, the city acting either on a citizen's complaint or on the initiative of an inquisitorial process begun by her own officials.

A person accused of a serious crime was secured in the *Loch*, the prison cells located in the cellars underneath the town hall, while the circumstances of the crime were established or his accuser was examined and the charges substantiated. Should they prove false, the accuser faced severe punishment, often the penalty set for the offense for which he had denounced the other. But if the investigation indicated that the crime was probably committed as charged, the procedure turned against the defendant. In case he admitted his guilt at once the inquest was over. But if he did not, he was straightway subjected to examination by torture to make him confess. For according to the justice of the time, confession was needed for conviction. Without it a man could not be judged guilty. Hence the torture.

Torture had been a part of German jurisprudence since the middle of the fourteenth century, probably brought in from Spain. The object was to extract confessions, the legal assumption being that an accused man who did not confess immediately was recalcitrant and only torture would loosen his tongue. There were safeguards, however. Only the Council could order the torture applied, and the order was given only if suspicion of guilt was at least reasonable. Second, statements made while under physical duress did not really count, and a confession to be legally valid had to be made a second time, freely and before several of the *Schöffen* members of the Council. All this suggests that a rather careful preliminary investigation of the accused and the charge against him reduced the possibility of an innocent man owning to crimes he had not committed while being tormented in the torture chamber. Justice in the sixteenth century was not altogether negligent of its duty to protect the innocent.

First, the suspect was questioned intensively by two examin-

Forms of Torture. From Ulrich Tengler, *Layenspiegel*, 1509.

ing judges while a pair of secretaries took down the record. This was then read to the Council at its next session, where further steps were ordered. If torture was authorized, the suspect was taken to a vaulted chamber where the instruments and their manipulators awaited him. Very likely the sight alone of these fiendish devices caused him to lose heart; only a hardened criminal would fail to take fright in the face of a collection of pain machines that in the course of time had become standardized due to their success in doing the job for which they were intended. Again he was invited to confess. A moment later he felt the thumbscrew, first loosely attached, barely touching his thumb, then, unless he spoke, it was tightened. After the thumbscrew came the windlass. His hands, crossed behind his back, were bound to a winch in a wall-mounted frame and his body raised to the ceiling while wooden and stone blocks of increasing weight were tied to his feet. Two big stones were expected to produce internal bleeding. Next, still keeping his silence, he was strapped to a ladder and rolled back and forth on a spiked drum. Then came the "fire," candles or torches applied to the arm pits. This was the ordinary sequence, but there were variations: the "cradle," a seat-like contraption fitted with spikes, the *"Kranz"*, a leather and metal band with a screw device to tighten it around the forehead, red hot tongs to pinch the flesh, and a few others. Order and application of these instruments were laid down by the Council; no initiative was allowed the torturer and his assistants. A thin tunnel drilled through the ceiling of the torture chamber to the floor of the Council Chamber immediately above it enabled the councillors to keep an ear on what was going on below.

Against these pains, and the virtual certainty of being maimed for life, few victims could hold out, though we do hear of men who did, and there were occasional complaints that all a guilty man had to do to go free was to refuse to confess under torture. On the other hand, not a few were apparently driven by their agony to commit suicide in their cells, severe though the judgment of sixteenth-century society, Lutheran as well as Catholic, was on those who laid hands on themselves. Most, however, broke down and confessed. Recorded by a secretary, the confession was placed before the Council. There might be a delay while

Methods of punishment and execution. From Ulrich Tengler, *Layenspiegel*, 1509.

corroborative evidence was gathered and witnesses heard, but usually the Council voted at once on verdict and punishment. It also ordered a judicial session to formalize proceedings. Though this session again heard the evidence and the confession, the accused was already convicted when he entered the tribunal room. Acting out a precise protocol, the accused faced the judges (the thirteen *Schöffen* of the City Council), charge and confession were read, the judges present at the torture certified that a second confession had been freely made, the bench was polled for the verdict, and sentence was pronounced.

Serious crimes—murder, treason, sexual offenses, highway robbery, arson—nearly always brought the death penalty, but the manner in which this was carried out reflected a judgment upon the character of the culprit and the nature of his crime. A murderer was hanged or broken at the wheel. Arsonists and rapists were beheaded, thieves always hanged. Wizards and counterfeiters and sodomists were usually burned at the stake, traitors drawn and quartered. Occasionally a death sentence was commuted to expulsion from the city. But only in the rarest instances were prison sentences given. Prison served principally as a place of detention during trial, and few people were maintained there long at public expense. Only an occasional drunken rowdy was jailed and only if he could not pay the fine. Still, the cells in the *Loch* and in the tower on the *Burg* never seemed to lack occupants. Nuremberg's chronicles record a steady incidence of offenses, from petty theft and hooliganism to murder and treason. There was much for the courts to do.

As it happens, the man who for forty years was Nuremberg's public executioner has left us a diary of his work along with his comments on the men and women on whom he practiced his craft.[22] Franz Schmidt was an intelligent man, unhappy over the disdain in which the profession he had inherited from his father was held by the complacent burghers of his city. He felt sorry for some of his victims and sought to alleviate, or at least shorten, their sufferings. But he was also proud of his skill at hanging and bone breaking, and glad of the approbation of the crowd attracted to his display of it. Schmidt gives us vivid glimpses of executions. Felons were taken to the designated place beyond the walls in a cart, or they were dragged there on a sled. A

procession of officials, clergy, and citizens preceded the victim
and trailed behind him. Prayers were said, the sacrament given,
and the prisoner got a "strengthening drink" as a last comfort—
perhaps it was really a drug to numb him. Then the execution by
sword, stake, metal bar, or drowning. All this amid the noise of
the crowd and the smell of frying pork sausages from butchers'
stalls put up for the occasion. It seems horrendously barbaric to
us now. But persons guilty of the kinds of crimes punishable by
death were judged asocial and deserving of the rightful wrath
of their fellow citizens. Hence the harsh penalties and the brutal
methods of execution.

The social reprobation represented by the sternness of the
law, and the rewards of life held out by the city at work and play
—these are the two poles that defined the burgher's existence
and spurred his actions. They accord with the view of human
nature current among those who thought about such things. Men
were capable and productive when firmly directed but easily led
astray and quick to backslide. The kind of government the city
provided was the only setting in which man could prosper himself and benefit his fellows. The city offered what was, in all
likelihood, the best environment yet devised for the maintenance
of that delicate balance of freedom and discipline, of individual
fulfillment and social purpose, without which life was thought to
be neither good nor useful, pleasing neither to man nor to God.
Other political systems exploited man, indulged him, or left his
capacities idle. The self-governing city alone encouraged him to
do the best that was in him.

At least this is how it looked to those who surveyed the urban
scene from within, during its good years. The historical judgment
may be a bit less flattering. But no modern critic would deny
that the independent city of the fifteenth and sixteenth centuries
evolved a political and social environment in which its citizens
could and did live productively and, by and large, happily.

SIX

Learning and the Arts

The Cultural Environment—Artists and Intellectuals—Education: the "Poet's School" and the *Gymnasium*—Libraries—Humanism and the Classical Revival—the Nuremberg Humanists —Regiomontanus, Celtis, Pirckheimer—Scholarships and Popular Interests—Geography: Martin Behaim and Johann Schöner —Chronicle-writing—the *Nuremberg Chronicle*—Printing and Publishing—Music and Musicians—The Mastersingers—Hans Sachs—Painting and Sculpture—Woodcut and Copper Engraving—Realism in Art—Nuremberg's Golden Age of Art: Wolgemut, Stoss, Vischer, Krafft—Albrecht Dürer and his Students—After Dürer—the Endurance of the Medieval City.

In Nuremberg nothing flourished as luxuriantly as commerce, but literature and the arts were not absent. It is true that contemporaries sometimes voiced exaggerated opinions of Nuremberg's importance as a seat of culture. We hear of a "Florence of the North," a "German Athens," a community of enlightened men and women who first opened their doors to the new learning. This was the elegant bombast of ceremonial orators and other professional flatterers whose phrases were meant to please, not to describe. A few of their claims have survived into modern times, but these are usually based on the life and work of Albrecht Dürer in Nuremberg. Dürer was a superbly gifted man, but he was unique. He towered over his fellow artists in his native city, and no other intellectual nor literary man there reached his stature.

Still, much was going on in Nuremberg in nearly every field of intellectual and artistic endeavor. Quantitatively at least, there was some justification for comparing Nuremberg to the golden cities of other lands and ages. Like all her other blessings, this abundance reflected Nuremberg's stellar commercial position, which was a great lure to men who had something to write, paint, print, or say. Her central location in Germany made her a meeting point for interesting men from all over Europe, while her political importance as the site of imperial diets brought an unceasing stream of dignitaries and patrons of great influence. Her commercial ties prepared a world market for sculptors and painters, printers and engravers. In Poland, Hungary, and Bohemia, Nurembergers designed stained glass windows and carved gilded altars which the wealthy installed in their favorite churches. (The years before the Reformation saw an enormous boom in these tokens of munificent piety.) They decorated burgher houses and princes' mansions, painted family portraits, and cast memorial brasses. A flourishing production of woodcuts and copper engravings was centered in Nuremberg as nowhere else and reached markets in the faraway corners of the continent.

Locally, also, artists found much to do. Throughout the late fifteenth and early sixteenth centuries, while the city was gaining in wealth and growing in size, new buildings and expansion of old ones claimed the attention of architects and artists. Private affluence expressed itself in country villas and town houses, family chapels, libraries and music rooms. Nuremberg artists lived in a pervasive atmosphere of successful business, and it affected their habits. Dürer was an efficient promoter of his own and his students' work, and Veit Stoss, the sculptor, paid regular visits to the great commercial fairs of central and eastern Europe to obtain commissions for his studio. On the other hand, Nuremberg's fame as a place in which one could buy nearly everything under the sun, or have it made to order, drew many visitors, among them scholars and scientists. And her patrician government, comfortably conservative and as steady as it was vigilant, was assurance of the political and economic stability indispensable to men who rely on patronage for their livelihood. Nuremberg's firm social order, built on good laws and guarded by an ever-watchful Council, proved a beneficial environment for artists and workmen alike. It was not a climate in which to introduce bold new concepts or experiment with new styles. But in sixteenth-century Germany inclinations did not in any case run in that direction. It

was an environment in which to raise to excellence, perhaps bring
to perfection, what had been long prepared and securely founded.

For the artist such a conservative setting was no disadvantage.
Artists tended to be traditionalists not only because the market
demanded it (patrons would never have condoned radical deviations from familiar norms) but by training as well, for they had
emerged as "artists" out of the deeply rooted world of the medieval craftsman: apprenticeship, journeyman, itinerancy, masterpiece, and the rest. Solid, slowly matured artisanship was a good
foundation to fall back on when orders must be turned out swiftly
or a mass market supplied, or when an assistant's work had to
make do for the busy master's. It was also a brake on willful individualism, for the medieval artisan's congenital distrust of innovation was indelibly stamped on him after he had spent a decade
or more of his formative years in painstaking and highly competitive training. In any case, a great deal was still to be done within
the accepted conventions. Techniques were not beyond further
refinement. New media invited exploration. A Dürer engraving, a
carved altar by Veit Stoss, a stone crucifix by Adam Krafft do not
conceal their kinship with the works of more modestly gifted
colleagues. Nor do they deny their debt to past generations of
honest craftsmen. But in their effortless perfection of technique
and in their deep and moving intensity of feeling they bear no
less conspicuously the distinguishing marks of genius.

For the literary and scholarly intellectual, on the other hand,
the situation was less happy. He, too, profited from the city's
wealth and prestige. But a social and political climate that put so
little value on independent thinking and did its best to discourage
adventurous minds from reaching untested conclusions was
bound to exert a stifling effect on thought. It was not only that the
governing patriciate held down the lid with its anxious determination to keep things as they were. All of society, that is to say
all the groups and associations and fraternities of which urban
society consisted, shared the Council's distrust of new things.
From the mastersingers with their mass of punctilious rules
guarded by official watchdogs, to the small band of humanists who dissected and criticized each other's books; from the
physicians, so vain of their professional reputations, to the Protestant theologians who knew truth when they saw it, men spoke

and acted by codes according to which they approved and censured. The new, the different was everywhere regarded with suspicion. Nuremberg was emphatically an unintellectual society.
Learning was much praised, to be sure, and scholarship esteemed.
Councillors pointed with pride to Willibald Pirckheimer, the leading scholar among them. They maintained a public library and
did not starve the schools of funds. Visits by Konrad Celtis and
Regiomontanus caused much gratification. But not a single
thinker, poet, or scholar was able to impress his mind upon the
city's civic personality. Nuremberg would have been exactly
what she was had no one written a book there or, for that matter,
read one.

Let us begin our survey with education. Young scholars in
fifteenth-century Nuremberg attended one of four Latin schools,
called trivial schools because they gave instruction in the basic
subjects of the *Trivium*. Each was attached to one of the city's
main churches, but actual direction had long ago fallen to the
Council. They were good schools, as was to be expected of a society so solicitous of its citizens' welfare, and the Council made frequent use of its right of inspection. Occasionally it subjected the
whole system to more or less sweeping reform. In 1485, for example, a new school order was issued incorporating the recommen-
dations of an appointed commission. Curriculum, discipline, and
masters' duties were stipulated down to small details. Young boys
of six or seven studied under a special master who tutored them
six hours a day in the alphabet and drilled them in simple Latin
phrases. Teaching was not confined to Latin (this was one result
of secular influence on the schools), and masters were required
to give pupils daily practice in writing German sentences. For
older boys the learning day was shorter, for they played a part in
divine service and attended choir practice. They memorized their
Donatus and Alexander of Villadei (authors of the two most
widely used Latin grammars) and recited a daily passage from
Horace or Cicero. After the mid-day meal they wrote Latin sentences and analyzed them. There was also some practice in cal-
ligraphy. Senior classes did *explications de texte* on selected
ancient writers and on a few moderns like Enea Silvio, whose
style and vocabulary were recommended for imitation. Some be-
ginners' instruction in logic rounded out the program.

Many people thought these procedures old-fashioned and in-
capable of preparing the sons of the upper classes for the roles
they were to play in business and political life. In the last years of
the fifteenth century, therefore, the Council was persuaded to
establish a new primary school under purely secular auspices. It
was hoped that Konrad Celtis would agree to become its rector
(Celtis had been in Nuremberg for his coronation as poet laureate
in 1487 and was gaining admirers all over Germany), but he had
no taste for such a sedentary occupation. A lesser man was obtained for the post, Heinrich Grieninger, like Celtis a scholar of
the ancient authors on whose books he had lectured in Munich.
Thus the new school could be named a "poet's school" to suit the
demands of men of modern literary tastes who liked to think of
their schoolmaster as a "poet" rather than a "magister." There was
a small circle of such men in Nuremberg (we shall meet them
presently), and they continued to urge the authorities to make
improvements: adopt better language textbooks to replace the
Doctrinale (which, as Grieninger wrote, "stultifies young minds")
and introduce wider selections from the classics including Greek.
Willibald Pirckheimer was the spokesman for this group, and an
effective one owing to his connections among the patricians.
When the poet's school gave up the ghost after a few years' struggle, the victim of attacks from the churches and lack of support
from the well-to-do who preferred to have their sons educated by
private tutors, Pirckheimer turned to the improvement of the
older schools. In 1510 he and the prior of St. Lorenz persuaded
the Council to call Johann Cochlaeus as rector of the Lorenz
school. Cochlaeus, born in a village near Nuremberg, had attended the poet's school briefly, then gone to the University of
Cologne. Soon after assuming his new position in the city he
began to publish excellent textbooks on grammar, music, geometry, and geography and base his teaching on these. But in 1515
he resigned to be tutor to Pirckheimer's nephews and accompany
them to Italy. From there he went to other posts to become in the
1520's the celebrated antagonist of Luther. At the Sebald School
another graduate of the University of Cologne was rector, Johannes Romming, an active scholar too and author of a respectable
number of pedagogical treatises and school editions of classical
writers.

Meanwhile the Council had appointed a new commission to survey the schools. A new *Schulordnung* laid down admirable principles of administration and instruction: separation of age groups with a more flexible program for the youngest boys, special tutorials for gifted pupils, vigorous drill in grammar and vocabulary lightened in the afternoon by "pleasant chapters from Aesop and Terence or similar authors who are not only useful to know, but also delightful to read." Everything said in class must be translated into German in order to stop the deadly habit of mindless Latin memorization. Weekly inspection by one or two commissioners assured compliance with the rules and exemplary performance.

This was in 1511. A little more than a decade later the acceptance of the Reformation necessitated still another reorganization in order to adjust the schools to the new religious purpose. In view of the Council's earlier educational policies, this latest reform was little more than a continuation of trends long under way. A new school, the *Gymnasium*, was organized, and Philip Melanchthon himself was persuaded to plan its curriculum and come down to speak at the opening exercises in 1526. Melanchthon was easily the ablest pedagogue in Germany at the time. Under his tutelage formal education began at last to coincide with both the intellectual and ethical needs of the individual and the requirements of civic society.[1] Learning, he taught, must satisfy the claims of religion, but it must also serve moral and political ends. Curriculum and books were chosen with these aims in view. Prescribed readings included Erasmus, Virgil, and much Cicero; the Bible and selections from the Fathers; also a generous sampling of history from Livy and Tacitus. Under its first rector, Joachim Kammermeister, or Camerarius to give him the elegant name he preferred, the *Gymnasium* was assured of sympathetic guidance in the two traditions, classical and Biblical, upon which Melanchthon looked as a revivifying force. Camerarius was a disciple and friend of Melanchthon's (Melanchthon's students were to be found teaching in Protestant schools and universities all over Germany, propagating the influence of the man they loved and admired), and he stayed on for ten years to give the new school its direction. Not merely a teacher and administrator, he was also an indefatigable philologian. He edited and translated

Aristotle, Plato, Cicero, Plutarch, Homer, Sophocles, Herodotus, Thucydides, Xenophon, Euclid, Galen—to name only the most important of the ancient authors on his list. He wrote biographies and history as well as treatises on pedagogy. He translated Dürer's *Four Books on Human Proportion* into Latin and prefaced it with a life of the author. Most of these works were published after he had left Nuremberg, where teaching and administrative duties left little leisure for writing. But his dedication to literature and his disciplined intellectual habits must have been pervasive in the school while he directed it. Other teachers at the *Gymnasium* were Eobanus Hesse, a poet of some distinction, and Johann Schöner, who had already made a great name for himself as an excellent mathematician and astronomer and as one of Germany's most notable geographers.

Unfortunately, the intellectual excitement which these men brought to the school's first decade did not last. In the thirties and forties of the sixteenth century the *Gymnasium* languished and lost many of its best pupils and masters.* Some observers thought this typical of the plight of learning in Nuremberg. Public funds were spent only where absolutely necessary, and not many in the Council were convinced that preeminence in the arts was worth the money. Among humanists and literary men, Nuremberg enjoyed an unenviable reputation as a city of misers without respect for anything that did not yield a tangible profit. "Money is King among us," Pirckheimer wrote in 1527 to Johann Cuspinian in Vienna, who at once replied to commiserate and assure his friend that things were no better elsewhere. But he had expected more of Nuremberg, he added.[2] Some people experienced the councillors' penny-pinching at first hand. Celtis was one of these, for he got a paltry eight gulden for his fine *Norimberga*, the description of the city he dedicated to the Council in 1495. A glance at the manuscript should have told the councillors that Celtis had made them an unusual gift. But though they liked the flattering portrait of their city, they treated it as the work of an itinerant hack. Celtis had anticipated the snub. The *Norimberga* contains not a single reference to an intellectual life in

---

* The *Gymnasium* was transferred to nearby Altdorf in 1571. In 1577 Rudolf II made it an academy, and in 1622 it became a full-fledged university.

Nuremberg, and his silence on this point is conspicuous testimony of his opinion of councillors and townfolk. Celtis was not one to sulk silently over an affront to his vanity. He poured his resentment into a biting ode to the stingy Nurembergers who gave him eight whole gulden for all his work on their behalf.[3] By 1500 it had become general knowledge that generosity to authors was not one of the virtues of the government at Nuremberg. That is why Pirckheimer warned Cuspinian against dedicating his history of the Roman consuls to the city councillors. They do not know enough to appreciate such gifts, Pirckheimer said. Criticism failed to move the councillors from their chosen path, however. They were not ashamed to be accused of turning every penny twice and placing monetary matters uppermost. They saw no disgrace in that.

In any case, the protests referred only to public policy. Privately a good deal was being done to promote learning, for example: libraries. Some noted personal libraries existed in Nuremberg, among them the famous collection of Hartmann Schedel, a municipal physician since 1481 and an omnivorous consumer of books. Hartmann was the younger of two Schedels in Nuremberg; his cousin Hermann, also a medical doctor, had studied in Leipzig and Padua and practiced in various parts of Germany before taking a post in Nuremberg. Wherever he stopped he visited libraries and copied all that he could, mostly in his own hand. His shelves in Nuremberg held medical and legal tomes, chronicles, treatises on astronomy and astrology. He owned volumes of St. Jerome's letters and writings of Petrarch, Boccaccio, Filelfo, and Enea Silvio. He also had the classics: Terence, Juvenal, Horace, and many others. Upon Hermann's death his books were dispersed, but many came into the possession of his cousin who proved a good disciple, for he had spent every free moment during his student years in Padua and elsewhere copying everything in sight. When he settled down in Nuremberg, Hartmann had the basic works in philosophy (his original field of study) and also volumes on every subject germane to the polyhistor he fancied himself to be. He bought or copied all the Cicero he could get; he had Einhard's *Life of Charlemagne*, also the *Divine Comedy*, and Enea Silvio's *Europa*. He amassed medical, geographical, and astronomical tracts and collected Greek inscriptions, intending to publish a monograph on these later in his life. Unlike his cousin (and many other fifteenth-century bibliophiles) he did not scorn printed books. His friends, knowing his passion, made him presents of books, as did his patients in the monasteries and convents in and about Nuremberg. His catalogue listed more than six hundred volumes, but it was not complete, for he was never able to keep up with his acquisitions. All of Schedel's books, incidentally, were intended for use. He had no interest in costly illuminations or fine bindings.[4]

Hartmann's books, too, were scattered after his death in 1514, but the core of his and his cousin's libraries was added to the budding municipal library. This collection had originally been a purely functional reference shelf for lawyers and diplomats. Occasionally the Council authorized the purchase of a needed volume; once or twice a municipal jurist bequeathed his personal library to the city. In 1430, for example, Konrad Konhofer left the city one hundred and fifty volumes and this prompted the Council to furnish a spare room in the town hall as a *Librei*, with presses along the walls and desks to which the most frequently used books were chained. This library was open to all who wished to read there or look up a reference. It was a lawyer's library primarily, but it grew in range as private citizens took an interest in it and bought collections as they became available—Regiomontanus' library, for example, which was acquired in 1522. Later in the 1520's the dissolution of the monasteries brought in substantial additions, and very cheaply too. The Dominicans offered up some splendid fourteenth- and fifteenth-century manuscripts; St. Catherine's yielded a collection of German mystics; St. Aegidius' handed over a number of books by classical and modern Italian authors, many of which had originally been purchased from Hartmann Schedel. All these were incorporated in the town library, which numbered, in the 1550's, some four thousand volumes and was competently directed by a *Pfleger* appointed by the Council.

The Schedels' passion for books and their industry in acquiring them had therefore borne some fruit in Nuremberg. As professional men with years of study and practice abroad, with correspondents among the learned of Germany and Italy, their interests might be expected to be more sophisticated than those of local men of affairs. Medicine was still a theoretical pursuit in the fifteenth century and encouraged detached habits of thought. Men who had studied it were likely to rise above the demands of daily business and give free rein to their minds and fancies.

This was true of jurists as well; in fact among Roman lawyers one could find some of the most open-minded men of the time. All of Nuremberg's jurisconsults had studied abroad, most of them in Italy. Before going to Nuremberg they had served at the courts of princes and bishops and had seen something at first hand of the great struggles between emperor and barons, popes and kings, cities and feudal lords. The experience had broadened their minds and multiplied their points of view. In Nuremberg, as in other cities where lawyers were kept from direct responsibility in the conduct of public business, they lived at some remove from affairs, writing memoranda and preparing briefs and opinions. They were therefore apt to take a somewhat abstract view of things and place theory on a par with practice. The speculative approach was, in any case, natural to them, for they had been conditioned to it by their legal training, Roman jurisprudence, particularly as taught in Italy, being a theoretical subject and one which favored rational methods. This, of course, was just what the city councillors feared and why they excluded lawyers from their innermost confidences. They distrusted theory and suspected lawyers of excessive sympathy with alien influences. They were right in their suspicion, though wrong in their dread of the consequences. German jurists did exhibit an enlightened interest in intellectual variety and were open to suggestions from every source.

This intellectual inquisitiveness disposed them to be immediately receptive to what is usually called the classical revival. Here again their professional training had prepared the way. Justinian's code and the writings of the Roman jurists were the modern legist's working documents. In pondering the legal problems raised and interpreted there, the student touched the concrete circumstances in which ancient law had operated. To explore these he was obliged to reach into the fields of history, geography, and biography. Beyond these, in turn, beckoned the wider world of humane letters. Moreover, because it was the lawyer's task to speak in public, as advocate and often as diplomat, he had to be trained in the art of rhetoric, and rhetoric was the gateway to the whole realm of Latin and Greek literature. Enough of this literature was readily at hand to sustain his initial interest and whet his appetite for more. Once exposed to it he was likely to become a devotee for life, often spending as much time and energy on his classical studies as in the pursuit of his professional career.

No one who has sampled the literature of ancient Rome and Greece needs to have the vigor of Renaissance classicism justified, nor the enthusiasm in which its work was carried on. Even slight acquaintance with it conveys an impression of extraordinary subtlety of intellect and of a virile and high-spirited civilization. No matter what a man's interest, he could find there an embarrassment of intellectual riches: stirring examples from history, political ideas to set him thinking about problems of civic administration, thoughts on soldiering and citizenship, a disciplined and infinitely resourceful language, and above all explorations of the deepest problems of human life and nature. Much of this literature had always been available, much more was known by title but was not at hand or was to be seen only in inferior copies of uncertain provenance. What could be more inviting than a grand reconnaissance of the entire corpus of ancient letters in order to repossess it? The early fifteenth century seemed the right time to undertake this task. In the cities of northern and central Italy political and social conditions had created a volatile milieu where inherited ideas no longer compelled respect. As early as the fourteenth century men like Petrarch had read Cicero and Livy with a more comprehending sympathy and had written about their discoveries with uncontainable excitement. Their elation quickly spread to others. Patrons encouraged the search for manuscripts and supported scholars who studied them. Rediscovered texts and newly appreciated authors were introduced into the academic curriculum, where they became the specialty of the humanists, as the propagators of classical letters were called. City governments and princely rulers competed for the services of men versed in Roman and Greek history. At public ceremonies and occasions of state classical oratory became indispensable. North of the Alps both opportunity and incentive for a classical revival had so far been lacking. But given the nature of the subject it was bound to come. In this movement the jurists of Germany led the way.

Nuremberg's leading jurist in the early fifteenth century was Gregor Heimburg, who had degrees in civil and canon law from Padua and made a brilliant career as lawyer and diplomat, not only in Nuremberg where he took service in 1430 but also in the councils of secular and spiritual lords whom he represented in intricate and sometimes sensational cases. His local renown stemmed from his vigorous advocacy of Nuremberg's claims against the Margrave Albrecht Achilles in the late 1440's and early 1450's. He pleaded successfully, but when litigation was over he switched sides and entered the service of the Margrave. Princely government offered greater scope for the application of Roman jurisprudence to politics, and life at court must have suited him better than the stuffy atmosphere of Nuremberg, where, despite his fame and the social privileges accorded to doctors of the law, he was kept at elbow's distance from the hub of affairs.[5] While Heimburg lived in the city he seems to have been the moving spirit of a little group of men who talked about books and ideas not strictly limited to their professional concerns. Most of them were lawyers: Heinrich Leubing and Martin Mair (the latter destined to become a prominent Bavarian and imperial politician). One or two were laymen: the municipal secretary Niklas von Wyle, for example, was the translator of popular works of ancient and Italian humanist literature into German. None of these men remained in Nuremberg long enough to alter the city's cultural tone, but they did introduce the discussion of topics which had been exciting literary men in Italy for some time. This they did among themselves for their own profit and enjoyment. They did not think it necessary to present their new-found pleasures as a saving message for all.

The arrival of Hermann and Hartmann Schedel added two enthusiasts to this small band of fledgling humanists in Nuremberg. Both Schedels were distinct late medieval types: avid bibliophiles and accumulators of information but undiscriminating and a little naive in the trust that knowledge in large enough quantities produces wisdom. However, their studies had made them aware of the changing trends of scholarship and given them a taste for new ideas. Hermann's letters reveal something of the minds of these men who saw themselves as purveyors of the new learning. The letters are full of the latest news and gossip about books and writers. They raise abstruse problems of philology and carry on lengthy historical and philosophical arguments. Their formal and, by our taste, swollen phrases—most of them lifted straight from the approved classical authors —mark the two men as practitioners of that brand of classicism which tried at all costs to force modern thought into Ciceronian moulds. Hartmann had a respectable knowledge of ancient literature, and his library included a good selection of the classical books available at the end of the fifteenth century. As he had copied most of them by hand, he must have known their contents intimately. He also collected coins and bought engravings of ancient monuments. These were the things he cared for most. He certainly gave more thought to them than to his medical practice. In time his zeal began to make an impact on his contemporaries. Sigismund Meisterlin, the chronicler, practiced letter writing in the grand manner and ransacked monastic libraries for manuscripts of missing ancient authors. The patrician Hans Tucher built a library and collected portrait coins of Roman emperors. He had enlargements of the portraits drawn on a poster and displayed it in the town hall. He also commissioned a collection of biographies of the emperors taken from Suetonius and other ancient authors.

None of this was more than dabbling in erudite pastimes known to accord with the tastes of humanist intellectuals in Italy. A more solid scholarly undertaking might have been sparked by Regiomontanus, who settled in Nuremberg in 1471. Regiomontanus (Latin for Königsberg, a town in Franconia where he was born Johannes Müller) was an established and well-known scientist and man of learning. He had been commissioned by King Matthias Corvinus of Hungary to begin systematic observations for improved planetary tables, and this he set out to do in Nuremberg where special instruments could be built according to his designs. He also planned to use the resources of Nuremberg's printers and woodcut artists to publish scientifically usable editions of all the available records of astronomical observations. Since each of these editions required thousands of mathematical figures to be specially cut in wood, this was a formidable project. Regiomontanus was a severely professional scholar, and he had much to teach the local intellectuals. He was a widely cultured man, knew Greek well, and had a far more realistic grasp of ancient civilization and its potential impact on modern thought than the humanist dilettantes of the Schedel group. But he remained in Nuremberg only four years before going on to Rome to help Sixtus IV with his calendar reform, and during his stay his uncommunicative nature and secretive habits kept him a stranger to all but two or three favored intimates. He published several highly important astronomical works during these years, and when he left Nuremberg (and died soon afterwards) his books and papers remained behind. But his learning was too specialized to benefit local humanism at this point, and his personality was too saturnine to make an impact on Nuremberg's cultural life.

Humanism in 1500 could take several directions in a city like Nuremberg. It might so seize the minds and elate the spirits of her leading citizens as to transform fundamentally both the aims and the conduct of public affairs. This, of course, did not happen in Nuremberg. Of her governing burghers only one, Willibald Pirckheimer, had both inclination and aptitude to accept and profit from the new learning. Only he recognized the political and moral influence that antiquity might exert upon the present, but he also knew that Nuremberg was not receptive to this influence. Most of his colleagues did not understand this; they lacked not only knowledge but even the interest. Nor is it easy to see how these hard-headed patricians with their calculating and literal minds would have drawn inspiration from a letter of Cicero or a chapter from the history of Thucydides. Thus the greatest impact humanism might have on a society, the fundamental alteration of its image of itself and the face it presented to the world at large, was absent. The revival of learning did not even bring a change to Nuremberg's epistolary and diplomatic style, except to the language of law, as we have seen.

Secondly, humanism might express itself in greatly expanded and accelerated scholarly pursuits. Nearly everywhere in Europe scholars were at work to collect manuscripts of ancient and medieval authors, collate them to find the best readings, edit them, translate Greek into Latin, and emulate the ancients in writing works on philology, history and geography, music, mathematics and science, poetry and literature. Nuremberg had her modest share in this great endeavor to put knowledge, particularly knowledge of the ancient past, on a secure foundation. Nuremberg's historians tend to make much of these early attempts to prepare a home for the classical revival; of one citizen, we hear that his house was adorned with frescoes of the Seven Sages and the Nine Muses; others wrote letters in the Ciceronian epistolary style or substituted the classical *tu* for the conventional *vos* in addressing one another. Hartmann Schedel is the representative man of this type of neophyte local humanism, a dilettante, though exceedingly earnest in his attachment to the cause of learning.

Serious humanist scholarship in Nuremberg has its origin in the impetus provided by the man who has been called Germany's arch-humanist, Konrad Celtis. Celtis visited Nuremberg on several occasions, first in 1487 when, as we saw earlier, Frederick III awarded him the poet's silver laurel in a ceremony intended to revive the poetic laureations of ancient times. In the same way Enea Silvio Piccolomini had been honored, also by Frederick, more than forty years earlier. But in 1487 the occasion was peculiarly revealing of the tenuous political and intellectual conditions in the Empire: Frederick, a refugee from King Matthias of Hungary whose troops had conquered his hereditary lands and driven him from Vienna, bestowed the laurel on a young poet who at the time had written nothing more than a few occasional verses and an adacemic treatise on poetics. It was not long, however, before Celtis began to substantiate what had then been an empty gesture. His Latin poems, notably the *Amores* published later on in Nuremberg, established him as one of the few neo-Latin poets of talent in Germany, and his many imaginative schemes for collaborative scholarly enterprises, propagated with unflagging energy wherever he happened to be, made him for a time the prime mover of organized learning in Germany. He traveled too much to bring any of his larger projects to fruition, and his temper was too mercurial to put up with the sustained labors of philology and history. But his enthusiasm was catching and the few books he did complete—an edition of the dramas of the tenth-century nun Roswitha, and the description of Nuremberg—were models of their kind and paradigms to more than a generation of followers.[6]

Nuremberg was a sort of headquarters for Celtis. He returned time and again to see his friends, enjoy their ample hospitality, and talk about philosophy, geography, education, and a hundred other things.[7]. His circle consisted of the jurist Peter Dannhauser, who enlisted Celtis' help in preparing the results of his own scholarship for publication, and Sebald Schreyer (Latinized "Clamosus"), a prominent burgher, member of the commission to reform the civil code, and a generous patron of local artists and men of letters. Schreyer opened his house to Celtis and unsuccessfully tried to enlist him as the editor of a planned revision of Hartmann Schedel's *Chronicle*. The other members of the group were Johann Löffelholz, a respected jurist and diplomat and an active amateur scholar, the municipal secretary Georg Alt, who translated the *Norimberga* into German, and Bernhard Walther, the one man close to Regiomontanus during the latter's sojourn in Nuremberg and financial supporter of his ventures in printing. Walther considered himself the literary executor of Regiomontanus; he bought his library when it was put up for sale and somehow gained enough scientific knowledge to continue the observations and publications Regiomontanus had begun. Another scientist member was Johann Werner, chaplain in one of the local churches, but by vocation a mathematician and writer on astronomical and geographical subjects, among them a commentary on Ptolemy's *Geography* and a German translation of Euclid. In 1522 Werner published a collection of his mathematical and astronomical treatises, one of which, on the motion of the spheres, embroiled him in a controversy with Copernicus. Finally, there was Hieronymus Münzer, a physician and amateur geographer who had drawn the maps in Schedel's *Chronicle*. Most of these men were typical of the first generation of humanists in Germany. Their projects were much too ambitious to be practical and their goodwill nearly always exceeded their competence. But the momentum imparted by Celtis, and the bracing sense of freshness drawn from their intensive occupation

with the classics, carried them over most of the inevitable dis-
appointments.

If Hartmann Schedel is the representative of early humanism
in Nuremberg, Willibald Pirckheimer is the exception. Pirckheimer belonged to Celtis' circle (his letters to Celtis reveal how
close the two men's interests were) but personally he stood apart
from the dilettantish bustle of the others. His talents and training
were vastly superior to theirs, but he was not the sharing kind
and seems to have had little influence on the other members of
the group. Though he opened his house and his excellent cellar
to many an itinerant man of letters, even helping out with a sum
of money now and then, he was really a solitary figure, usually
at cross purposes with the world, intimate with no one. He worked
out of his own resources and rarely engaged in the give and take
so characteristic of the community of humanists. Probably he
felt uncomfortable in Nuremberg, as had his father, who, though
a patrician, could not as a doctor of law serve in his city's government and became instead legal adviser to the bishop of Eichstätt. Willibald himself did not complete his juristic studies and
could take his place in the Council when he settled down in
Nuremberg. He was an invaluable counsellor, and his earlier
legal and military and diplomatic experiences made him one of
the city's best administrators. But he did not get on with his
fellow patricians and drew little pleasure and few rewards from
his public service. Scholarship was his real vocation. He was an
excellent philologian and a fine editor and translator, especially
of the Greek and Latin Church Fathers. He put out editions
and Latin translations of Gregory of Naziànzus and John of
Damascus, of the moral treatises of St. Nilus and of the works
of St. Fulgentius of Ruspe, a follower of Augustine whose polem-
ical writings against the Pelagians interested Pirckheimer. Of the
pagan classics he translated Lucian, the Greek rhetorician and
satirist, also Theophrastus, Plutarch, and Xenophon. He published
Ptolemy's *Geography* with notes by Regiomontanus. His work
on Ptolemy led him into historical geography and to a monograph
on ancient place names in Germany and their modern derivatives.
He bought coins and medals and made a catalogue of them
(published after his death by his secretary). He wrote essays on
moral subjects, an autobiography, a dramatic personal account

of his experiences as commander of Nuremberg's contingent in the Swiss war of 1499, and a host of occasional pieces: all in all a literary output to do credit to a man of twice his leisure.[8]

Still another direction for humanism to take in 1500 was to offer artists fresh inspiration and new subject matter. In Italy the classicism of the Renaissance had been accompanied by a most extraordinary flowering of all the visual arts. Every German artist with eyes to see and the wit to understand should have found the work of the Florentine and Venetian painters an eye-opening experience. At the very end of the fifteenth century German artists at last began to do what German scholars and academics had done for half a century: they went to Italy in order to gain knowledge and acquire technical polish. Albrecht Dürer was the first of the German artists to make the pilgrimage to the other side of the Alps. He left Nuremberg in the autumn of 1494 for several months' stay; ten years later he went back for a second and longer visit. His activities while in Italy established a pattern for future generations of eager young artists. He sketched voluminously and systematically, copied Italian paintings and architecture, and recorded the scenery. He met the celebrated painters and drew them out in conversation, trying to pick their brains and profit from their experience. He responded to the more scintillating intellectual environment and the less constricted social milieu and enjoyed himself enormously. Back home again, his work recorded at once what he had learned. His entire conception of the human form and its depiction had undergone a change. He occupied himself with philosophical problems of art: measure, proportion, perspective, the inner *ratio* of natural shapes and forms and their representation on a two-dimensional plane. But his countrymen hardly noticed this. They knew him to be a splendid draftsman, but they viewed his work as a virtuoso performance in an established style. Only a handful of disciples benefited from his advanced ideas. The one man in Nuremberg with whom he shared his deeper thoughts was Pirckheimer. Dürer did not fret over this lack of understanding among his own kind. He was a true son of his milieu. He never thought of himself as a trailblazer, and his Italian experience did not make him one. It deepened his art, made it more reflective and—as we can see so clearly now—universal in meaning and appeal. But it did not replace or even overtly change the inherited manner. Traditional elements remained uppermost in all his work.

It was largely this tenacity of tradition that kept the new learning, and the new sensibilities generated by Renaissance classicism, from influencing Nuremberg's cultural life. The hold of tradition also accounts for the self-consciousness of Nuremberg's humanists and for much that was mere posture in their bearing. They felt their estrangement keenly; they talked about it at length and in often bitter terms: the stranglehold of the clergy, the stupid complacency of their fellow burghers, the miserly councillors, the crude nobility living for drink and the hunt, the dust-gathering pedants at the universities putting their students to sleep with wooly thoughts read from mouldering notes. This attitude explains the humanists' attempts to build for themselves a little republic of learning peopled by enlightened men with high-sounding (and often unintentionally funny) Latinized names and regulated by elaborate social conventions and formidable titles of address ("Your Humanity"). It also explains the tremendous commotion made over every contribution, no matter how slight, to the sum of erudition. With these matters the citizens of Nuremberg had nothing to do. Life in Nuremberg was taken up with honest work and with the enjoyment of the fruits of industry. Burghers and artisans saw no use in stuffing brains and books with recondite matter in dead languages. Nor was it any good brooding about the deep meaning of things. Theologians did that. Learning and the arts had their place, but they must apply to real and immediate concerns, and they must speak to people in their own language.

In such a predicament humanism in Nuremberg (as indeed in nearly all Germany) was bound to remain academic, a thing of books and antiquaries, not of life and citizens. The phrases of its adherents, especially their generous self-appraisal and their mutual approbation, sound curiously hollow in the utter social void where these men lived and worked. In Nuremberg culture was valued only if it was demonstrably useful and practical, and if it added material value or enjoyment to life. Thus the arts which flourished best were those that offered something of instruction or delight to people of ordinary tastes. Classics were turned into homespun German rhymes where Biblical patriarchs, Homeric heroes, and Teutonic warriors fought like pikemen and spoke like shoe makers, bringing the plots of myth and epic into shop and living room. In 1515 a Latin poem on a favorite theme, the Choice of Hercules, was translated by a city official and amateur chronicler, Pangratz Schwenter, to illustrate in the common tongue and in respectable classical form the plain but enduring rewards of virtue. Similarly, mathematics and astronomy served the everyday purposes of weather observation and astrology. Many a serious scientist stretched his income by writing prognostications: Johann Schöner, for example, one of Germany's leading mathematicians and geographers. Georg Nöttelein, the noted cartographer (and organist at St. Lorenz), wrote predictions for every day of the coming year:

War-like noises and tumult in the city. The enemy destroys much property in the countryside. A distinguished citizen dies. Beware this day of neighbors and apprentices. The weather: unsettled but warm.

Regiomontanus was known in all Germany for his *Ephemerides,* an almanac giving the daily positions of sun, moon, and planets for the years 1475 to 1506. Equally popular were his calendars which he published two generations in advance, covering the years 1475 to 1531. They indicated the phases of the moon and gave the lengths of days, also eclipses seen locally and the movable feasts.

But of all the sciences, geography stood highest in popular favor at the time. Nearly everyone's curiosity had been aroused by the Portuguese and Spanish voyages and by reports of exotic animals and plants and of weird and fascinating human beings. Such reports followed close upon the voyages, first in broad sheets and hastily done woodcuts, later in travelogues and memoirs, and finally in collections of voyages and full-scale descriptions of new countries. Within Europe, too, much was still being discovered, and travelers, cartographers, and draftsmen were at work plotting the courses of streams, portraying towns and mountain ranges, describing picturesque scenery. Travel literature was much favored as popular reading, not only for descriptions of strange customs and places and exciting tales of capture and imprisonment, but also for flora and fauna seen in far-away countries and vivid accounts of exotic habitats. No wonder there was interest in seeing the new countries displayed on maps, and great pressure on the map makers to stay abreast of events. At the same time, laymen needed to learn something of meridians and degrees and lattitudes and the climatic zones. Reports of discoveries came almost monthly, sometimes of a new-found bay, sometimes a whole island. Geography had never been as exciting as it was in the late fifteenth century.

Nuremberg had her own participant in this rapid geographic advance. He was Martin Behaim, a merchant's son sent on business to Lisbon where he somehow (probably by passing himself off as a disciple of Regiomontanus and brandishing a copy of the *Ephemerides* to prove it), gained a reputation as astronomer and sailed on a voyage down the coast of Africa. During a visit to Nuremberg in 1490 he was invited, as a world traveler and eyewitness to the discoveries, to share his knowledge with his fellow citizens by making a globe and tracing on it the shape of the world as it was then known, including the outcome of the latest Portuguese voyages. The Council agreed to foot the bill, and Behaim set to work.

The result was his famous *Erdapfel*, not the first globe ever, but one of the earliest modern ones and certainly the most beautiful. Its beauty was not due to Behaim himself, but to the painter Georg Glockenton who inked and lettered Behaim's design onto the thirteen parchment segments cut to fit the globe. Scientifically the job was not up to much. In fact, it was a good way behind geographical standards prevailing in Behaim's own day. Most of its information came from such standard sources as Ptolemy, Strabo, Pliny, and Marco Polo. The globe even fails to do justice to the current state of African exploration, the subject on which Behaim had been supposed an expert.[9] Only a few years later, far better maps, some of them by Johann Schöner, were to circulate in Nuremberg, showing the islands of the New World as well as a more accurate outline of Africa. But the burgher who approached Behaim's "earth apple" on its stand in the town hall got from it a much more realistic grasp of the shape of his world and the relationship of its parts. He could spin the hollow sphere on its metal axis and see the contours of Asia, Europe, and Africa pass before his eyes; rivers and mountain ranges standing out in clear colors. It was far better than the old wood-cut maps in the chronicles.

There were, of course, pragmatic reasons for following the rapid spread of geographical knowledge with interest. Commercial profit was always the strongest incentive to extending known boundaries, and the trading ships were never far behind the vessels of the discoverers. In Nuremberg, the Imhof and the Hirschfogel were among the first to answer the call for foreign capital issued by the Portuguese in 1505. This made the reports of new voyages a matter of urgent practical concern. A geographer like Johann Schöner, incidentally one of the first to refer to the New World as America (in his admirable textbook on cosmography and geography published in Nuremberg by Johann Stuchs in 1515), kept himself informed on the very latest Portuguese and Spanish explorations and combined these data with his mathematical knowledge to produce reliable maps. He, too, was a maker of globes, on one of which he traced in 1523 the route of Magellan's circumnavigation of the earth which had been completed only a year earlier. It was in part due to Schöner's reputation that Copernicus' *De Revolutionibus Orbium Coeles-tium* was given to a Nuremberg printer, Johann Petreius, for publication in 1543. Copernicus' friend Joachim Rheticus went to Nuremberg to supervise the printing, but he had to leave before completion, and his place was taken by Schöner and Andreas Osiander, the Protestant reformer who had an interest and some competence in astronomy. It is not difficult to see that Copernicus' unsettling conclusions disturbed Osiander deeply. In Nuremberg's conservative religious climate, the new theory must have seemed twice as explosive as it really was. Osiander therefore urged Copernicus to present his new system not as an accurate description of the actual universe, but as a mere hypothesis to explain the phenomena. Copernicus rejected the plea, but Osiander had the last word. He replaced Copernicus' preface to the work with one of his own, unsigned and naturally taken to be by the author. In it he urged readers to entertain the theory of heliocentricity as nothing more than a hypothesis which "need not be true nor even probable." It was Johann Kepler who later exposed Osiander's trick. Osiander was in difficulties over other matters too, as we saw earlier. He was not the obscurantist he has been made out to be. He only meant to avoid trouble. It was not so extraordinary, incidentally, that a theologian and preacher should also be a competent scientist. Osiander's fellow reformer Thomas Venatorius, the preacher at the Hospital Church since 1523, was a fine mathematician and philologian who won his place in the history of science by preparing the first edition of the works of Archimedes in the original Greek, published in Basel in 1544.

Chronicle writing furnishes another example of how a lively popular tradition may keep a subject from losing its appeal even as it enlists the collaboration of erudite scholars. In Nuremberg (as in other cities) it had long been the habit of prominent citizens to record notable events from their private and public lives, making no distinction between the two worlds of personal and public affairs. A sense of history was natural to these family-conscious burghers for whom all things—business practices no less than political and social prerogatives—were questions of tradition. Where so much reference is made to the past, to the "good old customs," there is bound to arise a practical interest in the facts of history. Family chronicles were the earliest expression of this historical interest. Nearly every patrician family kept such a record, lists of births, deaths, trips taken, money spent, property acquired, and similar matters interwoven with news of Council sessions, wars, visits of dignitaries, fires, inflation, epidemics. These chronicles were carried forward through the generations, forming concrete links with the past. When something of historic importance happened in the city, someone usually took it upon himself to set it down. Thus the visit of Emperor Frederick III in 1442 is recorded in a few pages combining description of the festivities with an inventory of expenditures incurred. Wars, too, found their historians, anonymous writers usually, but men who had been eyewitnesses to the battles and had access to the documents.

Out of such fragments evolved the city's chronicles. By arranging the pieces in order and treating private notes as public records, by bridging gaps in the story with reconstructions based on documents or, in their absence, on conjecture, it was possible to compile a more or less coherent account of Nuremberg's history. At the same time attempts were made to push the city's history back into the past and collect the legends describing her origins and early growth. No one discriminated between fact and fancy in connecting these distant times with the present, and in the recital of recent events, too, errors and contradictions abounded. But judicious, not to say critical, weighing of the evidence was never an objective of these amateur historians. They wished only to make their ties to the past tangible and to have the results set out in writing. Many people tried their hands at these compilations, clerics as well as laymen, officials and private citizens. Some wrote in Latin, but most wrote in German. Their language is simple, functional, often picturesque. Their work does not qualify as formal history; it is too sketchy and leaves too many questions unasked. On the other hand it introduces us directly to the streets and houses of the city where the events had taken place.[10]

Needless to say, no learned historian could be satisfied with that, and in the 1480's a qualified historical scholar resolved to put historiography in Nuremberg on a sounder footing. Sigismund Meisterlin was a preacher at the church of St. Sebald, but he was also an avid and, for his day, very able historian. During his previous tenure of a similar post in Augsburg, he had written an excellent chronicle of that city. In Nuremberg there was even more to be done. "Let us throw out all the fables and rumors," he wrote, "for these disfigure history, which seeks only the truth."[11] The truth, he thought, lay somewhere in all those old records and boxes of charters, and only a critical study of them could extract it. To this procedure Meisterlin brought a sound guide: the methods of recent Italian historical scholars, notably Flavio Biondo and Enea Silvio. The books of these masters suggested something of the discipline of sound history, as well as the manner in which the results should be presented. Meisterlin borrowed freely from the Italian workshop. He undertook topographical studies, learned to relate events to their geographical sites and to the larger political arena beyond the gates; he wrote about manners and customs and commented on the development of the city's constitution. Above all, he showed how events moved forward through time, creating a historical momentum and proceeding with a kind of logic of their own. His friends Hermann Schedel and Sebald Schreyer encouraged him in his studies, and he set to work, beginning with a biography of Nuremberg's patron saint and going on to his major work, the *Chronicle of Nuremberg*. He wrote in Latin, translating into German as he went along. He was generally objective, but when it came to events which were, or were taken to be, topical, he was careful to let his narrative reflect the point of view of the men in whose interest he was writing. His is a patrician's interpretation of the rise and fortunes of Nuremberg; in fact it is a sort of official history. A test of this is his account of the rebellion of 1348; nothing Meisterlin says about it conflicts with the version that had for more than thirty years been the official one. Even so, the Council refused to give Meisterlin permission to publish his work, probably because he revealed too much about the operation of the government and its attitudes toward powerful magnates whose descendants might still make a lot of trouble. But manuscripts of Meisterlin's chronicles circulated, and his work became the start of serious historiography in Nuremberg. Celtis' *Norimberga* of 1495 is its immediate successor.

Before that, however, Nuremberg was to produce what was unquestionably the most popular history book of the late Middle Ages in Germany, Hartmann Schedel's *Book of Chronicles*. A huge volume of over six hundred large pages, published in both a Latin and a German version in 1493, the *Chronicle* was a happy result of the joint efforts of scholar, artist, printer, and businessman. Such a combination was not unusual in Nuremberg. The idea for a lavishly illustrated history to appeal to a mass market seems to have first come to Michel Wolgemut, the noted painter and draftsman who was also the proprietor of one of Nuremberg's busiest artistic workshops. Wolgemut spoke of his plan to the printer Anthoni Koberger who was eager to participate in the venture (he had recently done excellent business with illustrated Bibles and saints' lives) but wanted financial backing to meet expenses. Sebald Schreyer and another burgher, Sebastian Kammermeister, agreed to advance the money. A contract bound the partners and arranged for the sharing of profits. When it came to selecting the editor for the text of the book, Hartmann Schedel was the natural choice. Early in 1492 everyone got to work, closely coordinating their respective duties in order to produce a really fine volume.

The *Nuremberg Chronicle,* as it has been called since its first publication, is one of those wonderful books from the first half century of printing that delight the eye as much as the mind. A large folio in size, printed beautifully on heavy paper which is as supple to the touch today as it was nearly five hundred years ago, the *Chronicle* lures the prospective reader by promising him visual pleasure along with his reading. Each page is attractively laid out, as Schedel, Wolgemut, and Koberger intended in their collaboration. The pictures make the most immediate as well as the lasting impression. This too was intended, for the *Chronicle* is above all a picture book, successor to a long line of popular picture sheets and illustrated pamphlets, the woodcuts telling the story in an attractively unfolding visual narrative. It is the story of the world and its successive empires and kingdoms. History begins with Creation. A majestic full-page woodcut of God the Father opens the volume. What follows is retold from Genesis amplified with maps and plans from Ptolemy. The *linea Christi* winds its way through the pages, descending from Adam to Jesus. Chapters from Pliny alternate with the Old Testament and give occasion to show a gallery of weird human types found around the earth. Maps display the world as it was when first created. Kings of Egypt and Assyria crowd the heroes of Greece; the cities of ancient Babylon share pages with Athens, Sparta, and Rome. Diversification in narrative and illustration is assured by telling the story on several levels, as it were: Biblical and pagan, Asian and European, ancient and modern. Allusions to contemporary places and personages are taken up and amplified into a paragraph or two. In short, the *Chronicle* displayed the whole panorama of the human past in text and pictures, bringing it all very close to the reader, for Nineveh looks much like any medieval town, and Juno is comfortably dressed in the linen cap of a German artisan's wife. This did much to remove the strangeness from far-away places and the distant past.

The *Nuremberg Chronicle* has been justly famous for its fine depictions of European cities. More than fifty of these are dispersed through the book; not all of them accurate, in fact several are downright fanciful, and a few are used several times to represent different towns. On the other hand, many of the drawings were evidently made from life, and they are beautifully reproduced, the grandest of them spread full width across the double pages of the book. Among all the cities of the world, it is Nuremberg that stands out as the most splendid, in a superb woodcut done by Michel Wolgemut himself. The comparison of cities for magnificence and strength was surely one of the favorite uses to which the *Chronicle* was put. But it it not merely for aesthetic reasons that city representations play so large a role in this book. The *Chronicle*'s world is the world of cities. Cities are the fixed points in the great stream of history. They orient the reader in time and place. All that has happened is seen through the city dweller's eyes as he contemplates (a bit smugly) the extraordinary events of the past from the security and comfort of his town.

The woodcuts pick out the most dramatic moments of this story: Seneca bleeding to death in his bath, Joseph urged toward an alcoved bed by the Pharaoh's wife, St. Stephen stoned by a pack of malevolent ruffians, a group of leering Jews caught in the act of a grisly ritual murder, the Holy Roman Emperor attended by the Seven Electors, and many, many more; over 1800 illustrations altogether.* Schedel takes the story up to his own time, leaves a few pages blank to encourage the reader to be his own chronicler of the remaining events before the end of the world, then brings the book to a close with a description of the Last Judgment. Though he rambles a bit and tends to confuse the trivial with the essential, Schedel is always informative and, by his own lights, impeccable in his scholarship. He took his material from the best available ancient and modern sources; much of it was copied straight out of the texts, sometimes without changing a word. And why not? It was not up to Schedel to improve on the authorities, and his *Chronicle* was not meant to be an essay in interpretation or an exercise in high style. Its view of life as reflected in text and illustrations is simple and thoroughly conventional, as the kind of public at which authors and publisher aimed no doubt demanded. Neither Schedel nor

* To be precise: 1809 illustrations printed from 645 woodcuts. Most of the repetitions are of stylized portraits.

Wolgemut felt tempted to stand above their readers and address them in the names of philosophy and art. The *Chronicle* was a book of facts, both verbally and pictorially; it was intended to be practical. Koberger provided it with a good index to facilitate spot reading and reference, and it must have served many a sixteenth-century household as its encyclopedia of world history.

Today, of course, only the intellectual historian is interested in its contents, and the *Chronicle* appeals mainly as a handsome example of early bookmaking. Nothing has so far been said about printing and publishing in Nuremberg, but it will be evident that by 1493 Nuremberg had attracted a flourishing printing industry. The early history of printing is everywhere full of uncertainties, and we do not know much about the first practitioners of the new craft in Nuremberg.[12] In 1472 one Heinrich Kefer, identified as a former resident of Mainz, settled in the city and was accepted as a citizen, which suggests that he had something of value to contribute to his adopted city. But even earlier, in the 1460's, there is mention of a Konrad Zeninger of Mainz and a Franz Vestenberger, both printers. No specimens of their work have survived, but it seems that there was a considerable demand for printed books because in the early 1470's we hear of several other printers in the city. By the time Anthoni Koberger appears on the scene in 1473, printing from movable metal type was a securely established profession.

Anthoni was a characteristic Nuremberg combination of craftsman and entrepreneur.[13] He belonged to an old family in the city (a circumstance which helped him greatly in building his firm), and all his forebears, and he himself before he turned to publishing, had been members of established crafts. In these they had, of course, been constrained by the usual conventions and rules. Printing, on the other hand, was too recent an arrival to have been subjected to government regulation. This fact enabled an audacious and resourceful man to strike out on his own. For administrative purposes the early printers were associated with painters and other free artists. No special code had been written for them; in fact, printing being so obviously on its way to becoming a thriving trade, and promising to serve the city in so many useful ways, the Council was inclined to give the new printers a great deal of elbow room. Koberger began in 1473 with a bilingual edition of Boethius' popular *Consolation of Philosophy*, a large and beautifully printed folio with the German translation set against each Latin chapter. By 1500 he had issued more than two hundred titles and his firm was known everywhere as the most enterprising publishing house of the time.

Koberger's secret was the formula that made the *Nuremberg Chronicle* such a success: large folios of popular or widely used works, handsomely printed and often beautifully illustrated. The best example of this type is his great illustrated German Bible of 1483. Scripture was the staple of the early printing industry; an enormous demand for complete Bibles both in Latin and in the vernacular kept most presses steadily at work. German Bibles had been published at Strassburg in 1466 (Johann Mentelin's edition of a fourteenth-century German translation was the first German Bible to appear in print) and in Augsburg throughout the 1470's. Johann Sensenschmid and Andreas Frisner had issued a handome Bible in Nuremberg in 1475 or 1476. Koberger himself had been publishing Latin editions of the Vulgate since 1475, some of them with woodcut illustrations.

But his German Bible was the most splendid of them all. It was issued in two large volumes, set in a beautifully legible type and with gilded initials. Above all, it had pictures, unlike the competitor volumes, over a hundred woodcuts (in most copies they are illuminated in water color) to illustrate dramatic moments in the narrative. One need only glance at a few of the pages to understand what a difference these pictures must have made to Koberger's readers. Scholars might be expected to face page after page of solid black type without distress. But the layman appreciated the refreshment to his eyes offered by the pictures, and he liked the vivid comment on the text. It must also have been comforting to see kings and prophets appearing in such familiar garb and furnishings. All this made the 1483 Bible a most popular work. A few years after this Koberger produced another success: a German translation of the *Golden Legend* with 262 woodcut pictures providing rich pictorial documentation for the suffering of the saints. It, too, came in a big folio and was distinguished by the same clear and inviting type as the Bible. Still later, in 1493, came the Schedel chronicle. These big picture books established a tradition in Nuremberg. When

Albrecht Dürer published his *Apocalypse* in 1498, off his own press but from Koberger's type, he placed text and woodcuts on facing pages, words and pictures complementing one another, but pictures infinitely more suggestive and bound to attract the major share of attention. Dürer could count on a market for his book; Koberger had prepared the ground for him.[14]

Koberger's list included the *Speculum Naturale* of Vincent of Beauvais, Pliny's *Natural History*, collections of sermons of the kind widely used by the clergy of the time, the *Sentences* of Peter Lombard and other popular school works, Latin grammars and vocabularies, Ptolemy's *Geography* in the Latin translation of Pirckheimer, civil and canon law, the Nuremberg legal *Reformation* of 1484, and many more. In other words, a varied but thoroughly conventional list. All of Koberger's books were familiar, established works with either a wide popular appeal or lasting academic demand. He put out large editions of up to two thousand copies, a huge number for the time. In his most active years his shop near the Church of St. Aegidius employed over two hundred journeymen and apprentices. A contemporary counted twenty-four presses going full time. Paper came from local mills—Nuremberg possessed what was probably Germany's oldest paper mill, built in 1390 alongside the river just outside the gate (it can be seen on Wolgemut's woodcut of Nuremberg, in the lower right-hand corner)—partly it was imported from Strassburg and other sources. Koberger used local die cutters to design and cut his punches; local workmen built his presses and made the barrels wherein the books were shipped, unbound, all over Europe. Nurembergers could buy his book from retailers in the city (called *Buchführer*, nowadays the word for "bookkeeper") and from itinerant peddlers. But most of his business was a long distance from home. An efficient sales organization saw to it that his markets were well supplied. He had factors residing in a dozen cities in western and eastern Europe and warehouses near all the major book marts. He put out advertising prospectuses and publicity sheets. When orders exceeded his capacity to handle them, he subcontracted work to other printers. He also invested capital with fellow publishers, notably the Amerbach and Petri of Basel. By the time of Anthoni's death in 1513, the firm had become a speculative enterprise as much as a printing house. His sons could not maintain it, and the firm went rapidly to pieces. Its last book was issued in 1526.

By then printing was so solidly established as one of Nuremberg's important trades that more than a dozen shops found enough work to coexist profitably. They were no longer as free as in Koberger's early days. Alarmed at the ideological dangers inherent in the mass dissemination of the written word, the Council reacted, typically, with precautionary legislation. A mandate in 1513 compelled printers, including wood block cutters, to register with the Council and swear an annual oath "that neither they nor their assistants will print, cut, or issue poems, books, engraved pictures or figures without first notifying the Council and awaiting the Council's decision." Disturbances before and during the Reformation brought even tighter control. But this did not keep new men from entering the profession. Many of the newcomers brought to printing their special skills in the professions for which they had been originally trained. Hieronymus Andreae, for example, called *Formschneider* for his fame as a maker of woodcut blocks, cut the model letters for Johann Neudörffer's famous *Fundamentals of Handwriting* of 1519 and printed among many other books Albrecht Dürer's two treatises on measurement with their many figures. Andreae had great influence as a cutter of metal punches, in fact his work, along with Neudörffer's letter designs, is thought to be mainly responsible for the long hold of Gothic type on German printing. Hans Guldenmund, a graphic artist, printed popular picture booklets and satirical broad sheets. Christoph Zell, once a block cutter, became a noted printer of maps. Collaboration between printers and artists continued, to the advantage of both. When Celtis' works were printed in the first years of the sixteenth century they were carefully produced in fine settings with wide margins, large type, and good woodcut illustrations. His edition of the six dramas of Roswitha was set in a beautiful antiqua with woodcuts by Hans von Kulmbach and other Dürer students and two frontispieces which may have been sketched by Dürer himself. The 1502 edition of Celtis' *Amores* and *Norimberga* had a frontispiece, several illustrations, and four pictorial maps based on Celtis' own drawings to describe the geography of his regional poems. The *Ludus Dianae*, a five-act masque Celtis had written and performed for Emperor Maximilian, was printed in 1501 with the music included. The publisher was Hieronymus Höltzel, one of the first type setters in Nuremberg to print music.

Music printing became in fact a bread-and-butter business for many publishers. They put out missals, chorales, and music books for schools and universities. So much music making was going on in Nuremberg that some printers were able to specialize in scores for voice and instruments, especially in tablature for strings. Hans Gerle (we have met him as a builder and player of lutes) composed practice pieces for viols and lutes; they were cut in wood by Hieronymus Andreae and published by him. Johann Petreius, the printer of Copernicus' *De Revolutionibus*, also printed Hans Neusiedler's well-known *Book for the Lute* containing method, explanation of tablature, and a selection of "fantasias, preludes, psalms, and motets" for the beginning player. In the 1530's music printers were kept busy with Luther's reform of church music. They published settings of the psalms and chorales for congregational singing. At the same time secular music became ever more popular, especially part singing and playing. Johann vom Berg and Ulrich Neuber printed three-, four-, and five-part songs, not only from Germany but from France, Italy, and the Netherlands as well.

Music in sixteenth-century Nuremberg responded to all the needs and tastes of the time. Music was traditionally the responsibility of churches and monasteries, where boys were trained for choral singing, and where organ and instrumental playing were cultivated. Each of Nuremberg's church schools offered scholarships to twelve choristers of good voices; musical activities rested in the charge of *ludimagistri* and *cantores* who taught and also played and sang. Native organ makers built excellent instruments, and each of the churches employed at least one good player. Indeed, St. Sebald boasted one of Germany's most renowned musicians as its organist: Konrad Paumann, a poor local boy, blind from birth, brought up by a patrician family to foster his remarkable talent. As organist at St. Sebald's, Paumann presided over the musical life of the city until his departure for the court at Munich in the 1450's. His epitaph there shows him surrounded by all the instruments he played,[15] but it is his fame as organist and organ pedagogue that makes him a memorable person. His *Fundamenta Organisandi*, a series of graded organ pieces to teach playing from tablature and improvisation, was considered the best organ method of the time.

Music was very much part of everyday life in Nuremberg. Musical sounds filled the air as trumpet and trombone makers tested pitch and tone, and viol builders tuned their fiddles and gambas. The city retained pipers and trumpeters for ceremonial occasions, also a player of portatives and three lutenists and a band of fiddlers to play at weddings and dances. Strolling musicians were always welcome and never departed without their reward. The dances of the gentry in the great hall of the *Rathaus* set the social tone for the city; presence at these great occasions not only distinguished a burgher but, as we have seen, defined his family as patrician. At such affairs music played a necessary and pleasing part, contributing to the pomp as well as the merrymaking of the festivities. Musicians might also be hired, though in limited numbers, to perform at private celebrations, particularly weddings. A number of musical societies existed to encourage performances and amateur music making. Thus the social habits of the well-to-do attracted many performers to Nuremberg, as did the city's fame as a center of instrument building. We hear of well-known players and composers who were second- or third-generation offspring of Nuremberg musicians. Johann and Melchior Neusiedler belonged to such a family, also the Gerle, Konrad and Hans, all of them viol players, lutenists, and composers. Hans Gerle was among the early lutenists who developed the system of notation called tablature, in which lines represented strings, and notes the places where the player stopped them. Helped by printers and instrument builders, these men laid the foundation for what was to become a flourishing school of baroque music in Nuremberg during the following century. At the same time academic music, partly mathematical and partly practical in approach, got its start with Johann Cochlaeus who was rector of the Lorenz school for a few years after 1510. While in Nuremberg, he published his *Tetrachordum Musicae*, a pedagogical compendium of musical theory and practice. It became a standard teaching manual and went through eight or nine editions.

Of course, the musical activity in sixteenth-century Nuremberg

best known to us today is the work of the mastersingers. This
brotherhood of artisans, brought together by a taste for rhyming
and singing, endeavored to practice poetry and music as a craft,
with rules and conventions like every other trade. Richard Wagner's great opera has established the mastersingers of Nuremberg
in the general vocabulary, but the striking portrayal he gives of
them is somewhat overdrawn. Much less attention was paid to
the masters in their own day than Wagner would have us think.
Patricians and the learned regarded them with mild amusement
or disdain. True poets and composers thought their efforts worth-
less, and practicing musicians found their conventions silly. In
any case, nobody knew very much about what they were doing,
for they practiced their art secretively, most likely in defense
against the jeers and malice of their detractors. It was only
when mastersinging fell into neglect in the late sixteenth century
that reliable news began to be divulged.[16]

By calling themselves masters, the singers called attention to
the fact that they had properly learned the method of their craft,
unlike laymen who sang and rhymed by no rules, as they pleased.
These rules had developed in the course of the centuries among
singing brotherhoods in Mainz, Worms, Strassburg, Ulm, Augsburg, Nuremberg and other places in southern and western
Germany. Most brothers came from the artisan class, and nearly
all the trades seem to have been represented, not only masters
but journeymen as well. Each town's brotherhood developed its
own rules, but there was considerable agreement, as all traced the
origin of mastersinging to Twelve Ancient Masters:

> Would you like to know
> Where long ago
> Master song came from?
> What city or town
> Gave it renown
> And what it takes its name from?
> It was here in Germany
> That master singing
> In the year 962 A.D.
> Had its beginning.
> Otto our lord

Held the Emperor's sword
With courage and might,
Leo the Pope
Was Rome's trust and hope
And ruled with foresight.
Then God in His wisdom and grace
Awakened twelve men (but each
In a different place)
Who wrote in high German speech
Such beautiful verse and song
That before long
Their art gained such fame
That all knew its name.

The Twelve Masters came from all walks of life. They included obscure men and the minstrel Walter von der Vogelweide, knights and clerics as well as a smith, a rope maker, a fisherman. They were said to have invented the "tones," or musical modes, each a row (*Reihe*) of notes determining the character of the song. Theoretically no singer was allowed to depart from these "tones," but variations did in fact occur. Many of these variations were attributed to singers who had established mastersinging locally. Nuremberg's own old masters were the twelve singers familiar from Wagner's opera.* One of them, Hans Folz, a barber or bathing master, had a salutary influence on his fellow singers in persuading them to broaden the range of their subjects to include secular topics as well as religious ones.

The prevalence of religious themes in early mastersinging points to the origins of these organizations. The early brotherhoods had practiced mastersong as an expression of their religious sentiments. Subjects were devotional and the modes derived from Gregorian music. But the environment of the towns and the mutual impact of convivial tradesmen on each other was bound to bring the encroachment of more worldly themes. When a new subject was introduced, a new "tone" was often devised as its musical setting. If approved by the masters, this "tone" was con-

---

* Wagner telescopes time by making the ancient Nuremberg masters contemporaries of Sachs, who is given as one of the twelve, which he was not. The original twelfth old master omitted by Wagner was Niclaus Vogel.

sidered established and might be borrowed by others. Some value was thus placed on originality of invention (though the variation among "tones" is not very great), and it became customary to award the title of master only to a singer who had composed a new "tone" and won approbation for it. Thereafter the "tone" was his, called by his name and by the title he gave it. These titles have been a rich source of ridicule of the mastersingers; they were simply descriptive tags, referring to the contents of the poem, but outsiders can hardly be blamed for laughing at the "Black Ink Mode" of Ambrosius Metzger, the "Short Monkey Mode" of Georg Hagens, or at "Writing Paper," "Bleached Ticking," "Pointed Drinking Shoe," "Early Muscat Grape," "Faithful Pelican," and "Fat Badger" modes.[17]

The Nuremberg mastersingers met in the church of St. Catherine's convent, usually on holiday afternoons and sometimes on Sundays. The first part of their sessions was ordinarily given to "free singing," where any member could step forward and perform on any subject he chose. Only one person sang at a time, and all singing was unaccompanied. There followed the "main singing," which differed from "free singing" in several respects. Only experienced masters could sing. Subjects were limited to the Bible. Proceedings were extremely formal; the singer sat in a great chair in the center of the room, and opposite him, behind a curtained partition, sat four "markers," seasoned members of the craft who examined the singer on obedience to the rules and marked his mistakes on a slate. Each marker had his stated duties. One listened for fidelity to the mode, the second referred to the chosen verse in Luther's German Bible to ensure that everything was said correctly, the third wrote down end syllables to check the rhymes, and the fourth kept his eye on the *Tabulatur*, the tablet on which the masters' rules were written. The day's prize went to the singer who had made the fewest mistakes.

Needless to say, such procedures could only result in a stultification of whatever creative sparks might have animated mastersinging in its early days. The *Tabulatur* was a formidable maze of injunctions and prescriptions. A poem (*Bar*, probably from Latin *par*, equal) must consist of separate strophes (*Gesätze*), each of which has a number of *Stollen* set to the same mode. A *Stollen* consists of several verses. A verse must not exceed thirteen syllables in length because it must be sung in one breath. The verse consists of the "tone" row with coloratura added so as to vary the monotony of the melody. Coloratura includes trills, scale runs, and other ornaments. In the use of these the singer was given some freedom to show his imagination and vocal skill, but he must use them in moderation. Masculine and feminine rhymes must alternate in stated order. An *Abgesang* set to a contrasting tune and using a different rhyme pattern must follow a stated number of *Stollen*. A last *Stollen* concludes the *Bar*. If any one of these laws was violated, an error had been committed, and there were dozens of other rules as well (thirty-four in the Nuremberg *Tabulatur*), including bad grammar, faulty diction, and heresy—that is to say, incorrect interpretation of Scripture. Obviously, subservience to the rules was the highest virtue. With so many do's and don'ts to observe, winning the prize must have been like running an obstacle course. A young apprentice singer would naturally seek out a master with an impeccable knowledge of the rules and an imperturbable conventionality of taste. Were he not properly trained to the rules, he would never pass his tests, win acceptance of his masterpiece, and become a master himself. Thus the system perpetuated itself.

Nevertheless, an occasional master with a strong mind and a streak of independence in him might wrench the system a bit. This is what Hans Sachs did in the 1550's and 1560's. As a very young man Sachs had apprenticed himself to a master of great local fame, Lienhard Nunnenbeck, a linen weaver and inventor of several new "tones." But Sachs' own temperament was too lively to keep him satisfied as a mere disciple. A prolific popular verse maker and playwright and a man well read and conversant with many fields. Sachs was too full of the day's news and the world's stories to accommodate himself to the approved subjects. Though hardly a poet in any meaningful sense of the word, he had a good ear, and as an inventor of tunes he was head and shoulders above his colleagues. His skits and rhymes had made him popular in the town; he could afford to speak out.

Sachs did not set out to reform anything; he merely expressed his superior talent. His songs are tuneful and their melodic line unfolds naturally. One feels that some relation between words and music is intended. The melody is meant to be sung expressively.[18] All this distinguishes his songs from those of the other masters, whose tunes plod along monotonously, trailing the words with a deadpan literalness. In a way, this inexpressiveness of conventional mastersong is astonishing. In Nuremberg the master-singers were apparently among the first to turn to the Reforma-tion; the words of their songs show how quickly they responded to Luther's writings and how closely they studied them. But one listens in vain for a musical expression of this experience. If the masters were moved or elated by the great event, their verses and tunes do not show it. Mastersinging itself must have engendered a happy enthusiasm in many of the men. Adam Puschmann, who was to give the first description of the movement later in the six-teenth century, spent a decade of his youth visiting the various centers of mastersong in Germany, then studied six years with Hans Sachs while plying his trade as a tailor. But if he was excited about it all, his poems do not reflect it. The system of rigid rules, while inimical to creative artists, did enable the ungifted, by using the rules as a prop, to turn out mastersongs like pins or bars of soap. Sachs labored as hard at his tune smithing as all the others. But his best songs—the "Silver Mode," for example, set to a sacred text in Latin and German—are attractive pieces of mu-sic.[19] Johann Neudörffer, the calligrapher and writing master who knew Nuremberg's cultural life intimately, thought that Sachs single-handedly resuscitated mastersong from near-extinction. But this is an exaggeration; Sachs was not all that good. He was much too prolific to succeed every time. In 1554, at the age of sixty, he made a catalogue of his master songs and set it in the rhyming pattern of a *Meisterlied:*

> The sum, total and addition
> Of my verse and composition:
> My master songs are numbered
> Thirty-eight hundred
> And forty-eight.
> All these I made
> By the mastersingers' rules and codes,
> Set to two hundred and forty-four modes,
> Of which thirteen are my own
> Invented by me alone.

All this in addition to "histories, dance songs, carnival plays, philosophic poems, one hundred and thirty-three comedies, and five hundred and thirty occasional poems." No wonder that there is much pedestrian chaff in his work. The pity of it is that Sachs had it in him to do better. Had mastersinging been less firmly wedged in Nuremberg's rigid caste system; had he, as an artisan and self-taught man, had entry to the houses of the educated; had he been able to aim his songs at a wider and less stuffy audience —he would no doubt have made his mark on German language and music. There was Luther's example to tempt and guide him. But the fact was that mastersinging in Nuremberg was so closely tied to the social position of its artisan practitioners that it could develop only within their own tight little world. It was too characteristic an aspect of the German urban scene to have survived its age as anything other than a historical curiosity.

Not so painting and the other visual arts. Nuremberg's artists, although urban craftsmen by training and outlook, succeeded in developing a style which lifts their work above its own time and place. Why that should be so is not easy to say with confidence. In part it was certainly due to sheer technical mastery gained through long training and practice, often reflecting the inherited bent of several generations of artisans. It may also be that the favorite forms of art of the time, woodcut and sculpture in wood and cast bronze, were media peculiarly suited to the German artistic temperament. There was, furthermore, the fortunate circumstance that the late fifteenth century saw a growing demand for art works of every kind. We even hear of a number of private collections of paintings and *objets d'art* in the houses of Schedel, Schreyer, and others. But these factors would not by themselves have brought on a great school of artists had it not happened that around the turn of the fifteenth and sixteenth centuries there occurred in Nuremberg one of those lucky conjunctions of individual artists of rich and varied talent which sometimes visits a society. The presence of these men in her midst is Nuremberg's most substantial claim to distinction.

Once again description must begin with the past. Like every medieval town of a certain size, Nuremberg provided steady employment for painters of religious pictures and sculptors in

stone and wood. Throughout the fourteenth century the rebuilding of the principal churches proceeded apace, requiring great
quantities of decoration. Much of this was mass produced and is
of indifferent quality: stiff figures, standard groupings, stereo-
typed faces, and so on. But scholars have been able to trace
schools of sculptors, that is to say masters and disciples continu-
ously at work and sharing certain unified characteristics of manner and technique. One such school is associated with the Church
of St. Sebald, another with St. Lorenz. The tall ornamental fountain built around 1360 for the market place displayed in its stone
effigies of pagan and Biblical figures some of the best work of
these schools. Glass painting also flourished, a highly specialized
craft in which the distinction between artist and artisan was altogether blurred. Carvers of wooden statues supplied much of the
interior decoration of churches and private chapels. Skilled nuns
at St. Catherine's and St. Clara's spent lifetimes weaving great
tapestries to adorn the walls of the main churches on holidays.
The demand for such work never ceased, and the schools continued to function, now and then producing an outstanding individual master rising above the rest and impressing his name on
his work and that of his pupils.

It was the same with painting. From the mid-fourteenth century on painters and miniaturists—anonymous to us, and not very
distinct from each other in their work—illuminated manuscripts
and documents, and painted altar pieces for the city's churches.
They worked in a direct and simple style. The human figure was
treated emblematically without much attempt at individuation.
But there was often an intense drama in the scenes depicted:
harrowing flagellations and descents from the Cross, cruel tortures inflicted on the martyrs. The range of expressions on the
faces of spectators to these scenes runs the gamut from tenderest
pity to bestial hatred.[20] Colors were bright and clear. Such paintings were most often examples of craft rather than of "art," rapidly turned out on demand and largely undifferentiated. But they
do reveal traces of an independent use of line and color and,
occasionally, of a personal vision of things.

Somewhat later than this, from about 1470 on, Nuremberg
began to develop a school of woodcut printing which, more than

any of the other media, grew into an indigenous form of expression. None of the local scriptoria had ever boasted a recognized group of illuminators, and in this absence the xylograph quickly became a favored method of book illustration in Nuremberg. In the beginning woodcuts were crude and heavy handed and fit for little more than devotional pictures for the illiterate. Technically they were very simple: drawings were traced on blocks of soft wood, pear usually; then the wood was cut away so that only ridges were left, to appear as black lines in the impression. On these early woodcut blocks the ridges were thick, and the spaces between them wide. Watercolor was often used to fill them; in fact many of the early block books were really coloring books, inviting the buyer to be his own illuminator. Playing cards were made in this way, also whole books with text and illustrations cut from one block. Most of the printings were votive pictures, much favored at the time, and broadsheets or fugitive pieces with a cartoon and a verse or two, or picture sheets telling a topical story in a series of simple pictures, much like a modern comic strip.[21]

A sixteenth-century observer would have been quick to note what was unsatisfactory about these early efforts. They were lacking in life-likeness, in verisimilitude. They were stiff, crude, "unnatural." It was not that realism itself was absent. In fact, tombstone effigies, for example, from the late fourteenth and early fifteenth centuries, astonish us with an uncanny naturalness of attitude and expression. Painters took a sometimes gruesome delight in painstakingly realistic depiction of physical details. But to a critic of Dürer's time this was not enough. He liked his art to be a mirror of life, the more faithful and exact the better. This was the rule by which praise and rewards were bestowed. Johann Neudörffer, who knew most of the local artists of his day and in 1547 wrote their biographies, like Vasari, knew what he meant by good art. Describing the miraculous skill of the sculptor Hieronymus Gärtner, he wrote:

He was most adept at carving free-hand from small pieces of wood about the size of an index finger such things as a cherry with its stem. But his greatest and most praiseworthy feat was that from the same piece of wood he cut a tiny fly seated atop the cherry, and its wings and little legs were as true to nature as if it were alive.

A familiar anecdote about Dürer told how his little dog, seeing a self-portrait in oil that had just been completed and was drying in the sun, ran to it to lick his master's face, getting instead fresh paint on his nose; and Dürer himself instructed the graphic artist to "execute everything most distinctly and painstakingly, and omit not the tiniest wrinkle and speck of dust, insofar as this is possible." When Christoph Scheurl wished to flatter Lucas Cranach in the most gratifying terms possible, he reminded him of the many instances when his paintings were mistaken for the very objects they depicted:

Once in Austria you painted a bunch of grapes on a table, and with such success that while you were out of the room a magpie flew in by the window and, upon discovering the illusion, tore at the painting with its claws and beak. In Coburg you painted a stag which caused the dogs to bay at it.[22]

This criterion determined the development of all the arts. Specialization of tasks was one of the results. In stained glass making, for example, artist and glass painter separated, the latter soon reduced to the respected but distinctly lower position of executant of the former's designs. Thus Dürer and his student Hans Baldung did the cartoons for the so-called Löffelholz window in the Church of St. Lorenz, but took no hand in the making of the glass itself.[23] In woodcut, too, artist and cutter, formerly one and the same person, split apart. Cutting the blocks to the artist's drawings became a highly skilled craft in which several Nurembergers excelled, most notably Hieronymus Andreae, whom we have met. This separation, in turn, enabled the artist to make great technical demands on the mechanical execution of his designs which became, in the hands of Dürer, enormously intricate and difficult. Dürer's later xylographs were cut by professional *Formschneider* not because Dürer could not have done it himself—he had had excellent all-around training in Michel Wolgemut's workshop and in fact did cut the blocks for his *Apocalypse* of 1498—but because he was a busy man and had expert workmen at his disposal. Dürer's great advances in woodcut technique, the introduction of modeling and the suggestion of light and shade by means of an almost infinite number of very fine lines[24] would hardly have been possible without this specialization. With these changes the woodcut was made to appear "natural" to its admirers. And it was the same trend to naturalness that prompted artists like Dürer to turn to copper engraving as an even more suitable medium for rendering life exactly as it was. This change did not eliminate the woodcut, which was in any case the most economical means of multiplying draftsmanship by publication and which had unique aesthetic properties that continued to fascinate artists, particularly Dürer. But it was possible to do things with the burin on a soft copper plate that could never be done in wood. In the hands of an expert craftsman an engraving could render hair, flesh, textile with breathtaking fidelity. Dürer's engravings show this preoccupation with the details of naturalistic realism. The little hare, the greyhound, the portraits and landscapes and studies of plants are marvels of art copying nature. With Dürer naturalism was a means to an end; his engravings are far more than mere copies of leafy trees and sunlight streaming through a window. But his contemporaries did not quite see that and admired him for his wizardry in conjuring living things onto a piece of paper.

The golden period of art in Nuremberg came during the last ten years or so of the fifteenth century—when Veit Stoss returned from Cracow, Adam Krafft was working on the tabernacle for the Lorenz church, and Peter Vischer made Nuremberg a synonym for superlative bronze sculpture—and the early decades of the sixteenth century when Dürer was the dominating figure in the city's artistic life. Most of the best work was still being done, as long ago, in shops and studios. Michel Wolgemut was the biggest operative; he was to painting and to the woodcut what Koberger was to printing; in fact the two collaborated closely, as we have seen. Wolgemut appeared in Nuremberg in the 1480's, married the widow of an older artist, Hans Pleydenwurff, and took over his studio, turning it into a thriving artistic enterprise. Aided by his stepson and disciple Wilhelm Pleydenwurff and by a large staff of journeymen assistants and apprentices, he engaged in large-scale production of paintings, woodcuts, frescoes, wood carvings, and glass designs. As with all such studio procedures, it is difficult, and for the layman impossible, to identify individual hands. Experts speak of a "Master of the Forchheim Altar" and a

"Master of the Landau Altar" among his staff, but in personality and technique his men were very much alike. Dürer left Wolgemut's studio as a journeyman in 1490, aged eighteen. He struck out on his own after that but continued to work for Wolgemut upon demand.

A similarly large-scale operation was carried on by Peter Vischer whose foundry down by the river was one of the city's interesting sights. There he mixed his copper, zinc, lead, and tin and turned out bronze castings for patrons all over the Empire and as far away as Poland and Hungary. Peter had inherited the shop from his father and was in his turn succeeded by his five sons. They specialized in beautifully modeled tomb plates and caskets bearing life-sized likenesses of the deceased. They executed commissions for the cardinals of Magdeburg and Cracow, the bishops of Bamberg and Würzburg and the counts of Henneberg and Hohenzollern. The Elector Frederick the Wise ordered a monument for his castle church in Wittenberg, and Maximilian I requested figures of King Theodoric and King Arthur for the colossal tomb he was erecting for himself in Innsbruck. He had asked for more than the two, but Vischer had time only for these. Vischer's best effort was reserved for the Church of St. Sebald at home: a splendid ornamental shrine to house the silver casket holding the remains of the city's patron saint. This work was commissioned in 1488 when Peter submitted a design as part of his masterpiece. But casting did not get under way until 1507 and was not completed until 1519. One of Vischer's younger sons, Peter junior, had spent his itinerant years in Italy, and his contribution to the tomb in its slowly emerging final form introduced an interesting note of tension stemming from classicist ideas absorbed abroad. But the general character of the work is traditional. Mythological and Biblical figures abound, and scenes from the life of the saint, and a portrait of the elder Vischer by his son, showing the old master in his leather apron and cap, holding punch and hammer in his strong fists.

Veit Stoss, the sculptor, presided over a busy studio and a large number of pupils and assistants to whom he imparted his superb skill in moulding wooden figures for those sumptuous carved altars which are one of the glories of German medieval

art. He had lived in Cracow for some years to complete the altar
for the church of St. Mary, a stunning work with its profusion of
carved and gilded statues, many of them larger than life size, its
reliefs of the life of the Virgin and of the Passion. In 1496 he returned to Nuremberg, bought a house, organized a workshop,
and settled down to the production of stone and wood sculptures
for local and neighboring churches. His crucifixes were especially
in demand, for Stoss was famous for his ability to reflect in the
Savior's features the shattering anguish of his Passion. But he was
equally adept at portraying sweetness and grace. His "Angelic
Greeting," a rendition of the Virgin saluted by the angels upon
the Annunciation, is one of the delights of the Church of St.
Lorenz, where it hangs suspended from the ceiling in its wooden
medaillon. Stoss designed a huge altar for the Church of the Carmelites where his son Andreas was prior, but it was left unfinished
when Andreas was expelled from the city during the turmoil of
the Reformation. He was invited, like Vischer, to contribute to
Emperor Maximilian's great tomb in Innsbruck. His reputation was truly international, and it continued to grow during the
years of his residence in Nuremberg.

Such widespread renown gave the councillors much pleasure.
It was the touchstone by which they assayed an artist's worth.
When his studio was hard pressed to fill orders from princes and
prelates in far-away capitals, the Council knew that their man
was good. The medallist Matthes Gebel is an example. Gebel
spent fifty years in Nuremberg in the course of the sixteenth century. He was probably the greatest, and certainly the busiest, of a
school of Nuremberg medallists that included several other masters like Hans Krug and Hans Schwarz. Nearly every patrician
family in the city commemorated its leading members with his
coins, but most of his work was done for notables throughout Germany. In recognition of his fame, Gebel was given citizenship and
many other honors. On the other hand Adam Krafft, the able
sculptor of the great stone tabernacle in the Lorenz church, never
quite gained the renown of Stoss and Vischer because his work
was limited to the local scene. Krafft's contract for the tabernacle
shows that he was regarded as little more than an ordinary workman. He had submitted the designs earlier and been selected by

a committee of burghers. The contract bound him to finish the job in three years and to do nothing else while at work on it, also to keep exactly to the original specifications. His reward, however, was munificent: 700 gulden for three years' work. Krafft and his assistants also did funeral monuments—a huge stone relief for the Schreyer family on the outside wall of St. Sebald's, for example—and religious and ornamental plaques for burgher houses, also epitaphs, tomb statues, crucifixes, and decorative reliefs like the "Seven Stations of the Cross." Krafft too portrayed himself and his favorite assistants in life-sized statues at the base of the tabernacle in the Lorenz church.

There is no doubt that Nurembergers took a great deal of pleasure in their artists' achievements. Artists were part of society; they shared its attitudes and agreed with its judgments. They were ordinary people and were regarded as such. To the Council they were first of all citizens like all others, subjected to the same sweeping controls and expected to act like everyone else. If they got into trouble with the law they were held to account with undiminished severity. Hundreds of council decrees show this to be so.[25] An artist's fame made him no exception to justice and discipline. When it was discovered that Veit Stoss had forged another man's signature on an "I.O.U." he was brought to trial and after confessing, branded on both cheeks. Law and social cohesion always came first with the Council.

But that was just the point. Nothing set artists apart from the rest of men, and nothing obscured their work from the appreciation of their fellow citizens. Artists never theorized about the purpose of art. That seemed too obvious to bear thinking about. If any of the humanists had taken an interest in the visual arts they might have written something about the artist's ability to confront man with the essence of reality and to make his experience intense and meaningful by concentrating it in the glance of a pair of eyes, the tilt of a head, or the folds of a garment. No one said such things in Nuremberg. But the responses were there just the same. At its most moving, the art of Stoss and Vischer and Adam Krafft communicates with a kind of wordless eloquence whose power lies in its intellectual simplicity and in an utter lack of self-consciousness. Art appealed to every man's senses. Its frame of reference was the workaday life of the medieval city with its profusion of impressions arising from the urban scene within and impinging from the wider world without.*

Albrecht Dürer's art, too, is contained in this frame, and yet Dürer does not quite fit the mould of the craftsman-artist. Much of Dürer's work was popular in every sense of the word. The woodcut cycles of the life of the Virgin and the Passion, the topical pictures (like the famous rhinoceros)—these suited a wide general demand and reflected common predilections. He had a flourishing business going in everything the contemporary art market required: Christopher pictures, saints, portraits in all the media, coins, wooden statues, and so on. He took up well-worn subjects like the Apocalypse (in a cycle of fifteen woodcuts done in 1498) and even though his genius transmuted and integrated the conventional elements into a clarifying vision, he never left the common ground where he and the public spoke to each other.

But there is more than that to the artist Dürer. In company with most of the truly creative men of our civilization, but quite unlike his contemporaries such as Wolgemut and Stoss, Dürer knew his gifts and was much intent on personal problems of development and expression. One need only study the extraordinary succession of self-portraits to feel this concentration on himself. The earliest of these portraits dates from his thirteenth year and is highly unusual, not only technically (a silver point drawing) but because young apprentices were not then encouraged to scrutinize themselves so indulgently. His most famous self-portrait, a frontal view of his beautiful face framed in luxurious dark brown curls, shocks one with its obvious allusion to the head of Christ; and the analogy is made even more explicit in the last of the self-portraits where he reveals himself six years before his death, in broken health, haggard, holding scourge and flail in his hands. He was a serious man (though not above humor and playfulness, as his letters and many of his drawings reveal). He tended to be reflective, even speculative, about his work.[26] He

---

* Nothing shows this universal appeal more convincingly than the woodcuts, and no one should deprive himself of the pleasure of examining at least a few of the more than forty portfolios of superb reproductions in the original sizes in Max Geisberg's *Der deutsche Einblatt-Holzschnitt in der ersten Hälfte des XVI. Jahrhunderts* (Munich, 1923 ff). The whole panorama of the sixteenth-century scene opens before us as we turn these leaves.

searched for ways of deepening his perception and intensifying the expressiveness of his art. Alone among Nuremberg's artists he stood on close terms with the city's intellectuals. To Pirckheimer he was bound by an intimate friendship, and he was one of the men who gathered round Johann Staupitz during his visits to the city. Such contacts, unavailable to most other artists, broadened Dürer's intellectual range considerably, even though to the end of his life he apologized for being an unlearned man. He had had little formal schooling. As the son and grandson of goldsmiths, he was apprenticed to the trade, but allowed to change to painting when his inclination became evident. At the age of fifteen he began a three-year apprenticeship with Michel Wolgemut who taught him all the branches of the artist's craft. In 1490 he began his migratory years which took him to many cities in Germany and, in the autumn of 1494 to Italy. The year 1495 saw him back in Nuremberg, married, and settled down to work.

All this time he had not been neglecting his studies. He learned Latin well enough to read Vitruvius in the original and he picked up a knowledge of basic geometry. He read widely, and his drawings and paintings reflect the expanding horizon of his mind. In Italy he had been impressed not only with the technical virtuosity of artists there, but also with their knowledge of the structure and processes of nature. His second journey in 1505 convinced him of the artistic superiority of Italians. This he attributed to their intellectual approach. They not only observed and copied, they also studied and analyzed. He resolved to do the same.

Thus Dürer became a theorist of art, the first in his own country, as he had been the first German artist to make the educational journey across the Alps. He bought Euclid's *Elements* and *Optics* and provided himself with a mathematical foundation. He went to Bologna to study what in 1505 he still called "the secret art of perspective." He examined some of Leonardo da Vinci's drawings and made copies. Somewhere he came across Leon Battista Alberti's celebrated treatise *On Painting* which, though not printed until some time later, circulated in Latin and Italian manuscripts wherever schools of Italian painters flourished. Dürer must have been powerfully attracted to Alberti's description of painting as an intellectual art and of the painter as a man above and beyond the other artificers, almost "another god." Dürer's life-long self-preparation for his career follows Alberti's advice to the letter: "The painter . . . should be a good man and learned in the liberal arts. . . . First of all I desire that he know geometry. . . . Artists should associate with poets and orators who have a broad knowledge of many things. . . . Never take the pencil or brush in hand if you have not first constituted with your mind all that you have to do and how you have to do it."[27] This describes Dürer exactly. There is little doubt of what it was that he sought in his investigations. He was looking for a device with which to solve the riddles still obscuring the design of natural things. He wanted to know the relationship of all tangible forms. Measure, proportion, perspective were the keys to the understanding of how things were constructed and arranged. Alberti had devoted the whole first of his three books to the mathematics of painting. Dürer too had come to realize that the artist, whatever his higher purposes, was first of all nature's copyist and could not do without a knowledge of mathematical properties and relationships.

The first fruit of Dürer's new quest was a treatise on geometry with the homely title, in German, *Instruction in Measuring with the Compass and the Ruler,* published in 1525. "Until now," he notes in the dedication of the book to Pirckheimer, "we have in this German land of ours set many a clever young lad to learning the art of painting, but we have taught him by rule of thumb without any foundation or reason. Though many have by means of much practice become skillful painters, they are thoughtless fellows, working on impulse alone." There is only one reason for this lack, says Dürer, ignorance of the art of measuring, which is the true foundation of painting. The Italians have long been aware of this, and that is why their country's art has in the past two hundred years been raised as high as it stood in the days of the ancients. To make a beginning, Dürer presents nearly all of Euclid before turning, in the third book of his treatise, to the application of geometry to architecture and painting. In many ways he had to turn over new ground, even invent German words to describe figures like a hyperbole. Text and drawings argue forcefully that designing a monument or cutting a letter in wood are not matters of practice and experience only but products of the application of strict mathematical principles. His fourth book introduces the geometry of the regular solids and, as a culmination, the technique of perspective with explicit drawings and instructions on how to become proficient in its use.

Three years later, in 1528, there followed Dürer's last work, the *Four Books on Human Proportion*, again dedicated to his friend Pirckheimer. It is a pioneering book, as he says himself in the preface. Not in the sense that he has invented anything new. If the ancient books on the art of painting were extant, he writes, nothing more would have to be said on the subject. But they are lost, and someone must do for modern times what the ancients did for their, "so that the art of painting may in due time be returned to its state of perfection." He addresses himself to German artists in particular. They are skillful enough in their use of color, he says, but they know nothing at all about the art of perspective, and "without right proportion no painting can be perfect." His book is a manual for the training of aspiring artists in this fundamental discipline. Everything is given its correct measure: each part of the body of a "long thin man," a "heavy stout peasant woman," a child, figures standing straight or bent at the waist, weight on both feet or shifted to one. All bodily relationships are made mathematically precise: eyes to the oval of the face, length of fingers to size of hand, knee cap to breasts, buttocks to skull, and so on. Of course, Dürer realized the dangers inherent in so schematic a device. Once you have got used to the idea of measure, he says, and have learned the correct method, you may draw and paint at will without first working out all the proportions. Lacking this knowledge, however, you cannot produce anything worthwhile. You may be an uninspired painter, but "as long as a thing has its right measure, no one will condemn it, no matter how badly it is done otherwise." Therefore the rules and models.

Needless to say, Dürer himself was above this sort of thing. He did not impose his prescription on himself when it came to the actual execution of his works. Despite his own words to the contrary, his instinct prevented him from using his theories as props on which to mount his art. For lesser men, Dürer's method was a blessing, and his books quickly became standard reading; imitations appeared within fifteen years of his death. But Dürer himself did not need the rational approach to painting he recommended to others. Great artist that he was, he kept his drawing free not only from mathematical construction but from every appearance of intellectualizing. Only in the famous *"Melencholia,"* an emblem of philosophic preoccupations popular with the learned of the time, did the cerebral predominate. In all else Dürer spoke with the forthrightness of the popular artist.

The woodcut suited this role exactly. Dürer knew this and devoted himself above all to its perfection. Much more so than his engravings, which are soft, polished, and, in a manner of speaking, Italianate, Dürer's woodcuts reflect and address the rough-grained, four-square character of the German public. Again he seems to have taken the words of Alberti to heart: "The work of the painter attempts to be pleasing to the multitude; therefore do not disdain the judgment and views of the multitude when it is possible to satisfy their opinions." Dürer's effort in behalf of the public met with success. His output was enormous: more than a thousand drawings, woodcuts, and engravings and nearly a hundred paintings.[28] Commissions for larger works came from all over Germany, from the mighty such as Emperor Maximilian (drawings for a prayer book, the designs for the colossal "Triumphal arch") and the elector of Saxony (a portrait and several paintings and altar pieces) and from merchants and burghers. In Nuremberg, the councillors consulted him on the modeling of coins and the construction of new buildings, and they asked him to do the frescoes for the ceremonial hall in the rebuilt *Rathaus*. In 1526 the Council accepted his paintings of the four Apostles in exchange for a gift of one hundred gulden; later on it purchased his "Adam and Eve" and two of his self-portraits. He operated a studio with pupils and assistants who helped him with his many commissions. Like all disciples, they tried to adopt the master's style and manner. A few favorites seem also to have been tutored in his theories on measurement.

No student, however, could approach the exalted visions of Dürer's last years when flawless technique was paired with a deep religious understanding to produce pictures of extraordinary beauty and power. Two great engravings in 1513, "Saint Jerome" and "Knight, Death, and Devil," open a sequence of masterpieces that became more intense with the Reformation to which Dürer turned with fervent commitment. He continued productive until the end, which came in 1528. By then he had reached the synthesis for which he had been striving most of his life. He had risen above the everyday demands of the workshop artist and achieved a style which satisfied at once the taste of the large and varied public he served and the needs of his own rich and refined artistic nature.

Dürer's impact did not entirely vanish with his death. He left a number of able students who continued his work in all the media he had employed. Several of them became renowned masters in their own right, notably Hans Baldung who had studied with Dürer for a few years and directed his studio while Dürer was in Italy. In 1509 he left to pursue his career as a highly individualistic painter and engraver. Most of the other disciples also moved away. Hans Schäufelin, his most productive pupil, went to Augsburg and Nördlingen. Sebald and Barthel Behaim were expelled as religious troublemakers in 1525 and never returned. Hans von Kulmbach, a hard working and gifted painter, resided in Nuremberg but predeceased Dürer. Only Hans Springinklee and Georg Penz remained in the city after Dürer's death. The former copied Dürer's manner so faithfully that some referred to him as "Little Dürer." Georg Penz had been expelled with the Behaim brothers, but he succeeded in rehabilitating himself and was allowed to return. He completed Dürer's wall designs for the town hall and settled down in Nuremberg for the rest of his life, a very busy painter, much honored and rewarded by the Council.[29]

But the golden age of the arts in Nuremberg had passed its apogee. From about the 1550's on, painting, sculpture, architecture, and the graphic arts receded to a state of ordinariness from which no outstanding master arose to renew them. Never again was Nuremberg to see such a constellation of talent as in the decades just before and after 1500. No doubt this condition was, in part at least, an aspect of Nuremberg's general regression as a city state in the later sixteenth and seventeenth centuries. Burghers ceased to support the arts,[30] not for lack of money but because their city's position was no longer commanding enough to compel continuing expression in architecture and the decorative arts. Not a major city now, lacking a prince or a prelate to impress his idea of majesty on her streets and buildings, Nuremberg passed through the succeeding centuries largely unaffected by changing styles and tastes.[31] Not far away the margraves of Ansbach and Bayreuth and the bishops of Bamberg and Würzburg raised splendid churches and palaces and filled them with marble, lacquer, gilt, and porcelain. Nuremberg remained what she had been.[32]

But this stagnation was not without its delayed blessing. All over Germany medieval towns fell to pieces as baroque mansions replaced timbered dwellings, and ancient structures hid behind neoclassic façades. Nuremberg escaped this depredation. For nearly four hundred years from the onset of her economic and political decline the medieval city stood intact, a living monument. It was left to the bombs of the second world war to accomplish in a stroke what the erosion of time and the shifting winds of fashion had been unable to do in centuries; they reduced the old town to rubble.

Reference Notes

The following abbreviations are used: MVGN, *Mitteilungen des Vereins für Geschichte der Stadt Nürnberg;* and BLVSt, *Bibliothek des litterarischen Vereins in Stuttgart.*

CHAPTER I

1. On the Holy Roman Empire in the late Middle Ages see Hajo Holborn, A *History of Modern Germany,* Volume I (New York, 1959). G. Benecke, *Society and Politics in Germany* (London, 1974). Also the two chapters in the *New Cambridge Modern History* I (1957), "The Empire under Maximilian I" and II (1958), "The Empire of Charles V in Europe." The best constitutional history of the Empire is Fritz Hartung, *Deutsche Verfassungsgeschichte vom 15. Jahrhundert bis zur Gegenwart* (7th edition, Stuttgart, 1959). On imperial reform attempts in the fifteenth century, see F. Hartung, "Imperial Reform 1485-1495," and K. S. Bader, "Approaches to Imperial Reform at the End of the Fifteenth Century," in Gerald Strauss, ed., *Pre-Reformation Germany* (London, 1972). On the creation of territorial bureaucracies, see H. S. Brather, "Administrative Reform in Electoral Saxony at the End of the Fifteenth Century," in *ibid.* On the humanist attempt to "illustrate" Germany, see Gerald Strauss, *Sixteenth-Century Germany, Its Topography and Topographers* (Madison, Wisconsin, 1959).

2. On German cities in the Middle Ages and early modern times, see Hans Planitz, *Die deutsche Stadt im Mittelalter* (Graz-Cologne, 1954). There is a vast and controversy-laden literature on the development of towns and urban institutions in Germany, much of it discussed in Planitz's book. A very useful introduction to the comparative history of German cities is the *Deutsches Städtebuch* (volume I, 1939, II, 1941, III-V, 1952 ff.), which takes up the political, social, cultural, economic, religious development of more than 2000 towns and cities in as many articles. See also Edith Ennen, *Die europäische Stadt des Mittelalters* (2nd ed., Göttingen, 1975); and on European cities generally, see J. H. Mundy and Peter Riesenberg, *The Medieval Town* (Princeton, N.J., 1958); Henri Pirenne, *Early Democracies in the Low Countries: Urban*

Society and Political Conflict in the Middle Ages and the Renaissance
(translated by J. V. Saunders, New York, 1963); Max Weber, *The City*,
a translation of part of his *Wirtschaft und Gesellschaft* by D. Martindale
and G. Neuwirth (New York, 1962): Edith Ennen, *Frühgeschichte der
europäischen Stadt* (Bonn, 1953); Fritz Rörig, *Die Europäische Stadt
im Mittelalter* (Göttingen, 1955.) English translation: *The European
Town* (Berkley, 1971). Also Chapter 1, "The Rise of Towns," in *The
Cambridge Economic History of Europe*, III (1963). Interesting comparative articles on cities, including German cities, may be found in the
Recueils de la société Jean Bodin, volumes VI-VII, *La ville* (Brussels,
1954-55). On Nuremberg itself, see the comprehensive collaborative
history edited by Gerhard Pfeiffer, *Nürnberg: Geschichte einer europäischen Stadt* (Munich, 1971), chapters 20-50, with bibliographies.

3. Published by G. W. K. Lochner, *Der Spruch von Nürnberg* (Nurem-
berg, 1854). Other encomia: Hans Sachs, *Ein Lobspruch der statt
Nürnberg* (1530), published among his works in the *Bibliothek des
litterarischen Vereins in Stuttgart*, Volume 105 (1870), 189-99. Helius
Eobanus Hesse, *Urbs Noriberga illustrata* (1532), published by Joseph
Neff (Berlin, 1896).

4. Published by Albert Werminghoff, *Konrad Celtis und sein Buch über
Nürnberg* (Freiburg, 1921).

5. There are several contemporary plans of the sixteenth-century city
which allow the modern student to orient himself. They are listed, and
one of them taken up in detail, in Karl Schaefer, "Des Hieronymus
Braun Prospekt der Stadt Nürnberg vom Jahre 1608 und seine Vor-
läufer," *MVGN*, XII (1896), 3-84.

6. Much surprising information about the pleasant aspects of city life can
be gained from the book (*Baumeisterbuch*) kept by one of these
architects, Endres Tucher, published in *BLVSt*, Volume LXIV (1862).

7. Nuremberg's remaining burgher houses are meticulously described in
Wilhelm Schwemmer, *Die Bügerhäuser der nürnberger Alstadt aus
reichsstädtischer Zeit* (Nuremberg, 1961).

8. On the population of Nuremberg, see Caspar Ott, *Bevölkerungsstatistik
in der Stadt und Landschaft Nürenberg in der ersten Hälfte des 15.
Jahrhunderts* (Berlin, 1907). On German cities generally: Erich Keyser,
Bevölkerungsgeschichte Deutschlands (2nd edition, Leipzig, 1941). On
the problems and conclusions of comparative European population
studies, see the fascinating volumes by Roger Mols, *Introduction à la
démographie historique des villes d'Europe du 14e au 18e siècle* (Louvain, 1954-56).

9. On the origins of Nuremberg and the controversies among scholars
about this, see Ernst Mummenhoff, *Nürnbergs Ursprung und Alter in
den Darstellungen der Geschichtschreiber und im Licht der Geschichte*
(Nuremberg, 1908). Much of the documentary material on which my
narrative is based appears in the five volumes of *Die Chroniken der
deutschen Städte vom 14. bis ins 16. Jahrhundert: Die Chroniken der
fränkischen Städte: Nürnberg* (Leipzig, 1862-74). Also in Lazarus Karl

von Wölkern, *Historia norimbergensis diplomatica* (Nuremberg, 1738). The *Nürnberger Urkundenbuch*, still incomplete, will contain the full documentary record. The best general history of Nuremberg in its early periods is Emil Reicke, *Geschichte der Reichsstadt Nürnberg* (Nuremberg, 1896).

10. Henri Pirenne, *Medieval Cities* (translated by F. D. Halsey, Princeton, 1925).

11. There is no comprehensive work on the municipal rebellions of the mid-fourteenth century in Germany. For an excellent discussion of political aftermaths of the uprisings, and an analysis of persevering patrician control over municipal politics, see Erich Maschke, "Verfassung und soziale Kräfte in der deutschen Stadt des späten Mittelalters, vornehmlich in Oberdeutschland," *Vierteljahrschrift für Sozial- und Wirtschaftsgeschichte,* Volume 46 (1959), 289-349; 433-76.

12. On the acquisition of Nuremberg's Territory, see Heinz Dannenbauer, *Die Entstehung des Territoriums der Reichsstadt Nürnberg* (Stuttgart, 1928).

13. See the discussion of Nuremberg's foreign politics in Eugen Franz, *Nürnberg, Kaiser, und Reich: Studien zur reichsstädtischen Aussenpolitik* (Munich, 1930), Part I.

14. A long and representative list of incidents is given in Johann Ferdinand Roth's *Geschichte des nürnbergischen Handels,* Volume I (Leipzig, 1800), 59-83; 138-250; 396-418.

15. Götz describes his feud with Nuremberg—and most of the rest of the world—in his autobiography, edited by H. S. M. Stuart, *The Autobiography of Götz von Berlichingen* (London, 1956).

16. In his *Lobspruch der statt Nürnberg* of 1530. See note 3, above.

CHAPTER II

1. The German text of Scheurl's epistle is published in *Die Chroniken der fränkischen Städte:* Nürnberg, Volume V (Leipzig, 1874), 785-804. The Latin text may be found in Johann Christoph Wagenseil, *De . . . civitate Noribergensi commentario . . .* (Altdorf, 1697), 190-201.

2. For a thorough discussion of the citizen oath, and a review of the abundant literature on it, see Wilhelm Ebel, *Der Bürgereid als Geltungsgrund und Gestaltungsprinzip des deutschen mittelalterlichen Stadtrechts* (Weimar, 1958).

3. For a comparison of Nuremberg's politics with constitutional developments in Italian cities and the theories put upon them, the following summary article will be useful: P. J. Jones, "Commune and Despots: The City State in Late Medieval Italy," *Transactions of the Royal Historical Society,* Fifth Series, Volume 15 (1965), 71-96.

4. Taxation in the territories, as distinct from cities, was, of course, thoroughly bureaucratic. The Bavarian Tax Instruction of 1554, for example,

included a questionnaire to be answered in writing by every tax payer concerning himself, his income, and his property.

5. See Adalbert Erler, *Bürgerrecht und Steuerpflicht im mittelalterlichen Städtewesen* (Frankfurt am Main, 1939).

6. See Julie Meyer, "Die Entstehung des Patriziats in Nürnberg," *MVGN*, Volume XXVII (1928), 31.

7. The role of merchants and merchants' associations in the formation of urban political institutions in Europe has been discussed by Karl Frölich, "Kaufmannsgilden und Stadtverfassung im Mittelalter," *Festschrift Alfred Schultze* (Weimar, 1934), 85-128.

8. On the emergence of the urban patriciate in Germany, see Hans Planitz, *Die deutsche Stadt im Mittelalter* (Graz and Cologne, 1954), 256-75. For Nuremberg patricians, Julie Meyer, *op. cit.*

9. For some recent Marxist interpretations, see Leo Stern and Erhard Voigt, *Deutschland in der Feudalepoche von der Mitte des 13. bis zum ausgehenden 15. Jahrhundert* (Berlin, 1964), chapters 1 and 6. Karl Czok, "Zur Volksbewegung in den deutschen Städten des 14. Jahrhunderts" in *Städtische Volksbewegungen im 14. Jahrhundert* (Tagung der Sektion Mediävistik der deutschen Historiker-Gesellschaft vom 21.-23.I. 1960 in Wernigerode, Berlin, 1961), 157-69. Hans Motlek, *Wirtschaftsgeschichte Deutschlands: Ein Grundriss* I (Berlin, 1957), 170-96.

10. The classical statement is by Otto von Gierke, *Das deutsche Genossenschaftsrecht* (Darmstadt, 1954), I, 249-78; 300-332. See also Walter Ullmann, *Principles of Government and Politics in the Middle Ages* (London, 1961), 215 ff.

11. Ernst Mummenhoff gives these dates, and many more relating to other families, in *Altnürnberg* (Bamberg, 1890), 19-20.

12. See the table of Council membership of patrician families for the years 1421 to 1440 given by Paul Sander, *Die reichsstädtische Haushaltung Nürnbergs* (Leipzig, 1902), 52-3.

13. There is a roster of nonpatrician merchants in Johann Ferdinand Roth, *Geschichte des nürnbergischen Handels* (Leipzig, 1800-1802) I, 307-96.

14. The Kress *Familienchronik* is in the Germanisches Nationalmuseum in Nuremberg. Christoph's portrait is reproduced in Eberhard Lutze, *Einst im alten Nürnberg* (Stuttgart, 1939), '53.

15. The most comprehensive description of the inner workings of Nuremberg's government is to be found in Paul Sander, *op. cit.*

16. Ernst Pitz *Schrift- und Aktenwesen der städtischen Verwaltung im Spätmittelalter: Köhn-Nürnberg-Lübeck . . .* (Cologne, 1959).

17. The *Amptbuchlin* for 1516 is printed in *Die Chroniken der fränkischen Städte: Nürnberg*, Volume V (Leipzig, 1874), 805-20.

18. Adalbert Erler, *op. cit.*, gives many examples of the application of this principle in practice.

19. Doubt has been cast upon the accuracy of the evidence as it has come down to us. Muffel appears to have been involved in private quarrels with fellow councillors, who may have framed him. All the evidence

is printed in *Die Chroniken der fränkischen Städte: Nürnberg,* Volume V (Leipzig, 1874), 753-77.

20. For details see L. Schönberg, *Die Technik des Finanzhaushalts der deutschen Städte im Mittelalter* (*Münchener volkswirtschaftliche Studien,* Volume 103, Stuttgart and Berlin, 1910).

21. For details of what follows, see Ernst Scholler, *Das Münzwesen der Reichsstadt Nürnberg im 16. Jahrhundert* (Nuremberg, 1912) and by the same author, *Der Reichsstadt Nürnberg Geld- und Münzwesen in älterer und neuerer Zeit* (Nuremberg, 1916).

22. See the full roster of municipal officials in the *Amptbuchlin* (Book of Offices) of 1516. Cf. note 17 above.

23. Carl L. Sachs, "Metzgergewerbe und Fleischversorgung der Reichsstadt Nürnberg," *MVGN,* Volume XXIV (1922), 1-260.

24. Henri Pirenne, *Early Democracies in the Low Countries: Urban Society and Political Conflict in the Middle Ages and the Renaissance* (New York, 1963), 86.

25. For a representative collection of portrait medals, including several by Hans Schwarz, of Nuremberg patricians, see Georg Habich, "Studien zur deutschen Renaissancemedaille," *Jahrbuch der Königlich-preussischen Kunstsammlung,* Volume 27, 1. Heft (Berlin, 1906), especially plates facing pages 45, 57, 60, 64.

26. Much sumptuary legislation has been collected by Joseph Baader, *Nürnberger Polizeiordnungen aus dem XIII. bis XV. Jahrhundert* [*BLXSt,* Volume 63 (1861)]. For a discussion of these and one of the few English-language books on Nuremberg, see Kent Roberts Greenfield, *Sumptuary Law in Nürnberg: A Study in Paternal Government* (Johns Hopkins University Studies in Historical and Political Science, Series XXXVI, No. 2, Baltimore, 1918).

CHAPTER III

1. Fritz Kern, *Kingship and Law in the Middle Ages* (Oxford, 1939). Part II.

2. See Guido Kish, *The Jews in Medieval Germany: A Study of their Legal and Social Status* (Chicago, 1949).

3. For Nuremberg statutes relating to the Jews see Joseph Baader, *Nürnberger Polizeiordnungen* . . . (*BLVSt,* 63 (1861), 321-6. For a discussion of the complex relations between Jews and their gentile hosts from the vantage point of Jewish law and custom see Jacob Katz, *Exclusiveness and Tolerance: Studies in Jewish-Gentile Relations in Medieval and Modern Times* (Oxford, 1961).

4. Jews were being expelled elsewhere in Germany and Europe too. See the chronological table of anti-Jewish actions in major cities from the 12th to the 16th centuries in *Encyclopaedia Judaica* II, 986-7.

5. I follow the argument presented by Friedrich Lütge, *Deutsche Sozial- und Wirtschaftsgeschichte. Ein Überblick* (2nd ed., Berlin-Göttingen-

Heidelberg, 1960), 177-85, and in greater detail in his article "Das 14./15. Jahrhundert in der Sozial- und Wirtschaftsgeschichte," *Jahrbücher für Nationalökonomie und Statistik*, 162 (1950), 161-213. See also the detailed investigation by Ernst Kelter, "Das deutsche Wirtschaftsleben des 14. und 15. Jahrhunderts im Schatten der Pestepidemien," *Ibid.*, 165 (1953), 161-208. Cf. also Heinrich Bechtel, *Wirtschaftsgeschichte Deutschlands* (2nd ed., Munich, 1951-52), and Jacques Heers, *L'occident aux XIVe et XVe siècles: aspects économiques et sociaux* (Collection "Nouvelle Clio," No. 23, Paris, 1963), Chapter II. An excellent agricultural history is B. H. Slicher van Bath, *The Agrarian History of Western Europe* (transl. by Olive Ordish, London, 1963).

6. Karl Pagel, *Die Hanse* (Braunschweig, 1952), 385 ff. See also *Cambridge Economic History of Europe* II (1952), 223 ff. on the Hanse, and chapters 4 and 5 generally for the development of European trade patterns in the late Middle Ages.

7. See Hutten's dialogue *Praedones* (*Dialogi Huttenici novi*, 1521) and Luther, *Address to the Christian Nobility of the German Nation* (many translations).

8. "Eine Predigt, dass man Kinder zur Schule halten solle," (1530) *Weimar Ausgabe* XXX², 517 ff. Luther tries to deflate the argument that high prices make it impossible for good men to accept low-paying scholars', or ministerial positions.

9. For a brief analysis of the inflation in the first half of the 16th century, see B. H. Slicher van Bath, *op, cit.*, 107-9.

10. A wealth of figures to illustrate the price rise in the early years of the 16th century is given by M. J. Elsas, *Umriss einer Geschichte der Preise und Löhne in Deutschland* (Leiden, 1936-40), where prices are given for a vast number of commodities in selected German cities. See also Bechtel, *op. cit.*, II, 85-97.

11. For a contemporary list of cities with which Nuremberg enjoyed reciprocal commercial privileges, see Ulman Stromer's *Püchel von meim Geslechet* printed in *Chroniken der fränkischen Städte: Nürnberg* I (1862), 99-100. On Nuremberg's economy generally see Wolfgang von Stromer, "Nuremberg in the international Economics of the Middle Ages," *The Business History Review*, vol. 44 (1970), 210-225, and the contributions by various specialists in *Beiträge zur Wirtschaftsgeschichte Nürnbergs* 2 volumes (Nuremberg, 1967).

12. On Nuremberg's trade routes, see Johannes Müller, "Der Umfang und die Hauptrouten des Nürnberger Handelsgebietes im Mittelalter," *Vierteljahrschrift für Sozial- und Wirtschaftsgeschichte* VI (1908), 1-38.

13. See Richard Ehrenberg, *Capital and Finance in the Age of the Renaissance: A Study of the Fuggers and their Connections* (London, 1928). This is a truncated translation of Ehrenberg's *Das Zeitalter der Fugger: Geldkapital und Kreditverkehr im 16. Jahrhundert* (Jena, 1896). See Book I, Chapter 2 of the English version for a discussion of some Nuremberg firms; Book I, Chapter 5 of the German original for a general

discussion of corporations. The best recent study of the Fuggers is Götz von Pölnitz, *Die Fugger* (2nd ed., Frankfurt, 1960).

14. For a general survey of the international economic agreements of German cities, see Jean Schneider, "Les villes allemandes au moyen age: Les institutions économiques," *Recueils de la société Jean Bodin*, VII: *La ville, institutions économiques et sociales* (Brussels, 1955), 403-82.

15. For a lively, but extremely unfavorable, picture of toll and traffic conditions in Germany at this time see Eli F. Heckscher, *Mercantilism* (transl. Mendel Shapiro, revised 2nd ed., London and New York, 1955), I, 56-78.

16. Published originally in Frankfurt in 1568. There is a facsimile edition, *Jost Ammans Stände und Handwerker* (Munich, 1884). Much more revealing than Amman's woodcuts are the copper engravings in Christof Weigel, *Abbildung der gemein nützlichen Hauptstände von denen Regenten . . . bis auf alle Künstler und Handwerker* (Regensburg, 1698). Weigel, who drew from life, portrays each artisan in a characteristic stance and shows in close-up the essential tools of his trade.

17. The Vasari of Nuremberg artists and artisans was Johann Neudörfer. See *Des Johann Neudörfer, Schreib- und Rechenmeisters zu Nürnberg, Nachrichten von Künstlern und Werkleuten daselbst aus dem Jahre 1547* (ed. G. W. K. Lochner, Vienna, 1875). More detailed biographies are contained in Johann Gabriel Doppelmayr, *Historische Nachricht von den nürnbergischen Mathematicis und Künstlern . . .* (Nuremberg, 1730).

18. Many of these are described and illustrated in the fascinating book by Ernst von Bassermann-Jordan, *The Book of Old Clocks and Watches* (4th ed., New York, 1964).

19. Endres Tucher's *Baumeisterbuch*, printed in *BLVSt*, 64 (1862). For an earlier example of an architect's record, see Ernst Mummenhoff, ed., "Lutz Steinlingers Baumeisterbuch vom Jahre 1452," *MVGN* II (1880), 15-77.

20. For a rather tentative discussion of municipal economic policies see Chapter 4, "The Economic Policies of Towns," in *Cambridge Economic History of Europe* III (1963).

21. Nuremberg's political decline in the 17th and 18th centuries has been examined by Eugen Franz, *Nürnberg, Kaiser, und Reich: Studien zur reichsstädtischen Aussenpolitik* (Munich, 1930), Book II.

22. See Richard Ehrenberg, *Das Zeitalter der Fugger . . .* II 147-221. The story of these financial crises has been omitted from the English version of the book.

23. See the memorandum addressed by Nuremberg merchants to their Council, dated 1571, printed in Johannes Müller, "Die Finanzpolitik des Nürnberger Rates in der zweiten Hälfte des 16. Jahrhunderts," *Vierteljahrschrift für Sozial- und Wirtschaftsgeschichte* VII (1909), 1-63.

24. There is an article on this interesting man: Gustav Aubin, "Bartolomäus

Viatis: Ein nürnberger Grosskaufmann . . . ," *Vierteljahrschrift für Sozial- und Wirtschaftsgeschichte,* 33 (1940), 145-57.
25. See Fritz Schnelbögl, "Paul Pfinzing als Kaufmann," *MVGN* 45 (1954), 372-86.
26. See Johannes Müller, *op. cit.* (note 23 above).

CHAPTER IV

1. See Heinz Dannenbauer, *Die Entstehung des Territoriums der Reichsstadt Nürnberg* (Stuttgart, 1928), 160. On the percentage of clerics in German cities generally see Philippe Dollinger, "Les villes allemandes au moyen age: Les groupements sociaux," *Recueils de la société Jean Bodin, VII: La ville, II: Institutions économiques et sociales* (Brussels, 1955), 371-401, especially 377.
2. Some of these, and other, complaints are given in Hans von Schubert, *Lazarus Spengler und die Reformation in Nürnberg* (Leipzig, 1934), 174-89.
3. Scheurl's collection of letters has been published: Franz von Soden and J. K. F. Knaake, eds., *Christoph Scheurls Briefbuch: Ein Beitrag zur Geschichte der Reformation und ihrer Zeit* (Potsdam, 1867).
4. Luther's reply: *WA, Briefwechsel* I, 85-7.
5. These, and other sermons and treatises by Linck, are printed in Wilhelm Reindell, ed., *Wenzel Lincks Werke* (Marburg, 1894). The reference is to page 112.
6. On the Reformation in Nuremberg generally, see Gottfried Seebass, "The Reformation in Nuremberg," in *The Social History of the Reformation,* ed. L. P. Buck and J. W. Zophy (Columbus, Ohio, 1972), 17-40; Gerhard Pfeiffer, ed., *Nürnberg: Geschichte einer europäischen Stadt* (Munich, 1971), chapters 25-27; Hans von Schubert, *op. cit.;* Adolf Engelhardt, "Die Reformation in Nürnberg," *MVGN,* 33-34 (1936-37), 36 (1939), a detailed but strongly pro-Lutheran account; Georg Ludewig, *Die Politik Nürnbergs im Zeitalter der Reformation* (Göttingen, 1893).
7. On the imperial cities and the Reformation, see the excellent study by Bernd Moeller, *Reichsstadt und Reformation (Schriften des Vereins für Reformationsgeschichte* No. 180 Gütersloh, 1962) English translation: *Imperial Cities and the Reformation: Three Essays* (Philadelphia, 1972).
8. Printed in *BLVSt,* 90 (1872), 368-86.
9. On this see Schubert's excellent biography, cited above, Note 2.
10. *Disputation zwischen einem Chorherren und Schuchmacher* (1524), a clever and sometimes very funny satire in which the common man evens the score with his former mentor by pulling out a Bible passage to squelch every stuffy clerical argument.
11. A fragment of a second satire on Eck, *De Eckio bibulo* was found among Pirckheimer's papers. On the question of authorship, see Hans

Rupprich, "Willibald Pirckheimer: Beitrage zu einer Wesenserfassung," *Schweizer Beiträge zur allgemeinen Geschichte*, 15 (1957), 92. On Pirckheimer see also Lewis Spitz, *The Religious Renaissance of the German Humanists* (Cambridge, Mass., 1963), chapter 8.

12. From the Council's reply to the threat of the Papal nunzio, Chieregati, in 1522, *Deutsche Reichstagsakten unter Karl V*, III (Gotha, 1901), 414. The sentiment was reiterated in a number of other communications.

13. The Council had this record published: *Handlung eines ersamen weysen Rats zu Nürnberg mit iren Prädikanten 1525*.

14. Edited by Josef Pfanner, *Die Denkwürdigkeiten der Caritas Pirckheimer* (Landshut, 1961). The memoirs include letters to and from the Council, preachers, and private citizens, as well as a running account of events.

15. On this point see the monograph by Bernd Moeller, cited in note 7, above.

16. On this, and the following points, see the article by Hans Baron, "Religion and Politics in the German Imperial Cities During the Reformation," *English Historical Review*, 52 (1937), 405-27; 614-33. Baron analyzes the politics of the imperial cities, especially Nuremberg, vis-à-vis the emperor and the princely territories, and examines the reasons for the divergent policies pursued by Nuremberg and Strassburg in the years after 1529. The story is told in greater detail by Eugen Franz, *op. cit.*, Chapters III and IV.

17. The list of cannons, hand arms, carts and gun carriages, crossbows, body armor, etc., etc. is still in existence. See von Dotzauer, "Das Zeughaus der Reichsstadt Nürnberg," *MVGN*, 16 (1904), 151-78. There was also an inventory of materiel distributed about the city. It is printed in *ibid.*, II (1880), 173-86.

18. The story of the war is told by Ernst Mummenhoff, *Altnürnberg in Krieg und Kriegsnot: I, Der zweite markgräfliche Krieg* (Nuremberg, 1916).

CHAPTER V

1. Giovanni Botero, *Delle cause della grandezza delle città*. Introduction.

2. For detailed information, given by the man responsible for the fire fighting apparatus, see Endres Tucher's *Baumeisterbuch* (*BLVSt*, Volume 64, 1862), especially pp. 140-9.

3. But not nearly as much as in later centuries. For a comparison with the horrendous conditions of working class existence in the nineteenth century, see the excerpts from the famous Chadwick Report of 1842: Edwin Chadwick, *Report . . . from the Poor Law Commissioners on an Inquiry into the Sanitary Conditions of the Labouring Population of Great Britain*, ed. M. W. Flinn (Edinburgh, 1965).

4. There is an interesting description of such an elaborate bath in Thomas Murner's symbolic *Badenfahrt* (New edition by Viktor Michels. *Thomas Murners deutsche Schriften* I,2, Berlin and Leipzig, 1927).

5. Has's poem is printed in *MVGN* Volume 16 (1904), 243-4.

6. Caspar Ott, *Bevölkerungsstatistik in der Stadt und Landschaft Nürnberg in der ersten Hälfte des 15. Jahrhunderts* (Berlin, 1907), 84.

7. Tucher's *Baumeisterbuch* provides much evidence for the rise in prices and wages in the period he covers, 1465-1475.

8. This appears from a careful study of the wages of municipal construction workers in the years 1503-1511 by Carl L. Sachs, *Nürnbergs reichsstädtische Arbeiterschaft* (Nuremberg, 1915).

9. On this problem generally, see John U. Nef, "Mining and Metallurgy in Medieval Civilization," *Cambridge Economic History of Europe*, volume II (1952), 469-73.

10. For a detailed discussion of Nuremberg's coinage, see the two books by Ernst Scholler given in note 21 to Chapter II, above.

11. There is abundant source material for wages and income. Just to give two published examples: Albert Gümbel, "Die Baurechnungen über die Erhöhung der Türme von St. Sebald in Nürnberg," *MVGN*, Volume 20 (1913), 10-94, giving construction costs and wages for the years 1481-1495; and the *Haushaltungsbuch* of Michel and Paulus Behaim, published by J. Kamann in *ibid.*, Volumes VI (1886), 57-122 and VII (1888), 39-168.

12. Willibald Imhof's *Unkostbuch* is ms *Amb. 64 in the Stadtbibliothek*, Nuremberg. Another bit of evidence on the wealthy is a list of one hundred rich Nurembergers compiled in 1500 by the father of Christoph Scheurl, the lawyer. We learn from it that three newly admitted citizens had brought into the city a fortune of 100,000 Gulden each, six had brought between 30,000 and 50,000, and twelve between 15,000 and 20,000. Scheurl's father listed himself as being worth 14,000 Gulden. It is most likely that the older families had fortunes considerably larger than these newcomers. Scheurl's list is given and commented upon by Helmut Haller von Hallerstein, "Grösse und Quellen des Vermögens von hundert Nürnberger Bürgern um 1500" in *Beiträge zur Wirtschaftsgeschichte Nürnbergs* vol. 1 (1967), 117-76.

13. For these laws see Joseph Baader, *Nürnberger Polizeiordnungen aus dem XIII. bis XV. Jahrhundert* (BLVSt, Volume 63, 1861), 87-90.

14. For an example of such a drawing see *MVGN* Volume 51 (1962), 96.

15. On the *Schembart* there is a book in English: Samuel L. Sumberg, *The Nuremberg Schembart Carnival* (New York, 1941).

16. A representative collection of carnival plays is published by Adalbert Keller, *Fasnachtspiele aus dem 15. Jahrhundert* (BLVSt Volumes 28-30, 46, (1853-1858). For a historical and literary discussion of the carnival plays, see Maximilian Rudwin, *The Origin of German Carnival Comedy* (New York, 1920) and Eckehard Catholy, *Das Fasnachtspiel des Spätmittelalters* (Tübigen, 1961) with a comprehensive bibliography. A few of Hans Sachs' plays have been translated into English: E. U. Ouless, *Seven Shrovetide Plays* (London, 1930, in prose) and, in verse, *Happy as a King, A Way with Surly Husbands,* and *A Charm for the*

Devil (London, 1932-35). Also Henry Gibson Atkins, *The Farmer in Purgatory* (London, n.d.).

17. There is an excellent discussion of the theater of Hans Sachs in Wolfgang F. Michael, *Frühformen der deutschen Bühne* (*Schriften der Gesellschaft für Theatergeschichte*, Vol. 62 Berlin, 1963).

18. On the various Germanic law books and their relations to one another, see Otto Stobbe, *Geschichte der deutschen Rechtsquellen* (Braunschweig, 1860-64), Volume I. On city laws in the Middle Ages, and the family groups into which they fall, *ibid.*, I, 482-551.

19. There is a good article on the Nuremberg "Reformation" of 1479: Daniel Waldmann, "Die Entstehung der Nürnberger Reformation von 1479 (1484) und die Quellen ihrer prozessrechtlichen Vorschriften," *MVGN* Volume 18 (1908), 1-98.

20. On legal books for the layman see Roderich Stintzing, *Geschichte der populären Literatur des römisch-kanonischen Rechts in Deutschland* (Leipzig, 1867), Chapters 6-9.

21. On Heimburg, and the position of the jurist in medieval cities and states generally, see Paul Joachimsohn, *Gregor Heimburg* (Bamberg, 1891).

22. Schmidt's diary has been translated into English: C. Calvert and A. W. Gruner, *A Hangman's Diary* (London, 1928). See also Theodor Hampe, *Crime and Punishment in Germany as illustrated by the Nuremberg Malefactors' Books* (transl. by Malcolm Letts, London, 1929).

CHAPTER VI

1. There is a good description of Melanchthon's educational ideas in Clyde Manschreck, *Melanchthon, the Quiet Reformer* (New York, 1958), Chapter 10-11.

2. Hans Ankwicz von Kleehoven, *Johann Cuspinians Briefwechsel* (Munich, 1933), Nos. 56, 57.

3. This is Ode No. 11 in Book III of his *Libri odarum quattuor* (ed. Felicitas Pindter, Leipzig, 1937), pp. 77-8.

4. The Schedel libraries are described in Richard Stauber's *Die Schedelsche Bibliothek . . .* (Freiburg i.B., 1908).

5. On Heimburg's interesting career see the excellent monograph by Paul Joachimsohn, *Gregor Heimburg* (Bamberg, 1891).

6. On Celtis' career see Lewis Spitz, *Conrad Celtis, the German Arch-Humanist* (Cambridge, Mass., 1957).

7. Celtis' correspondence mirrors these subjects of discussion between him and his friends: Hans Rupprich, ed., *Der Briefwechsel des Konrad Celtis* (Munich, 1934).

8. On Pirckheimer see the books cited in note 11 to Chapter IV, above. Also Hans Rupprich, "Willibald Pirckheimer" in Gerald Strauss, ed., *Pre-Reformation Germany* (London, 1972).

9. For a critical discussion of Behaim's globe, and a superb reproduction

of its segments, see E. G. Ravenstein, *Martin Behaim, His Life and His Globe* (London, 1908).

10. The Nuremberg chronicles have all been published. For reference see note 9 to Chapter I, above.

11. For a detailed discussion of Meisterlin's historical writings, see Paul Joachimsohn, *Die humanistische Geschichtschreibung in Deutschland. I, Die Anfänge: Sigismund Meisterlin* (Bonn, 1895). On general questions of historiography in Germany at this time, see the same author's *Geschichtsauffassung* and *Geschichtschreibung in Deutschland unter dem Einfluss des Humanismus* (Leipzig and Berlin, 1910).

12. On printing and book production generally, see L. Febvre and H.-J. Martin, *L'apparition du livre* (Paris, 1958).

13. On Koberger and his firm see Oscar Hase, *Die Koberger. Eine Darstellung des buchhändlerischen Geschaftsbetriebes in der Zeit des Überganges vom Mittelalter zur Neuzeit* (Leipzig, 1885). Hase, himself a publisher, was mainly interested in the business aspects of Koberger's activities and gives a vivid description of these.

14. See the magnificent facsimile of the *Apocalypse* with the German text, published by Eugrammia Press, with an introduction by Erwin Panofsky [taken from his Dürer biography], (London, 1964).

15. The epitaph is shown in the article on Paumann in *Die Musik in Geschichte und Gegenwart* Vol. 10 (1962), 970.

16. The first comprehensive description of the mastersingers and their activities was given by Johann Christoph Wagenseil in his *De . . . civitate Noribergensi commentario . . .* (Altdorf, 1697). An earlier account came in 1571 from Adam Puschmann, himself a mastersinger: *Gründlicher Bericht des deutschen Meistergesangs*, republished in *Neudrucke deutscher Literaturwerke des XVI. und XVII. Jahrhunderts* (Halle, 1888).

17. Nearly all the modes are named in Scene 2, Act I of Wagner's *Meistersinger,* where the apprentice, David, lectures Walther von Stolzing on the extreme rigors of learning the rules. For a concise analysis of the structure of mastersong poetry, see Otto Paul and Ingeborg Glier, *Deutsche Metrik* (4th ed., Munich, 1961), 95-99.

18. Five of Sachs' mastersongs have been faithfully recorded in the Archive series of Deutsche Grammophon, ARC 3222.

19. Sachs' *Silberweise* is given, in music and text, as No. 281 in Adam Puschmann's collection of mastersongs: G. Münzer, ed., *Das Singebuch des Adam Puschmann nebst den Originalmelodien des M. Behaim und Hans Sachs* (Berlin, 1906).

20. See the plates in *Die Nürnberger Malerei im XV. Jahrhundert* (*Anzeiger des Germanischen National-Museums* 1932-33) (Nuremberg, 1933).

21. These are described, and some are reproduced, in Karl Schottenloher, *Flugblatt und Zeitung* (Berlin, 1922), 128-51.

22. The Neudörffer quotation: Johann Neudörffer, *Nachrichten von Künstlern und Werkleuten* (ed. G. W. K. Lochner in *Quellenschriften für*

Kunstgeschichte und Kunsttechnik des Mittelalters, Vol. 10, 1875, p. 116). Neudörffer's biographies are entirely external and mostly uninformative. The Scheurl quotation: Christoph Scheurl, *Oratio doctoris Scheurli attingens litterarum prestantiam* . . . (Leipzig, 1509), prefatory letter to Cranach.

23. These window designs are beautifully reproduced and discussed in Karl Oettinger and K.-A. Knappe, *Hans Baldung Grien und Albrecht Dürer in Nürnberg* (Nuremberg, 1963).

24. See the discussion of these in Erwin Panofsky's superb *The Life and Art of Albrecht Dürer* (Princeton, N.J., 1955). Also: T. D. Barlow, *The Woodcuts of Albrecht Dürer* (Penguin Books, London, 1948). The most comprehensive discussion of woodcuts, aesthetic and technical, is to be found in Arthur M. Hind, *An Introduction to a History of Woodcut* (London, 1935) two volumes. On Nuremberg, see II, 368-89.

25. The Council's decrees relating to artists have been collected by Theodor Hampe, *Nürnberger Ratsverlässe über Kunst und Künstler im Zeitalter der Spätgothik und Renaissance* (*Quellenschriften für Kunstgeschichte und Kunsttechnik,* N.F., Vols. 11-12, 1904). [For the complicated history of the shrine (mentioned on p. 274) and the controversy surrounding the roles of the elder and younger Vischers in its completion, see Heinz Stafski, *Der jüngere Peter Visher* (Nuremberg, 1962).]

26. Durer's writings, including his letters, have been collected in a splendid volume edited by Hans Rupprich, *Dürers schriftlicher Nachlass* I (Berlin, 1956).

27. There is an English translation of Alberti's treatise: Leon Battista Alberti, *On Painting* (transl. John R. Spencer, London, 1956).

28. For a synopsis of Dürer's work in the graphic arts, see Joseph Meder, *Dürer-Katalog* (Vienna, 1932). The 1955 edition of Panofsky's Dürer biography (see note 24, above) has a fine selection of reproductions to illustrate Dürer's work. See also C. Dodgson, *Albercht Dürer* (London and Boston, 1926) for reproductions of all the engravings and etchings, W. Kurth, *Dürers sämtliche Holzschnitte* (Munich, 1935) for the woodcuts, and F. Winkler, *Die Zeichnungen Albrecht Dürers* (Berlin, 1936-39) for the drawings. The most recent collection is Karl-Adolf Knappe, *Dürer: The Complete Engravings, Etchings, and Woodcuts* (London, 1965) with most of the reproductions in the original sizes and a good biographical and critical introduction. On interpretations of the "Four Apostles," see Gerhard Pfeiffer, "Albrecht Dürer's 'Four Apostles:' a Memorial Picture from the Reformation Era," in *The Social History of the Reformation* ed. L. P. Buck and J. W. Zophy (Columbus, Ohio, 1972), 271-96. On Dürer and the city of Nuremberg generally, see the articles in *Albrecht Dürers Umwelt. Festschrift zum 500. Geburtstag Albrecht Dürer* (Nuremberg, 1971).

29. For illustrations of the works of all these artists, see the catalogue *Meister um Albrecht Dürer* (*Anzeiger des Germanischen National-Museums 1960-61* (Nuremberg, 1961) and the literature cited there.

30. We know, however, of two notable private collections in the late years of the sixteenth century. The first is that of Willibald Imhof, which incorporated the earlier collection of his uncle, Willibald Pirckheimer, and contained antiquities, coins, bronzes, marble busts, engravings, and paintings including several by Dürer and Cranach. The other collection belonged to Paul von Praun, the catalogue of whose stones, engravings, paintings (including Titians, Raphaels, Michelangelos, a Leonardo, and ten Dürers) ran to 500 pages. Praun lived alternately in Nuremberg and Bologna, but before his death he sent his entire collection to Nuremberg.

31. For a general impression of painting, sculpture, and the graphic arts in seventeenth- and eighteenth-century Nuremberg, see the catalogue *Barock in Nürnberg, 1600-1750 (Anzeiger des Germanischen National-Museums,* Nuremberg, 1962).

32. In the course of the nineteenth century Nuremberg grew into an industrial city and a railway center and became the second largest city in Bavaria. All the new residential quarters and, of course, the industries were situated in the new city, beyond the old walls.

ILLUSTRATION CREDITS

Index

299